HIGHER EDUCATION AND DISABILITIES: INTERNATIONAL APPROACHES

*For Claire, John
and Carole*

Higher Education and Disabilities: International Approaches

Edited by
ALAN HURST
University of Central Lancashire
Preston

Ashgate

Aldershot • Brookfield USA • Singapore • Sydney

© A. Hurst 1998

Published by
Ashgate Publishing Ltd
Gower House
Croft Road
Aldershot
Hants GU11 3HR
England

Ashgate Publishing Company
Old Post Road
Brookfield
Vermont 05036
USA

British Library Cataloguing in Publication Data
Higher education and disabilities : international
    approaches
    1.Handicapped students - Education (Higher)
    I.Hurst, Alan, 1944-
    378.1'9'827

Library of Congress Catalog Card Number: 98-71960

ISBN 1 85972 508 2

Printed and bound by Athenaeum Press, Ltd.,
Gateshead, Tyne & Wear.

Contents

Preface and acknowledgements

The idea of compiling the collection of papers which are contained in this book was prompted by my participation in a number of international conferences concerned with the development of policy and provision for students with disabilities in higher education since 1992. Over the years, colleagues with similar interests and working in other countries have become friends and it is to them that I owe a great deal. There is little point in listing them here since their names appear at the start of every chapter. They have been totally supportive of my efforts throughout the production of this book. For many, my requests coincided with busy times at work and yet they responded with speed and interest. Some of them have had to struggle with writing in a language which is foreign to them. As editor I have tried to adapt their own words sometimes in order to ensure fluency in English. In doing so I hope that I have done nothing to harm the original meaning and intention. If this has been the case, then the shortcomings are mine. I hope that all the contributors feel that their efforts have been appropriately recognised by the publication of this book.

There are some others whose help and support has been unstinting despite pressures from elsewhere. It is only fair to name these "unsung heroes" of the struggle to complete the book. I owe a huge debt to those I work alongside at the University of Central Lancashire both in the Department of Education Studies under the relaxed and friendly leadership of the Head of Department, Ken Phillips and also in Student Services where John Greer has always been equally warm and welcoming. Colleagues in the Disability Services Section led by Catherine Badminton have been supportive in ways which they perhaps did not recognise but which I value enormously. Outside the University, members and staff of Skill : National Bureau for Students with Disabilities first under the direction of Deborah Cooper and more recently Barbara Waters have also provided me with ideas. I have been grateful especially to Skill's Assistant Director, Sophie Corlett, for her suggestions.

As the production process gathered speed others have been helpful beyond what might reasonably be expected. The editorial staff at Ashgate Publishing and especially Jo Gooderham and Anne Keirby have been incredibly understanding when deadlines have had to be put back as other more pressing responsibilities have had to take precedence. I would like to thank Valerie Polding for her very conscientious editorial work and helpful comments on achieving consistency between the papers. The final production of the text has been the responsibility of Joanne Kirk. I can say nothing which conveys accurately my debt to Joanne who has had to cope with almost every eventuality and has done so with a smile and a willingness that was undeserved. At a late stage Katie Pethiyagoda made a valuable contribution despite her other commitments. Finally I must mention the members of my family to whom I dedicate this book. I am sure that in the months and weeks leading to the final version of this book, they would have it to be called "The Lost Weekends" but that seems too much like another text. I hope that they feel that their sacrifices have been worthwhile.

To everyone associated with the book in any way whatsoever I offer my very sincere thanks.

Alan Hurst
February 1998

Notes on the contributors

The editor

Alan Hurst began his career in teaching after completing a first degree in history and sociology and a PGCE at the University of Hull. His first post involved teaching history in a grammar school in the Manchester area. He became Head of the History Department at the School and, having had a year's secondment to complete a Master's degree in Education, he started teaching in higher education at the Poulton-le-Fylde College of Education. This became part of what was then Preston Polytechnic and is now the University of Central Lancashire. Even whilst working at Poulton Alan became involved with a working group concerned with students with disabilities and became a member of what was then the newly formed National Bureau for Handicapped Students and is now Skill: National Bureau for Students with Disabilities. Since those early days his involvement with disabled students has grown. He completed his doctorate in 1990 at the University of Lancaster and was awarded the title of Professor in recognition of his work with disabled students. He has been invited to give presentations and chair conferences throughout the UK and in other parts of the world. He first book called 'Steps Towards Graduation' was published by Avebury Press in 1993 and looks at how people with disabilities gain access to higher education. He has contributed papers and book reviews to many other publications. He is a member of the Higher Education Funding Council's Advisory Group on Students with Learning Difficulties and Disabilities and was elected to the chair of Skill in 1996 and 1997. More recently he has been invited to become a member of a new standing committee on equal opportunities, access and widening participation which is being set up by the Higher Education Funding Council for England following the recommendations of the Dearing Committee.

Other contributors

Betty Aune was formerly Assistant Director of the Disability Services Office at the University of Minnesota, Minneapolis, and is now a lecturer at the College of St. Scholastica, Duluth, Minnesota, USA.

Gayle V. Gagliano is Director of the Training, Resource and Assistive Technology Centre at the University of New Orleans, New Orleans, USA.

Adolfus Juodraitis is a Dean of Faculty at the University of Siauliai, Lithuania.

Liisa Laitinen is an adviser for students with disabilities at the University of Helsinki, Finland.

Renate Langweg-Berhorster works for Deutsches Studentenwerk, Bonn, Germany.

David A. Leitch is a lecturer at St. Mary's University, Halifax, Nova Scotia, Canada.

Elena Mendelova is a lecturer in the Department of Mathematics, the Comenius University, Bratislava, Slovak Republic.

Carmel O'Sullivan is Dean of Women Students, University College, Dublin, Ireland.

Juozas Petrusevicius is a lecturer in the Department of Languages at the University of Siauliai, Lithuania.

Des Power is Professor in the Centre for Deafness Studies and Research in the Faculty of Education, Griffith University, Queensland, Australia.

Maria Pilar Sarto Martin is a lecturer in the Department of Pedagogy and Research in the Faculty of Education, University of Salamanca, Spain.

Cheryl T. Saucier was formerly working in the Training and Rehabilitation Service at the University of New Orleans, New Orleans, USA and is now Director of the Hoover Eye Institute, Baltimore, Maryland, USA.

Jenny Shaw works in the Regional Disability Liaison Unit located at Deakin University, Malvern, Victoria, Australia.

Despina Sidiropoulou-Dimakakou is a careers counsellor at the University of Athens, Greece.

Willem Temmink is a professional social worker and is a study adviser/counsellor with Handicap and Studie in Utrecht, the Netherlands.

Myriam Van Acker is Head of the Student Advice Service at the Catholic University of Leuven, Belgium.

Piet Vriens is a student counsellor working in the Student Advice Centre at the University of Amsterdam, Amsterdam, the Netherlands.

Majken Wahlstrom is the National Co-ordinator for Disabled Students based at the University of Stockholm, Sweden.

Joan Wolforth is the Co-ordinator of the Office for Students with Disabilities at McGill University, Montreal, Canada.

Introduction

Within the plethora of published materials about aspects of education, one group of learners appear to have been neglected. These are students who have disabilities and/or learning difficulties and who enter higher education. In some ways this is a surprising omission. At the level of schools and the compulsory education sector there are a number of research studies and other works about integration of learners with disabilities in mainstream provision. For those with an interest in inclusive education, they would find that within higher education, inclusion already occurs. There is little if any discrete provision along the lines of that found in other sectors. Moving on up the age scale, the debate on learning support for students in further education has been prominent for many years and has been given added momentum in the United Kingdom since the publication of the Further Education Funding Council's report called "Inclusive Learning" (The Tomlinson Report - FEFC 1996). In recent years the higher education sector has had a strong interest in improving access for and widening the participation of under-represented groups. Even here, it is only during the decade of the 1990s that some detailed attention has been given to people with disabilities (see Hurst (1993) for a list of sources and Hurst (1996) and also Cooper and Corlett (1996) for a discussion of policy developments since 1990). What is equally interesting is that a similar level of neglect can be found in other countries although it is only recently that this common feature has become more evident. This has resulted from those with an interest in developing policy and provision for students with disabilities meeting each other more frequently at international conferences and being in closer, more immediate contact through developments in information technology such as electronic mail.

The origins of this collection of chapters can be traced back to some particular conferences. In 1992 there were three significant meetings. In chronological order, the first of these took place at the Sorbonne University, Paris and was organised by the French government. A small number of participants from outside France gave papers although the main focus of the meeting was on the experiences of students with disabilities in French universities. Soon afterwards, there was an international conference organised by Waseda University, Tokyo. This was very similar to the French event in that there was a relatively small number of participants from outside Japan. The third meeting was organised by the University of New Orleans and used the facilities of the University of Innsbruck in Austria. Whilst there was a preponderance of plenary sessions and workshops delivered by colleagues based in the United States, there was an important series of meetings involving staff from other countries. This first conference was very successful and it was repeated in 1995, this time with an increased number of participants from outside the United States. (There is to be a third conference in Summer 1998.)

Alongside these world-wide gatherings, there have been international developments on a smaller scale. Within Europe, under the auspices of an international forum on student guidance (FEDORA), a group of colleagues from several countries have met regularly, spent time visiting each other, and developing materials which could be useful to students with disabilities (see the chapter by Hurst on international exchanges which comes later). There is a general feeling that knowing more about what happens in other countries is extremely valuable for both personal professional development and also for prompting progress and improved practices to support students with disabilities. Because of this and because this valuable information was in danger of either being restricted to those able to attend the meetings at best or being totally lost at worst, the idea for this collection emerged. Invitations were sent to a large number of colleagues in many different parts of the world. Many have responded and the results can be read in the following chapters. Unfortunately, many others could not find the time to respond. Thus, sadly there are no accounts of developments in several European countries: Austria, Denmark, France, Italy, Norway, and Portugal. It should not be inferred that what is happening in these countries is not interesting and that there are no initiatives. In fact, it would be possible to compile a second collection to include contributions from colleagues working in these countries. There are some other important gaps. No accounts were forthcoming from colleagues working in the African, South American and Asian continents. Again, it would be useful to find out more about how policy and provision is developing in countries which themselves are starting to change.

The accounts that follow result from the willingness of many colleagues to respond to my request for contributions. When making the request, a number of possibilities emerged. Apart from being of interest to those working to develop policy and provision for students with disabilities and/or learning difficulties, the collection might appeal also to those with an interest in comparative education. To meet the needs of this group, it might have been better to insist that contributors followed a standard brief. For example they should be asked to include details of the structure of their national education system including factual information about age gradations, qualifications etc. To impose such uniformity might have been helpful but it might have stifled much of the originality of approach which can be found in the accounts and which, in my view, makes them more stimulating.

Despite the breadth of coverage, the contributions do contain a number of themes which are common and which are of international concern and interest. In the second part of this introduction, attention will be drawn to some of these.

However, before moving on it is important to acknowledge that policy and provision for students with disabilities and/or learning difficulties does take place within different national contexts and different educational structures and systems.

Systems and structures of higher education: some basic comparisons

One significant difference is that between what have been described as systems based on "sponsored" and "contest" principles (Turner 1961). In brief, an analogy might be with a race. One system selects the runners carefully with the intention that all will have a chance to complete it successfully. The other allows anyone to enter the race and recognises that not all will finish it. Education systems which fit the former are those which exercise a significant degree of selection at a number of points throughout the learner's educational career. Taking England as an example and moving back in time to try to make the point more clearly, not too long ago children were selected for different types of secondary schooling on the basis of an examination taken when they were 11 years old. At the end of compulsory schooling, other examinations were used to determine access to different forms of education after the age of 16. The route with the greatest status was into the sixth forms of grammar schools which was then the key to entry to higher education. Even here, the use of the General Certificate of Education Advanced level examinations (GCE 'A' levels) allowed universities to select their students. Elements of this system remain although with the growth of comprehensive secondary education and widened access to higher education, perhaps they are less obvious. On the other hand, the end result of the selection procedures is that when students do enter higher education, the failure rate at the end of the first year of studies is low compared to other countries. The comparison is evident if one looks at systems where "contest" principles operate. Here there is much less concern with selection. Learners themselves choose to continue in the system and leave it only when they have to. For example, in many countries, there is a high drop-out rate at the end of the first year of university studies. Because students have obtained the basic matriculation requirements, they go to university but then find that they are unsuccessful.

Perhaps the most useful, recent comparative summary of European education systems has been provided by Tony Raban (Raban, 1997). He opens by discussing terminology which is important if misunderstandings are to be avoided. In particular he draws attention to the different meanings of the term "Diploma" which in some countries is the equivalent of what in England would be called a degree. Also, whilst many European countries refer to cycles of study, one of which is the third cycle, in England this would be called postgraduate study (and graduate study in the USA). In the United Kingdom, there are two cycles: one leading to a first degree which is where most students leave the system and one leading to a more advanced qualification. In some European countries - Germany, France and Spain would be good examples - there are three phases. The first consists of a broad programme of introductory studies, the second is more specialised and which is the level attained by most students, the third involves more advanced study, often including research and leading to the award of a doctorate. One other source of confusion must be noted since it is particularly relevant to the chapter on the Netherlands. Those who graduate from the non-university higher vocational education institutions are awarded a bachelors degree and yet, strictly speaking, this is not the equivalent of the English or American qualification.

Raban continues by discussing elements of the structures: method of entry, length and level of course, qualifications, control, and entry to employment, When discussing method of entry he notes the importance of selectivity in some countries along the lines outlined earlier. He draws attention to the fact that even within systems based on "contest" principles, some courses do have restricted entry since there is tight control on the number of places available. He comments that where the system is highly selective, there are other implications. For example, because students have to compete for places to study, they often go to universities away from their homes whereas when entry is open to all who matriculate, many will choose to study at the university nearest to their home and continue to live at or near home. From the point of view of students with disabilities and those working to develop policy and provision for them, this is of some significance. Also significant is the fact that in some countries, for example in England, restrictions on student funding have influenced choice of university with some students now choosing to study in the institution nearest to their home because it is less costly.

The lengths and levels of courses vary between countries although sometimes the length of a course cannot always be equated with the time taken to complete it. Raban gives examples of courses which last for four years but which take six years to complete. The additional time might be needed in some countries for work placement or indeed for military service. In all countries, financial pressures on both students and on state resources have led to a shared concern to complete courses in as short a time as possible. Some efforts have been made to introduce greater flexibility into the system. In England, there has been a move towards semester-based systems with modular structures and credit-based frameworks. Again, for students with disabilities and/or learning difficulties, these changes have not always been helpful. In modular structures, there is often the necessity to take formal examinations at two points during the year and so setting up any special facilities now has to be undertaken twice as opposed to just once under the old regime.

In considering control, Raban notes that more systems in the past were controlled centrally with the state setting out the content and level of courses. Some of the accounts in this book provide good illustrations of this - and of the recent shift to greater freedom in running their own affairs. This independence means that it has become more difficult to make comparisons.

This convergence in terms of independence is matched in the area of the transition to employment. In many countries, what students studied at university had direct vocational relevance. In England, this was less obvious and many employers were happy to see graduation as the certification of potential employees in terms of the acquisition of useful skills; employers followed this with their own programmes of more specific vocational training. This has changed somewhat with students and the institutions becoming more aware of the need for vocational qualifications. Where courses do not have a clear vocational linkage, efforts are made to identify transferable skills, for example in the use of information technology. Again, this does have implications for students with disabilities when they graduate. Apart from trying to persuade potential employers of the value and relevance of some qualifications, they might also need to overcome the documented resistance that many employers in several countries have towards employing people with disabilities.

Raban ends his account with a review of different approaches to student guidance, all of which do have implications for students with disabilities and/or learning difficulties. He identifies a number of times when students need advice and guidance: on entering higher education (choice of courses and of institution), academic advice during the course (subject choice, study-related problems), personal problems (accommodation, finance, health) and careers advice. There is a basic issue to be explored first of all since in some countries universities have not regarded it as their role to be responsible for some of these potential areas of difficulty. Sometimes, they have seen it as the responsibility of the students themselves or other sectors of society (for example schools should offer advice on entry, the state careers service for advice on employment, the state health service for medical advice, and so on).

In connection with the provision of information, students with disabilities and learning difficulties do have additional needs which the general prospectus might not include. There is a requirement too that the information should be available in accessible formats, for example in Braille. Institutions in many countries recognise this and make efforts to provide relevant information. Perhaps the concern which all institutions in all countries have addressed is advice about the curriculum, its structures, modes of delivery, and strategies of assessment. Where there might still be differences are in the allocation of responsibilities. In some countries, for example in England, advice about academic affairs is seen to be a part of the normal duties of members of the academic staff. In other countries, for example in Germany or the Netherlands, responsibility rests with a section of the central services supporting students. Considering this in relation to students with disabilities, the strengths and shortcomings of each method are not clear. In England, as academic staff are faced with more students and less time, providing any extra support for some students becomes more difficult. However, the tutor might well be more familiar with the academic issues involved than a colleague based in a central service. Advice, help, and support with problems of a personal nature such as those relating to finance or health are usually the responsibility of a central student services section although the models on which these are organised do differ both between institutions in the same country and also in terms of typical patterns between countries. Thus, services providing counselling or student accommodation or advice about careers are sometimes part of a fully comprehensive section of an institution and sometimes they operate entirely separately.

One service which has become much more important for many students in recent years has been advice about opportunities to spend time studying at an institution in a different country. Many students benefit from participation in a range of international exchanges and visits. It is important that students with disabilities and/or learning difficulties are also able to take part. In order for this to become a realistic possibility and to try to increase the chances of success, it is necessary for staff working with these students to become more knowledgeable about policy and provision in other countries. This is one of the major justifications for the publication of this collection of papers and it is to these which we now turn. Study abroad is also the focus of the closing chapter.

Higher education and policy and provision for students with disabilities in different countries: an overview

Before offering a brief summary of each of the contributions, it is necessary to say something about the order in which the contributions appear. Having considered a number of ways of organising the chapters and rejected many of them, the simple approach of placing them in alphabetical order by country has been adopted. This also adds to the variety of content and could make the book more interesting for its readers.

The collection opens with two chapters from Australia. In the first, Des Power explores several issues of policy which are replicated in other countries. These include the concern for the under-representation of people with disabilities in higher education and the strategies used by central government to provide funding. He identifies a number of dilemmas faced in other countries. For example, some debate has occurred about establishing what might be described as "centres of excellence" in order to meet the needs of different groups of students with particular impairments. A related issue is about how limited funds might be used to their best effect. On the one hand, there is the case for allocating additional finance to institutions with a proven track record; on the other hand, perhaps increased participation might result from providing financial assistance to institutions which have made only limited progress. Doing this would risk offending those institutions which have already invested in policy and provision out of their own resources. An interesting aspect of the Australian situation is the development of national guidelines on standards of service provision. The trend towards a national approach is evident in other countries and there are signs in England that a similar strategy is emerging. One aspect of the Australian situation shared by many other countries is the introduction of anti-discrimination legislation. The need for this is explored by the second Australian contribution from Jenny Shaw. She explores the social context in which attitudes to disability are formed and reviews the need for programmes to change the attitudes of staff and to develop the knowledge and expertise of those staff working to develop policy and provision for students with disabilities and/or learning difficulties. This is a concern which is expressed in many other contributions and is taken up in some detail in one of the chapters about the situation in England.

Myriam Van Acker's account of the situation in Belgium explores two major concerns. Having noted the importance of changes in the school sector, she begins by discussing issues relating to finance especially for institutions developing high quality policy and provision. Only a small number of institutions have made progress and this has been undertaken because of their commitment to students with disabilities. It has been done at their own expense; they have been given no additional funds for their efforts. Students with disabilities are aware of where support is available and so they direct their applications only to those places. The consequence of this is that the demand on the limited service is increased and since there is no commensurate increase in resources, the overall quality and effectiveness of the service might be diminished. In her description of the developments at the Catholic University of Leuven, Van Acker outlines the system of personal assistance available to those students who need it. The involvement of non-disabled students on a daily basis can do much to break down prejudice and negative attitudes.

The first of the two chapters from Canada highlights the lack of information about students with disabilities in higher education. As in other countries, Joan Wolforth notes how difficult it is to obtain both quantitative and qualitative data and the importance of having such information for arguing in favour of developments. There are strong parallels with the situation in other countries - for example in relation to anti-discrimination legislation and the development of national standards of service provision. Wolforth makes the specific point that there is a need for more research and so it does seem appropriate that the second paper from Canada describes a small investigation. David Leitch also takes up the point about the need for statistical data. His investigation is a valuable one and could be replicated elsewhere. His first concern was to discover the numbers of students with disabilities attending courses in higher education institutions in Canada. He found that since there were many different definitions of disabled students and different approaches to collecting statistics, establishing valid and reliable data was very difficult. Equally interesting is the information derived from the attempts of the research worker to make contact with the person responsible for students with disabilities in the various institutions. The problems involved in trying to get in touch with this individual could well be encountered in other countries. More significantly, they could be very discouraging for potential students with disabilities wanting to find out more about policy and provision.

In describing the situation in Finland, Liisa Laitinen draws attention to several concerns which are commented in other accounts. Firstly, she notes that entry to university is selective. Secondly, she points out that many of the buildings particularly at the long-established institutions such as the University of Helsinki are old and present difficulties in terms of access for wheelchair users. The University is also based on a number of sites which adds to the problems. Thirdly, Laitinen makes special mention of issues surrounding support for students who are Deaf and students with specific learning difficulties. Finally, after completing their courses successfully, she highlights the lack of employment opportunities for disabled graduates.

The development of policy and provision for students with disabilities in universities in Germany has been an important feature of the higher education system. Renate Langweg-Berhorster provides a detailed account of what disabled students can expect from the institutions in which they study. This covers finance, living accommodation and advice. The last-mentioned is of particular significance in this chapter since this is the first in which there is mention of a national organisation which is available to help disabled students. As will be seen from later chapters, there are national organisations in a small number of other countries: the Association for Higher Education and Disability (AHEAD) in Ireland and also in the United States although the two are not linked formally, Handicap and Studie in the Netherlands, and Skill: National Bureau for Students with Disabilities in the United Kingdom. The organisation which is described by Langweg-Berhorster is Deutsches Studentenwerk (DSW). It is different from these others in that it works with aspects of support for all students. The other organisations work only with students with disabilities.

In contrast to the situation in Germany, policy and provision for students with disabilities and/or learning difficulties in Greece is at an early stage of development. The chapter by Despina Sidiropoulou-Dimakakou is useful for indicating how much the progress that has been made in some countries might be in danger of being taken for granted and how much of a struggle there is to initiate change. Apart from the shortage of specialist trained staff and the availability of assistive technology, Sidiropoulou-Dimakakou sees the key to moving forward as a change in attitudes. In the Greek context, the change needs to occur not only in staff working in higher education specifically but also within the population in general. In the case of Greece, there is a need to locate the development of policy and provision within the broader social and educational context, one in which disability has been associated with feelings of guilt and embarrassment and kept hidden. A recently published comparative study of inclusive education in Greek and English schools suggests that despite considerable difficulties the process is underway and so the point will come in the near future when learners with disabilities who have passed successfully through the school sector will be looking to further their education at the higher level (Vlachou 1998).

Moving on to consider the situation in Ireland, Carmel O'Sullivan's account is another one in which progress with inclusive education in schools is seen as having implications for policy and provision in higher education. As more children pass through schools successfully, more are likely to want to take up places at universities. However, in contrast, to this, O'Sullivan also has a concern with those who might have not taken up earlier opportunities or indeed were going through the school system when opportunities to enter higher education were extremely limited. This 'second chance' approach is one which can be found in many other countries as efforts have been made to improve access for under-represented groups and to widen participation in higher education. The chapter describes an access programme and its objectives at University College, Dublin.

The chapter by Adolfus Juodraitis and Juozas Petrusevicius on Lithuania is especially valuable since it represents a country which has gained its independence relatively recently and is only just starting to develop its own structures and systems in all aspects of social life. The importance of the broader context cannot be emphasised too much. This would also include the cultural context since the situation with regard to people with disabilities is similar to that in Greece. Since gaining independence from Russia, the country has had to pay special attention to its economy and even after seven years there is still much to be done. Overall, Lithuania is not a rich country and this is reflected at all levels of the education system where there is a clear shortage of resources of all kinds. That does not mean that nothing is being done. On the contrary, there is a strategy emerging which will be interesting to observe. In developing policy and provision for students with disabilities in higher education, the importance of the experiences within the school sector have been seen as important. Also, Juodraitis and Petrusevicius argue that ensuring that there are close contacts with countries in Western Europe is important since they feel that much can be learnt that way. Already, such contacts are having an impact. For example, there are more students with disabilities on courses at their own institution than in the past as the university begins to take into consideration the needs of these students.

The account describing policy and provision in higher education for students with disabilities in the Netherlands echoes many of the concerns expressed by other contributors. Thus, Willem Temmink and Piet Vriens comment on the impact on higher education of changes in the school sector, the lack of staff training and staff development opportunities for those working with disabled students, and the valuable work undertaken by a national organisation, in this case Handicap and Studie. They go on to make other interesting observations. For example they note the difficulties in securing employment experienced by many disabled people after they graduate. This occurs despite efforts made to ensure that employers do not discriminate but as Temmink and Vriens point out, one significant employer which does not appear to welcome disabled employees is the government itself. A second important point to emerge from this chapter is about the attitude found in some institutions and which is found elsewhere. There are some institutions which argue that they need not develop policy and provision for students with disabilities since they receive no applications from this group of students. This is an interesting variation on the "which comes first - the chicken or the egg" argument. If students know that they will receive no support they will not apply and so the institutions which do not make any attempts to make progress in recruiting students with disabilities can continue along the same track.

Elena Mendelova's chapter displays strong parallels with the Lithuanian one. The Slovak Republic is a new country and so there is much to be done in all aspects of society. As will be evident from Mendelova's account about Bratislava, some progress has been made. In particular, she describes developments to support students with visual impairments. Perhaps this should not be a surprise. To meet the needs of students with mobility impairments could be very costly indeed in terms of alterations to old buildings etc. Giving high quality support to Deaf students would also be a major problem since there is a shortage of trained interpreters. As with the Lithuanian situation, an important contribution to progress has come through international links, in this case through the TEMPUS programme and working with experienced colleagues from the

University of Karlsruhe in Germany and the Royal National Institute for the Blind in England. For Mendelova, the need now is to develop awareness of disability amongst staff and to provide training.

Spain is another country which is only now starting to improve policy and provision for students with disabilities in universities. Pilar Sarto begins her chapter with a description of the important changes to the education system which have occurred in the last 20 years. Some of these have been implemented only recently and their impact has yet to be felt. Much of Sarto's contribution is about developments at her own university, the University of Salamanca. This is one of the oldest in Spain and its general environment and location within the city contribute to some of the difficulties faced by students. In particular wheelchair users and others with impaired mobility find the steep hills, cobbled streets, and narrow pavements hard to negotiate. Many of the buildings are old and have the protected status of historic monuments which makes improving access difficult. Nevertheless, undaunted by these factors, efforts have been made to make progress. The chapter discusses the survey carried out amongst students to find out their views about the university. Incidentally, it is interesting to note that in contrast to others, little attention is given in this chapter to students with specific learning difficulties.

In describing the situation in Sweden, Majken Wahlstrom provides further evidence that there are issues which are common in many other countries. For example, she comments on the shortage of interpreters and the difficulties of meeting the needs of Deaf students in higher education. A second issue concerns students with specific learning difficulties. Thirdly, she notes that some students with disabilities study on a part-time basis. There are also some unique aspects of the Swedish context. Firstly, there is the role occupied by Wahlstrom herself. The government has established the post of National Co-ordinator for Disabled Students which is intended to bring about a significant level of planned development. Secondly, the system of funding institutions involves a well-established practice of taking an fixed percentage of the annual budget for undergraduate students and using it to support policy and provision for disabled students. Finally, the need for staff training and staff development for those working to support disabled students has been addressed in an original way. Given the lack of appropriate staff development opportunities in Sweden itself, it is planned to organise a seminar with the University of Central Lancashire in England in early 1998 to make use of the programme of specialist courses developed there (see the chapter by Hurst which describes the programme in some detail).

Having mentioned the University of Central Lancashire, this provides a good link with the next two chapters, both of which have been written by Alan Hurst, editor of the collection, and which focus on the United Kingdom. In the first chapter he tries to balance an account of national policy developments with a case study of their impact on policy and provision at one institution, the University of Central Lancashire. In relation to policy a key concern is with the allocation of funding, both to students with disabilities and to the institutions which try to support them. He reviews some recent short term national funding initiatives which have been introduced in England and comments briefly on the developments in Northern Ireland, Scotland, and Wales where different approaches have been tried. The University of Central Lancashire was one of the institutions which made successful bids for additional funding and Hurst explores the projects which were financed from the special initiatives. A third project is underway and will end in late 1999 and this is also described. It is clear from this chapter that the speed of progress has increased in England and that other developments (for example the extension of anti-discrimination legislation) could ensure that the momentum is sustained. (For a review of developments which have occurred since the preparation of this book see Hurst in press.)

The second chapter has been included because it takes up an important issue mentioned by several contributors to this book. This is the issue of training and staff development opportunities for those working with students with disabilities and/or learning difficulties. One of the projects for which the University received additional funding was to devise a programme of courses and qualifications for this group of staff. The ways in which this was approached, especially the close involvement of experienced staff working in other institutions, the structure of the programme, the curriculum content, and the strategies for entry and assessment are discussed in some detail. Linked to this there are the needs of other staff who have contact with disabled students in the course of their daily duties. Thus, Hurst discusses progress with the most recent special initiative project aimed at delivering basic awareness raising for all members of the university before the end of 1999. In many of the accounts, it is suggested that more progress might be forthcoming if attempts were made to provide more information to staff so that they might then change their attitudes. The account from the University of Central Lancashire could be useful to others who are considering ways of promoting more positive attitudes amongst their colleagues.

The two chapters which end the collection of national accounts consider the situation in the United States of America. In some ways, the alphabetical ordering by country has had an important consequence in that the country which is regarded as having made most progress is left until the end of the book where it can come as a kind of climax. What has been done in the USA is often seen as the target at which many should be aiming. Whilst it cannot be disputed that policy and provision in many universities in the United States is far in advance of what can be found anywhere else, the two chapters here indicate that many important issues are still to be resolved. Betty Aune bases her account on her experiences at the University of Minnesota. The University has a well-established service with a range of full-time specialist staff. Particular attention has been given to advice about careers and employment. In her account she mentions university staff who have disabilities, a group who are often overlooked and yet who might be powerful allies in promoting change. The areas of difficulty mentioned by Aune include the provision of qualified interpreters to work with Deaf students, the development of service standards and guidelines, and the special circumstances of students with psychiatric problems, students with learning disabilities, and students with disabilities from the ethnic minority communities.

Gayle Gagliano and Cheryl Saucier take up the American situation by looking at the impact of anti-discrimination legislation, especially the Americans with Disabilities Act 1990. They then move on to explore a number of different models of service delivery before considering in detail, policy and provision at the University of New Orleans. As with Minnesota, this is a well-developed aspect of the university and in addition to a specialist adviser based in the main Student Centre, there is a service providing training, assessment and rehabilitation for people with disabilities. This facility is used by outside organisations although having it on campus is extremely helpful. In 1997 it moved into a new purpose-built block which has won prizes for the ways in which its design has taken into account the needs of users with a range of impairments. Before ending their account, Gagliano and Saucier identify their own list of current concerns. These are similar to the ones mentioned by Aune namely meeting the financial needs especially of Deaf students and their interpreters, and the definition, diagnosis, and special arrangements offered to students with learning disabilities.

Closing comments

After the end of the chapters containing national accounts, there is a further contribution from Alan Hurst. One of the aims underlying the compilation of this collection is that staff working with disabled students will be better informed about aspects of policy and provision in other countries. This could be helpful when students with disabilities express interest in participating in foreign visits and international exchanges. This short concluding chapter explores some of the issues surrounding study abroad and provides some practical suggestions for those involved.

The idea of students with disabilities doing what their non-disabled peers do and grasping the growing number of opportunities to spend time in another country forms a suitably optimistic note on which to close this introduction. As more disabled students enter higher education, it is likely that more will want to spend time overseas. That this is happening is a sign of the progress made and that gradually this once-neglected group are becoming fully included in all aspects of the higher education experience. If the chapters in this collection make some small contribution to this, those who have taken time to write about their own country will feel that their efforts have not been wasted.

References

Cooper, D. and Corlett, S. (1996), 'An overview of current provision' in Wolfendale, S. and Corbett, J. (eds), *Opening Doors: Learning Support in Higher Education*, Cassell: London.

Further Education Funding Council (FECE) (1996), *Inclusive Learning: The Report of the Learning Difficulties and/or Disabilities Committee* (The Tomlinson Report), Her Majesty's Stationery Office: London.

Hurst, A. (1993), *Steps Towards Graduation: Access to Higher Education for People with Disabilities*, Avebury Press: Aldershot.

Hurst, A. (1995), 'Equal opportunities and access: developments in policy and provision for disabled students 1990-1995' in Wolfendale, S. and Corbett, J. (eds), *Opening Doors: Learning Support in Higher Education*, Cassell: London.

Hurst, A. (in press), 'The Dearing Report and students with disabilities', *Disability and Society*.

Raban, Tony (1997), 'An update of European guidance and education systems' in Van Esbroek, R. et al., (eds), *Decision-Making for Lifelong Learning*, VUB Press: Brussels.

Turner, R.H. (1961), 'Modes of social ascent through education: sponsored and contest mobility' in Halsey, A.H. et al., (eds), *Education, Economy and Society*, The Free Press of Glencoe: New York.

Vlachou, A. (1998), *Struggles for Inclusive Education*, The Open University Press: Buckingham.

1 Disability services in Australian universities

Des Power

Recent Changes in Australian Higher Education

In 1988 the then Commonwealth of Australia Minister for Employment, Education and Training, John Dawkins, created what has been described as a "revolution" in Australian higher education, introducing a Government policy "White Paper" (Dawkins, 1988), the implementation of most of which had the effect of abolishing the former "advanced education" sector composed of institutes of technology and colleges of advanced education (most of which were teachers colleges) by amalgamating some of them with existing universities and setting in train changes in the funding and modus operandi of others which eventually allowed them to become universities in their own right. By 1995 the number of higher education institutions in Australia (now all called universities, except for the perverse Royal Melbourne Institute of Technology which elected to retain its previous name) had been reduced to thirty-eight in the "Unified National System", most in state and territory capital cities (the larger of which typically have three or four universities each), but with some in regional cities. All of these are set up by State and Territory Acts of Parliament and are theoretically self-governing, funded for their ordinary teaching, research and administrative activities by grants to the states and territories by the Commonwealth Government. (There are only two private, i.e., non-Government-funded, universities in Australia, both with small numbers of students compared with the state universities.)

With Commonwealth funding, despite much rhetoric to the contrary, has come increased Government control over many university activities, more marked since the "Dawkins Revolution". The Commonwealth has a great deal of control over university activities because recurrent funds for teaching, administration and services are tied to student numbers via an agreed "Educational Profile" for each university, an agreement which controls the range of courses for which each university can obtain Government funding at undergraduate and some postgraduate levels. In addition, universities are allowed under regulations introduced in the 1996 Budget by a new Liberal (i.e., conservative) Commonwealth Government elected in March, 1996 to charge fees for an additional 25 per cent of undergraduates above their Government-funded quotas and most postgraduate courses are now eligible to be offered to fee-paying students. It is not yet clear what this might mean for services to students with disabilities.

Government equity initiatives

The Government, through a number of its agencies, especially the National Board of Employment, Education and Training and the Higher Education Council (policy and advisory authorities) has also attempted to influence university policy and practice in a number of areas. One of the most important of these has been access to university for students in "equity target groups". In an influential policy statement, "A Fair Chance for All: Higher Education that's Within Everyone's Reach" (Dawkins, 1990), the Government moved to establish policy in this field, including setting of objectives, numbers, targets, and implementation strategies to provide more equitable access to universities for a number of groups. The target groups were socially and economically disadvantaged people, Aboriginal and Torres Strait Islander people, women (especially in higher degrees and fields traditionally difficult for women to enter), people from non-English-speaking backgrounds, people in rural and isolated areas, and (the focus of this book) people with disabilities.

In this paper the Government laid out "Objectives, Targets and Strategies" to improve access to higher education for these groups. In the case of people with disabilities the Objective was "To increase the participation in higher education of people with disabilities", and the Target was "To double the present [1990] commencing enrolments of people with disabilities by 1995, including an improvement in professional and vocationally-oriented courses of 30 per cent by 1995". At the time of writing, data are not available to determine whether these targets have been achieved, though informal opinions indicate that there seems to have been significant movement towards them.

The paper also laid out "Strategies to Achieve the Objective and the Targets". For students with disabilities the strategies were to include provision of:

- Special equipment and facilities;
- Advisers/contact people to help students with disabilities;
- Promoting distance education opportunities;
- Modifying materials and curriculum;
- Flexible timetabling and course requirements; and
- Information to students with disabilities about services available.

The paper, in regard to special equipment and facilities, advised about the need for finding out early in the enrolment stage what the special needs of students with disabilities might be, but was not particularly helpful in other ways; it merely noted that such activities were often expensive and that institutions "could concentrate their resources by specialising in courses for students with a particular kind of disability or related groups of disabilities". (This suggestion would seem to run counter to the notion of providing relatively open access to universities for students with disabilities because it would force students to go to the universities where the facilities were, rather than where the course of their choice was. With limited funding, there will always be in the relatively small Australian higher education sector a tension between the provision of high quality support and implementing it where the students wish to attend, particularly with high cost items such as attendant care, Braille/low vision services, sign language interpreting, etc.) Regarding advisers/contact people the paper noted that "students with disabilities face a range of frustrations and difficulties not experienced by other students" so that advisers or contact people "can help here".

It was also pointed out that greater provision of distance education opportunities and support for students with disabilities within such programs "may be the solution to some problems students with disabilities have, such as physical access and transport", but wisely goes on to note that "distance education will not be the choice of all students with disabilities, particularly those who may wish to remedy the isolation from the community that has resulted from their disabilities". In 1993 the State and Commonwealth governments established the "Open Learning Technology Corporation (OLTC)", one of the major aims of which is to improve access to education for students with disabilities. The Commonwealth Government had earlier commissioned a research study into the possibilities of "open learning" for students with disabilities (better called "flexible learning"; Johnson, 1995), the report of which has been published in summary form as "An Enabling Vision" (OLTC, 1994). A conference centering on this theme was held in early 1995 to assist the OLTC develop a Workplan for its activities for students with disabilities. At the time of writing (September, 1996) little seems to have come of these initiatives.

The Commonwealth Government had earlier established "Open Learning Australia", a consortium of universities which develops and provides distance education opportunities via television, radio and print distribution and in 1994 the beginnings of "OpenNet" which will eventually supply access to the Open Learning courses and the "Infobahn" of the future. It is hoped that several initiatives in flexible learning for students with disabilities at all educational levels will eventually flow from these activities.

With regard to modifying materials and curriculum the paper made the important point that "many materials and teaching processes in the higher education curriculum have been designed without people with disabilities in mind. Institutions should examine their courses to arrange the changes needed to increase their accessibility for students with disabilities, particularly in laboratory and practical work requirements". On flexible timetabling and course requirements the paper made the commonsense point that "for people with disabilities, getting to and from lectures, tutorials and library can be time-consuming and present logistical problems not encountered by non-disabled people" so that "timetabling arrangements be as flexible as possible" and "course requirements, such as completion within a certain time, do not present unnecessary barriers to people with disabilities". Finally, the paper states that information about higher education opportunities and possible sources of support for realising these opportunities are not easily accessed by prospective students with disabilities and so attention should be paid to making necessary information more widely available in a range of accessible formats adapted to the requirements of people with disabilities.

Another important initiative of the Commonwealth Government was to fund a survey by Andrews and Smith (1992) of the "Additional Costs of Education and Training for People with Disabilities" in universities and technical and further education colleges. This extensive survey gives valuable data on the costs to universities of providing various kinds of services to people with disabilities, and new data on the numbers of such people in universities which indicated that their numbers had increased considerably since the Ashby, Taylor & Robinson report in 1985. Detailed costing of various services were provided which (not unexpectedly) found sign interpreting, vision impairment and attendant care services to be most expensive. Andrews and Smith recommended a hierarchy of three groups of costs of disability services to university providers. The first level was "relatively 'low cost'" services which best fit within the generic services provided by all universities, and which could be considered to be of "no special cost" to universities because they could be absorbed into their regular student services provisions. Level Two could be provided by universities from their own funds, "but their nature and cost suggest they be regarded as 'additional' services which should be considered for special funding". Of central importance for people with disabilities and disability service providers was their recommendation about Level Three support which was of such high cost that special assistance as regards funding should be provided either to the university or the student. The former Labor Government had not acted on these recommendations and the new Liberal Government has not yet announced its intentions in this regard. Students with disabilities and disability service providers await some movement by the Government on the important issues raised by the Report.

Government funding programs

During the Labor Government period this policy statement was followed by a number of initiatives in equity programs and policies, as well as incentive funding via grants for specific targets through the "Higher Education Equity Program (HEEP)" to which universities may make bids to set up programs for people in equity target groups based upon the priorities in the university's published Equity Plan. Two models have been used for providing funds under this program. Typically, in the first, funds would be granted to a project to undertake specific support programs for designated equity target groups. A requirement of funding of programs under this model was that the university granted funds for a particular program will continue that program from its own recurrent grant after the end of HEEP funding (typically for a minimum of three years for major programs). A number of programs for students with disabilities has been established through this funding that might not have been able to be put in place without it (e.g. the Deaf Student Support Program at Griffith University). In the more recent model, universities are given a grant based largely upon past performance in achieving equity targets and each university may then determine what projects it will fund in line with its own priorities in its Equity Plan. As noted further below, this latter model has led to some complaints that "the rich get richer", and weaker programs are not provided with funds to improve their performance. Another feature of the latter model has been the funding of consortia of universities (typically in convenient geographical locations) to undertake larger programs across regions. The "Tertiary Initiatives for People with Disabilities (TIPD)" funded to the eight state universities in Queensland is one example of such a program. TIPD has received about Aus$400,000 to provide models of regional access and outreach services, development of models for employment of graduates with disabilities, and other activities which none of the universities individually might have been unable to undertake. It seems likely that the "consortium model" of joint activity will be further developed in coming years. (The new Commonwealth Government in its 1996-97 Budget announced the continuation of the HEEP Program, though what the future may bring is as yet not clear.)

Universities are also now required to establish and provide to the Government "Equity Plans" which specify their commitment to aspects of service to the equity target groups mentioned above and to report annually on the outcomes of their attempts to implement these plans. A certain amount of pressure on universities to do better in equity programs has thus been generated by the availability of funds (Aus\$5.14 million in 1994), and also the publication by the Government of university Equity Plans (or the lack thereof!; Beazley, 1993) and notice being taken of activities (and good performance financially rewarded) both in the HEEP funding and in the "Quality Assessment Program" for universities instituted by the Government which has led to the publication of quasi-"league tables" in this area. There has been some controversy over both these programs and their impact on university disability services. Under both types of funding universities considered to have good programs for, say, disabled students, are rewarded with more funds, but those who do not do so well, receive less or no funding. While this undoubtedly has encouraged some universities to do better for students with disabilities than they might otherwise have done, it has been pointed out that some universities have not done much at all, in part at least because of lack of funds, and that the funding might be better targeted to the lower performing universities in order to assist them to improve their programs. No resolution to this debate is in sight at the time of writing.

National guidelines for university disability services

In 1994 the Commonwealth Government National Board of Employment, Education and Training (1994a) commissioned the present writer to develop a set of "Guidelines for Disability Services in Higher Education". This document, while its guidelines are not mandatory and cannot be imposed upon universities, will hopefully have an impact in making available to universities examples of good practice for disability services from Australia and around the world. The document provides Guidelines on Outreach and Recruitment, Admissions and Enrolment, Support Programs, Physical Access, Personal Assistance and Vocational Guidance and Placement. It also surveys some "special issues" such as whether disability support services should be separate or included in generic student services (coming down eventually in favour of inclusion in generic services wherever possible, but noting that some needs are so specialist and/or intensive in demand that they should be specially provided for). It also comments on the "ownership" of programs and notes that students should have as much control as possible over their support programs, surveys some aspects of the use of nomenclature in the area which may be offensive to people with disabilities, and stresses the importance of "getting in early" to provide for students with disabilities' needs, the difficulty of which can be minimized if courses and materials are designed from the beginning with students with disabilities in mind.

The document also provides extensive appendices with models of policy statements, disability committee constitutions, outreach programs, "Disability Disclosure" forms, assessment guidelines, campus and building physical accessibility checklists, models for interpreting and notetaking services and other aspects of university disability services.

In 1996, the Commonwealth Department of Employment, Education, Training and Youth Affairs (DEETYA) commissioned the present writer and three colleagues to develop a "Code of Best Practice" for disability services in tertiary education. Again, this Code will not be mandatory, but universities and colleges will be asked to subscribe to it and commit themselves to its implementation over a period of time. At the same time, the Ministerial Council on Employment, Education, Training and Youth Affairs (MCEETYA; the Council of the Commonwealth and State ministers in these areas) has set up a Working Party to develop "Disability Standards" for education at all levels, including universities, which will be promulgated under the Commonwealth Disability Discrimination Act. These Standards will set required service and access levels and will be legally enforceable under the provisions of the Act, thus for the first time providing real teeth for people with disabilities and service providers to demand their rightful opportunities. All concerned are looking forward with interest to the publication of the Standards.

Aspects of the present scene

In its "Summary Report: Equity in Higher Education: Institutional Equity Plans, 1992-94 Triennium" (Beazley, 1993) the Commonwealth Government reported on the impact of its policy urgings and funding incentives upon programs for the designated equity target groups. As far as students with disabilities were concerned 34 of the then 37 universities reported to the government that they considered this group a priority in their equity planning and service provision. It is not possible to gauge the extent or quality of such programs from the data now available, but at the least it would seem that most universities are now aware of the need to have plans and programs in place for students with disabilities. Despite this, only 29 of the 34 universities reporting students with disabilities as an equity priority area had support programs for such students in place! Eighteen of them reported that they had special admissions arrangements for students with disabilities. Thirty of them reported that they provided special equipment and facilities, but again the extent of such provisions is not known. Anecdotal evidence would suggest that in some cases the level of such support is quite minimal. Twenty and 22 universities respectively reported that they had awareness and staff development programs in place, but only ten stated that they had policies about the critical area of modification of curriculum and materials and only 14 had flexible course arrangements; a state of affairs which would be a serious impediment to equity of access for many students with disabilities. The difficulty of providing services in the disability area may be indexed by the fact that while 34 universities declared people with disabilities a priority equity area, only nine of them achieved the target numbers they had set themselves.

These findings would indicate that while one might be wary about the quality of some of them, disability support programs have proliferated and improved considerably in the environment described above. Before 1989 coherent policy driven disability support programs in universities were not common; rather, disability services were often marginal in university activities, those that existed being the result of dedicated work by interested individuals or lobby groups rather than a result of deliberate planning. People with disabilities have many "horror stories" to tell of their attempts to enter universities in that era (Power & Stephens, 1990; Watson & O'Connor, 1995) and of the struggle they had to obtain equitable access to academic and social life of the university if they did get in. As a result, people with disabilities were greatly under represented in universities at this time (for example, a 1985 survey found that while people with physical disabilities represented seven per cent of the Australian population, the proportion of students with any disabilities in all post-secondary institutions was only 0.17 per cent; Ashby, Taylor & Robinson, 1985).

This situation slowly began to change in the late 1980s, partly as a result of the Government reports, policy and program initiatives outlined above, partly because of increased militancy by people with disabilities themselves in asserting their rights, partly because of the passage by Commonwealth and most State Parliaments of a series of "Anti-Discrimination" Acts which prohibited discrimination on the grounds of disability against people in their attempts to access community benefits, including, inter alia, education, and partly because community attitudes and understanding of the needs and capacities of people with disabilities were slowly changing towards increased acceptance of their right to higher education and their ability to benefit from it, with consequent benefits to themselves and the community generally, both socially and economically.

Within this context, the present situation for people with disabilities attempting to enter higher education is considerably better than it was ten years ago, but it is still far from ideal. A small number of universities have direct entry where students apply to the university itself, but in most states there is a co-ordinated system for applications where prospective students apply to a central body which allocates places in university courses in that state on the basis of criteria supplied by each university, decided mostly by the intra-statewide ranking of all students from the results of examinations during the final or last two years of high school, with non-immediate school leavers' scores being intercalated using complex formulae. In some states special provision is made to raise the score of people with disabilities if they meet a number of criteria about being disadvantaged in their academic progress by their disabilities. Some universities also have "special entry" provisions under which people with disabilities can apply for individual consideration for entry to courses, even if they do not meet the usual entry criteria. Increasingly, the central state admissions agencies are co-operating with university disability service providers by including a question/s on the application form about the presence of disabilities for which the applicant may require special assistance. In Queensland, for example, the people so self-identifying are forwarded by the Queensland Tertiary Admissions Centre a confidential detailed questionnaire about their needs which is sent on return to the Disability Service Provider in their chosen universities. This enables the Service to contact the student early to determine how needs may best be met before disabilities become a barrier to obtaining full benefit from the academic and social life of the university.

One of the most obvious manifestations of all this activity in recent years has been the development by several individual universities and consortia of (mostly large metropolitan) universities of numerous documents outlining "good practice" in developing policy and providing disability services. Models for policy and practice are now widely available, as are resources for staff development activities (especially strategies for better teaching and consulting for students with disabilities), notetaker training and deployment, alternative assessment procedures, campus accessibility checklists, outreach, admissions and enrolment procedures, etc. A number of documents, videotapes and other materials for use in outreach programs to assist students with disabilities in becoming aware of the opportunities available for them have been produced in several states. Statewide networks of providers and consumers of disability services exist in most states and a national organisation of disability service providers has been established, a newsletter regularly distributed and a national computer network set up (O'Connor, 1994). Three national conferences ("Pathways") of consumers and providers have been successfully held and another is planned for late 1998.

One University's activities

Griffith University in suburban Brisbane, the capital city of the state of Queensland (population about one million), is typical of the middle-size universities established in the expansion period of the 1970s with a typical range of faculties (except medicine). It expanded very rapidly in the "Dawkins Reform" era mentioned above (1989-93) from 6,000 students on one campus in a basically "science/humanities" university in 1988 to 20,000 students on five campuses in 1996. It now includes several professional schools (among them education, leisure management, engineering, law, psychology, nursing and other health sciences), the Queensland Conservatorium of Music and the Queensland College of Art, as well as continuing a wide range of sciences and humanities offerings. Although these mergers have placed some strains on the infrastructure of the University, it is generally conceded to have emerged from them very well, being considerably strengthened by the additions of the past few years.

Griffith University is a good example of the impact that the Government policies and programs outlined above have had on university disability service provisions. It is generally considered to be one of the leading universities in Australia in making support available for students with disabilities, having several innovative programs supported by either Government seeding money or its own recurrent funds. In 1993 it received the second-highest funding nation-wide from the HEEP program under the rewards for excellence in equity programming mentioned above.

Its programs are driven by an explicit policy document widely circulated in the University, implemented by a central Office of Disability Services which provides direct assistance to students with disabilities from a central Disability Support Fund, and by close Faculty consideration of the needs of students with disabilities through a designated Disability Liaison Officer in every Faculty. Policy and program oversight has recently been revamped by making the "Disability Advisory Committee" responsible to the Equity Committee of the University Council which oversees all equity activities of the University. (The Disability Advisory Committee, membership of which includes students and staff with disabilities, is responsible for policy and programming for both students and staff with disabilities.) An active program of upgrading buildings to provide adequate access for students with disabilities is under way and new buildings meet or exceed national standards for access.

At the direct student service level the University provides interpreting, tutorial and aids support for deaf and hard of hearing students, a notetaking service for any students who require it temporarily or permanently, Braille and large-print and screen magnification facilities for blind and low vision students, curriculum development and alternative assessment practices advice to staff, and counselling support from a specialist Disability Support Officer. Two electric scooters have recently been bought to enable students to move more readily around nominated campuses. An active staff development program on issues to do with better support for students with disabilities exists. In most areas efforts are made to "mainstream" support services into those provided for all students, though it is acknowledged that some services are so specialist that special provisions need to be made.

Conclusion

From the above survey it can be seen that the Australian university system has become more accessible to students with disabilities than it was a decade ago, more resources and funding for disability programs are available, more programs are in place, technological support is increasingly easing difficulties for students, "flexible learning" programs and distance education are providing more opportunities than previously and some universities are providing quite well for their students with disabilities. Nevertheless, more needs to be done. People with disabilities are still under represented in universities and public and university awareness and outreach programs must continue to point out opportunities. Funding is still limited and the issue of who shall receive the funding (program and/or student) has yet to be resolved. With goodwill and increased awareness these issues may be solved in the next decade to provide even more opportunities for students with disabilities to benefit from all aspects of a university education.

References

Andrews, R. & Smith, J. (1992), *Additional Costs of Education and Training for People with Disabilities.* Department of Employment, Education and Training, Canberra.

Ashby, G., Taylor, J. & Robinson, M. (1985), *Assistance for Disabled Students in Post-secondary Education.* Brisbane College of Advanced Education, Brisbane.

Beazley, K. (1993), *Equity in Higher Education: A Summary Report: Institutional Equity Plans 1992-94 Triennium.* Department of Employment, Education and Training, Canberra.

Dawkins, J. (1988), *Higher Education: A Policy Statement.* Department of Employment, Education and Training, Canberra.

Dawkins, J. (1990), *A Fair Chance for All: Higher Education That's Within Everyone's Reach.* Department of Employment, Education and Training, Canberra.

Johnson, R. (1995), 'Open Learning: Its role in the future of education'. In *Proceedings of the Open Learning Technology Corporation's "Enabling Vision 95" Conference.* Open Learning Technology Corporation, Adelaide.

National Board of Employment, Education and Training (1994a), *Guidelines for Disability Services in Higher Education.* Australian Government Publishing Service, Canberra.

National Board of Employment, Education and Training (1994b), *Resource Implications of the Introduction of Good Strategies in Higher Education for Disadvantaged Students*.   Australian Government Publishing Service, Canberra.

O'Connor, B. (1994), *Students with Disabilities in Post-secondary Education: An Australian Perspective on Policies and Practices*. Paper delivered at the International Conference on Excellence and Equity in Education, Toronto.

Open Learning Technology Corporation (1994), *An Enabling Vision*. The Open Learning Technology Corporation, Adelaide.

Power, D. & Stephens, M. (1990), *Outreach and Enrolment Programs for Disabled Students in Higher Education in Australia*.   National Board of Employment, Education and Training, Canberra.

Watson, R. & O'Connor, B. (1995), *Pushing or Riding Brooms: Clearing or Cluttering Pathways to Tertiary Studies for Students with Disabilities*. Paper delivered at the Conference: Ensuring an Inclusive Curriculum: From Practice to Vision, Brisbane.

2 "A fair go" - the impact of the Disability Discrimination Act (1992) on tertiary education in Australia

Jenny Shaw

Introduction

The Australian Human Rights and Equal Opportunity Commission's Disability Discrimination Act (1992) - commonly known as the DDA, was enacted in 1992 to eliminate "as far as possible discrimination against people with a disability with respect to employment; education; accommodations; access to premises; the provision of goods, facilities and services; transportation; land transactions; administration of Commonwealth laws and programs; and implementation of existing laws" (DDA 3(a), pp. 20-28). The premise of the Act is that people with a disability have "the same fundamental rights" and "the same rights to equality before the law" as others (DDA 3(b) and (c)). The DDA has had a significant impact for service providers within tertiary institutions but it is still questionable how important the DDA, as a tool for change, is, to tertiary students with a disability.

This chapter has been written from the perspective, experiences and observations of a disability service provider within the Australian tertiary education sector. It is not written from an academic nor legal perspective, but rather from first hand experiences of working within the tertiary education culture to provide an inclusive educational experience for students with a disability. This chapter will introduce readers to the history of the enactment of the Australian DDA, the culture in which it was placed and the impact the DDA has had on the Australian tertiary education sector.

Unlike the Americans with Disabilities Act (ADA), on which the Australian act is based, the DDA was initiated and proclaimed by the Commonwealth government - one could say for the good of people with a disability. It did not rise out of grass roots disability organisations. It was not discussed, there was no public debate, it was not publicised and, in fact, most people, even those with a disability, did not know it was happening. This is in contrast to the way in which the ADA came into being. It can be said that the Australian DDA was, and is still, to a certain extent, not owned by people with a disability. It was given to people with a disability as a gift, to assist them to get "a fair go" ... herein lies the difference between the culture of the U.S. and Australia and the effectiveness of disability discrimination legislation.

"A fair go"

Allow me to explain the significance of what it means to get "a fair go". The Australian "fair go" culture is based on the reliance and assumption that society will look after our well being and that everyone will get an even slice of the cake. To ensure that this happens ultimately means that Australians, including people with a disability, are dependant on the good will of others, namely government politics and private organisations, to ensure that they get "an even slice of the cake". Getting "an even slice of the cake" is not seen as a natural right. Add the assumptions and attitudinal factors that the general community have about disability, which are discussed shortly, to this equation and we then need to ask, do Australian people with a disability get "a fair go" and do they get "an even slice of the cake"?

The "fair go" culture is vastly different from the U.S. civil rights based culture from which the ADA was conceived and grew, before being transplanted via the DDA to Australia. Consequently the way in which the DDA has been accepted and utilised by Australian society and in this particular case, the tertiary education sector, is quite different from the way in which the ADA was embraced by the citizens and tertiary education institutions of the U.S.

Before going any further let us now ask some questions - what impact does the Australian "fair go" culture have on the lives of Australians with a disability? What perceptions and beliefs about disability does our society hold? How inclusive and empowering is our culture? In other words how well are people with a disability cared for, how appropriate are society's attitudes and goodwill, and how much of the cake do people with a disability actually get?

Disabled people in Australian society

People with a disability in Australia, as in most countries of the world, are marginalised and suffer extraordinary levels of exclusion, prejudice and misunderstanding; and of course poverty. Nancy Crewe in her article "Freedom for Disabled People - the Right to Choose" says, "no law forbids people in wheelchairs to ride public buses or to enter public buildings for example, but the steps at their entrances serve as more effective barricades than laws." (p. 358). Jenny Morris reiterates this point in her book "Pride Against Prejudice". Here she says

> we receive so many messages from the non disabled world that we are not wanted, that we are considered less than human ... the very physical environment tells us we don't belong. It tells us that we aren't wanted in the places that non disabled people spend their lives - their homes, their schools and colleges, their workplaces, their leisure venues (p. 26).

Morris goes on to say that there are a number of assumptions that the non disabled world holds about people with a disability. For people with disabilities:

> lives are burden and barely worth living ... that we crave to be normal and whole ... that we don't have any real or significant experiences ... that we desire to emulate and achieve normal behaviour and appearances in all things ... and ... that we should put up with any inconvenience, discomfort or indignity in order to participate in normal activities and events. And this will somehow 'do us good' (pp. 19-21).

One of the most profound assumptions that she identifies is that for people with disabilities the "only true scale of merit and success is to be judged by the standards of the non disabled world." Further to this she states there is an assumption that ... "normal is right, to be desired and aspired to ... The more energy and time we spend on over achieving and compensatory activity that imitates as closely as possible 'normal' standards, the more people are reassured that 'normal' equals right" (p. 101).

We also need to remember that people with disabilities are members of this same society as the rest of us, and they too can internalise and project similar attitudes towards disability issues. How often do we see people rely on charitable organisations, rather than pursuing strategies which will increase their choices and inclusive lifestyle options?

Returning now to the Australian Disability Discrimination Act (1992) - yet again this reflected the same notion that others will provide and care for us. The "fair go" notion was at play once again - this time disguised as a gift from the Australian Commonwealth government. Along with the passing of this legislation the Commonwealth government allocated a mere Aus$500,000 budget to meet the staffing and education expenses for the whole of Australia. This alone has been a major restriction in limiting the effectiveness of this important piece of human rights legislation. It has also created huge time delays for the resolution of claims of discrimination - sometimes up to 3 years.

The responsibility for the administration of the DDA lies with the Australian Human Rights and Equal Opportunity Commission (HREOC).   HREOC is currently undergoing some major changes as a result of the announcements made in the Commonwealth government's May 1997 budget. These changes include HREOC's funding over the next four years being slashed by 43 per cent, which will lead to staff numbers being cut by a third. Specific commissioners will be abolished and stricter legal procedures will be introduced requiring the use of the costly Federal Court system to effect decisions that cannot be reached via the conciliation process. We now need to ask whether people with disabilities will be able to afford to use the DDA to effect change and redress discrimination. Will a generic commissioner be able to represent disability issues without falling into the entrenched societal assumptions that have always limited people with a disability?

Tertiary education in Australia

Keeping in mind the notion of the Australian "fair go" culture, combined with the universal prejudices, assumptions and attitudes towards people with disabilities, let us now transfer this understanding onto the tertiary education sector. Students with disabilities enter the tertiary education system with a locus of responsibility for their educational and social experiences lying firmly with the often inappropriate goodwill of others - living in accord with society's expectations of them as people with disabilities. Too often students with disabilities encourage others to make decisions for them or even to allow them to take responsibility for their educational experience. I recall an extreme example of the way in which a person with a disability will often allow others to control their lives. A student came to me for advice about what subjects he should select for the coming academic year. I encouraged him to look at the most ridiculous combination of subjects. Subjects that I knew were of no interest to him. He looked at me quizzically and asked why he had to do those subjects. The reason I did this was to provoke him and to highlight the need for him to make the decision, not me nor anyone else. His decision needed to be based on his interests and career options. This student was pathetically dependant on others to lead his life for him and to pick up the pieces after him. His mother organised his life, his study routine, his time extensions and was the ever loving, always available mother.

Let us now turn our attention to the impact that the DDA has had on tertiary institutions. In general I would say that change has only recently begun, mostly initiated by complaints of discrimination and in very few cases the writing of institutional Action Plans. Only one complaint from a student with a disability against a tertiary institution has gone through to a public hearing, which enabled a judgement to be made and a precedent set. The result of this case now demands that students with a disability are able to graduate and progress like their peers. All other complaints against institutions have been resolved and thus the results generally remain confidential.

Provision within the DDA allows service providers, which includes tertiary institutions, to submit to HREOC, an Action Plan - a strategic, proactive document that promotes equity for people with disabilities. Action Plans are voluntary and will be taken into account if the service provider claims "unjustifiable hardship" in making accommodations for a person with a disability. An Action Plan must include:

- policies and programs designed to achieve and objects of the Act;
- communication of these policies and programs throughout the organisation;
- review of organisational practices to identify any discriminatory practices;
- mechanisms to evaluate the success of these policies and programs, including setting targets and goals;
- appointing personnel responsible for implementing the Action Plan; and
- any other measures consistent with the objects of the Act.
  (Parsons & Tait, 1994, p.11).

To date only two out of the 29 Victorian tertiary education providers have lodged an Action Plan with HREOC. Of the two institutions which have written and submitted Action Plans, both agreed that the educational impact in reviewing and challenging institutional policies and practices has had a significant impact in changing attitudes towards people with disabilities.

The general lack of knowledge and impact about the DDA from within the majority of the tertiary education community has meant that many direct and indirect discriminatory practices have yet to change. There is an assumption in Australia that because students with disabilities are able to access higher education then institutions are meeting their human rights obligations. As we all know, getting in and getting an equitable educational experience are two different things (for more details see Parsons & Tait, 1994, p. 11).

Direct and indirect discrimination

The DDA has defined disability in a very broad way and identifies two aspects of discrimination where breeches in the provision of access to education may occur. The aspects are termed "Direct Discrimination" and "Indirect Discrimination". "Direct Discrimination" is defined by the Act, as where, "the discriminator treats, or proposes to treat, the aggrieved person less favourably in circumstances that are the same, or not materially different, from those that the discriminator treats, or would treat, a person without a disability" (Parsons & Tait, 1994, p. 92). "Indirect Discrimination" is defined by the Act, as where,

> the discriminator requires the aggrieved person to comply with the requirement or condition with which a substantially higher proportion of persons without the disability comply or are able to comply; and which is not reasonably having regard to the circumstances of the case; and with which the aggrieved person does not or is not able to comply. (ibid., p. 92).

In relation to education, the Act states that

> it is unlawful for an educational body to discriminate against a student on the grounds of the student's disability or a disability of any of the student's associates; by refusing or failing to accept the person's application for admission as a student; or in the terms or conditions on which it is prepared to admit the person as a student, or, by denying the student access, to any benefits provided by the educational authority; or by expelling the student; or by subjecting the student to any other detriment. (ibid., p. 113).

It is my belief that most tertiary institutions understand what "Direct Discrimination" is, and infrequently directly discriminate against people or students with a disability. However, there is still a vast amount of work that needs to be done to ensure that "Indirect" discriminatory practices are addressed.

Shane Carroll, a Senior Lecturer in Law at the Victoria University of Technology states that "indirect discrimination is about disadvantage. It is brought about by treatment which appears to be neutral and fair, but which has an unequal or unreasonable effect, or impact, in the circumstances" (Carroll, 1992). Indirect discrimination is built into the system by being embedded within the organisational structure. Chris Ronalds, quoted in Carroll's paper, observed that as early as 1979 "Elimination (of indirect discrimination) requires a certain amount of restructuring of the existing system. It is obviously the most important type of discrimination to eliminate as the ramifications of any restructuring are much wider and deeper than the solution of an individual complaint". In fact, discriminatory practices are built into systems without any deliberate intent - although this does not deny that they have severe consequences and that they might be more difficult to eliminate.

Indirect discriminatory practices can be found in everyday activities on all tertiary education campuses. Does the institutional promotional material come in different formats? Is the application process accessible to all? Are the sporting and entertainment venues and activities accessible? Are lecture theatres accessible to both students and staff? Is the computer laboratory accessible and can the computers be accessed by a student who uses a wheelchair? Are the pathways around the campuses built with the correct gradient? The list is endless and can only be resolved when an institution takes an inclusive view to providing an accessible campus and program for its entire community. No longer is it appropriate to play "catch up" tactics.

Anti-discrimination and the role of the university Disability Liaison Officer

Let us now look at the ramifications of the DDA from the perspectives of the Disability Liaison Officer (DLO). Nearly all Australian tertiary institutions have employed at least one person to provide services and support for their enrolled students with disabilities - they are generally know as Disability Liaison Officers. The DLO has a multitude of roles. Apart from the provision of services for students with disabilities, the DLO is also a "watchdog" for physical access problems. They must ensure that the courses are presented in formats that are readily accessible to people with a variety of disabilities, that the assessment procedures are appropriate, that the selection and enrolment process are free of discriminatory practices and that academic and general staff are aware of disability related issues. They must be able to write reports and submissions, collate statistics, undertake research and represent and be answerable to their institution on disability related issues - a formidable task for any employee.

Prior to the enactment of the DDA most Disability Liaison Officers would have seen themselves as advocates for students with disabilities, requesting their institutions to be more responsive to the specific requirements of these students. Since the introduction of the DDA there has been a strong shift from a moral obligation to a rights based approach to the provision of an equitable educational experience. DLOs are now starting to be seen as an integral part of the institution and are beginning to be referred to for advice about compliance with the Act to ensure that students' rights are being met. The DDA is becoming a powerful tool, and in some cases a weapon, in the move towards the systemic change needed to create a more inclusive educational culture.

On interviewing six Victorian DLOs about the impact of the DDA on their work practises and not their institutions, all indicated that the DDA had changed their status. As one DLO said, "I am now part of the institution - I am no longer an outsider. It has given me more leverage, which doesn't require me to be righteous and indignant". All DLOs expressed concern about the DDA being a top down approach to change, yet again reiterating the way in which the DDA came about. The general consensus from DLOs was that there had only been one discrimination case against a university and its funding authority taken to HREOC that has challenged the core of the problems - the responsibility to ensure that adequate funding be available so that students with disabilities can study at the same rate of progress as their peers and can access the support in all aspects of university life, including post graduate studies.

The case described above came from HREOC earlier this year - 1997. Three students claimed discrimination by a tertiary institution and the Department of Employment, Education, Training and Youth Affairs (DEETYA). One undergraduate student had been restricted to support for only 60 per cent of his requirements. The other two students were post graduate students who were further down the prioritised list of support. This case was settled by conciliation the day before it was due to go to a public hearing. The case took 2½ years to get to this stage and would have set a precedent for the whole of Australia if the students had won at the hearing ... but alas, they capitulated at the last moment! One could ask why, but when you consider the Australian culture, demanding that your rights be met is at odds with the pervasive "fair go" culture.

When students are asked what is the most difficult issue about accessing university life the most common comment is - the lack of understanding that the staff have about disability and their attitudes towards them as students.

Remember the assumptions that society has towards people with disabilities, raised before! Those same assumptions and prejudices exist within our institutions of higher education. Students with disabilities are still not automatically seen as the part of the general community who will want to access tertiary education. The situation is changing, but slowly, then frequently only after being stung by a DDA claim, which understandably speeds up the process no end.

As indirect discriminatory practices are the cornerstone of the majority of the workload of DLOs it is necessary to challenge these practices in an informed and strategic manner. To prove indirect discrimination requires specific information to present a case. Moira Rayner, a current Commissioner with the Human Rights and Equal Opportunity Commission states that it

... requires access to statistical data, in many cases, because it is necessary to compare "proportions" of, on one hand, the number of people without the disability who can comply, as a proportion of the relevant base group without the disability; and the number of people with a disability who can comply with the requirement expressed as a proportion of the relevant base group of people with a disability. This requires organisation, confidence and resources (Rayner, 1995, p. 21).

DEEYTA, who provide the funding for higher education, only began collecting statistics, about the number of students with disabilities currently enrolled in the higher education system in the year 1995. Until then, issues relating to students with disabilities have always been put in the "too hard basket" and left unaddressed.

It is imperative that tertiary education be totally accessible to people with disabilities for many reasons and not just as a protection against discrimination. As Louise Granville says,

Education is an important area of public policy. This is evident not only in its ability to impact on an individual's quality of life in the form of facilitating access to employment and services, but also in its interconnectedness with other key policy spheres - e.g. income security and economic policy - which affect the ultimate health and well being of any community (Granville, 1995, p. 1).

For people with disabilities to get into decision and policy making employment requires a standard of education that only the tertiary system can provide. Once senior government and private company positions are occupied by people with disabilities, only then will we see generic policies that truly embrace disability.

Rayner concludes in her article "Fighting for the Rights"

... as McHugh J. commented in Waters V Public Transport Corporation (1991) EOC 92-390, anti-discrimination laws are not, and ought not be used as a political weapon for obtaining services for people with disabilities. Complaints of indirect discrimination in important areas of public service delivery - especially public transport and education - are a useful way of focusing attention on the issue, but one still based on fault by a particular respondent. That will probably not deter disability groups from taking up the Commissioner's exhortation, in Chapter 12 of her manual, "to use the Disability Discrimination Act ambitiously" (Rayner, 1995, p. 21).

This is an optimistic exhortation especially under the current weight of cultural expectations.

As long as students with disabilities remain collectively silent, entrenched attitudes and assumptions will not change. Disability Liaison Officers are only one voice in the system - other voices need to be raised - voices of student unions, past, present and prospective students with disabilities, friends and families need to form an alliance and be prepared to challenge the system to do better for them and demand that students with disabilities do indeed get "A Fair Go".

References

Anderson, E. (1995), *Issues and Barriers in Post Graduate Education for People who have a Disability*, DEET Co-operative Project, Deakin University, Geelong, Victoria.

Carroll, S. (1992), *Expanding Notions of Indirect Discrimination*, Disability, Discrimination and Justice conference, Griffith University, Brisbane, Queensland.

Granville, L. (1995), *Enabling Policies - Accessing Higher Education: the Socio-legal Response*, Outer Urban Research and Policy Unit.

Kosa, J. & Zola, I. (eds) (1975), *Poverty and Health*, Harvard University Press, Cambridge, Massachusetts.

Moodie, G. (1996), *A New Test for the Info Age*, The Australian, Sydney, New South Wales.

Morris, J. (1991), *Pride Against Prejudice*, The Women's Press, London.

Parsons, I. (1994), *Oliver Twist Has Asked for More*, Villamanta Publishing Services, Geelong, Victoria.

Parsons, I. & Tait, S. (1994), *Acting Against Disability Discrimination*, Villamanta Publishing Services, Geelong, Victoria

Rayner, M. (1995), *Fighting for the Right, Using the Law to Achieve Equality*, paper presented 4th International Abilympics Conference, Perth, Western Australia.

Rioux, M. & Back, M. (ed.) (1994), *Disability is not Measles*, L'Institute Roeher, Ontario.

Shapiro, J. (1993), *No Pity*, Times Books, New York.

Tait, S. (1995), *A User Guide to the Disability Discrimination Act*, Villamanta Publishing Service, Geelong, Victoria.

Tucker, B. (1994), 'Overview of the DDA and Comparison with the ADA', *Australian Disability Review*, Canberra.

Zola, I. (1983), *Independent Living for Physically Disabled People*, Jossey-Bass Publishers, San Francisco.

3 Supporting students with disabilities in Belgium

Myriam Van Acker

Introduction

Perhaps the first point to note when reading this chapter is that Belgium consists of two distinct communities. These are the French-speaking community and the Flemish speakers. What follows below considers the situation in the latter, based in Flanders towards the north and east of the country.

Within Flanders the system of higher education has two types. The "short type" involves a study period of three years. The "long type" takes either four or five years. Within the system, students who complete the first cycle (after two or three years) can be awarded a "candidature" diploma whilst successful completion of the second cycle (between two and four years) leads to a "licentiate" or the formal recognition as a chemist, engineer, or medical doctor. Each "type" has different possibilities in terms of courses. Students choosing either path can pursue courses in architecture, audio-visual and artistic studies, biotechnology, commerce, drama, industrial technology, management, and music. However only within the "short type" cycle is it possible to study paramedical sciences, social work, and teacher training. Education at this level is less theoretical than in the other path and is aimed at specific professions or occupations. Exclusive to the "long type" path are courses in applied linguistics and product development. The focus here is more theoretical and scientific involving the students' acquisition of high level skills. The "long type" education is not organised within the universities.

Within Flanders there are four universities which offer the two cycles. These are located in Antwerp, Brussels, Ghent, and Leuven. In addition there are three others (Brussels, Diepenbeck, and Kortrijk) which offer only the first cycle. All have different regulations and statutes since some are state universities and others are free and autonomous.

Entry to higher education follows after leaving high school. In Flanders, high schools are grouped into a number of networks Catholic schools have 12 networks which cover schools on 99 different sites. Autonomous high schools have five networks involving 42 sites. Provincial high schools have four networks bringing together 16 sites.   City high schools combine 14 sites into three networks.

To gain entry to university to study courses other than those in architecture and engineering, applicants must have a diploma of secondary education. (For these two subjects, there are entry examinations.) There is no selection process nor are there restrictions on the numbers entering. Applicants can choose where they would like to study. They can obtain a grant from the government although the amount available is determined by their parents' financial situation, particularly the value of their home if they own it.

Policy in higher education for students with disabilities

Within the schools sector, particular attention is given to the needs of disabled pupils.   They may study in special schools, segregated from mainstream provision, or they may be in mainstream schools, sometimes with the assistance of a support teacher. In recent times, when the high schools were grouped into networks, they were given additional funding by the government to organise services for pupils with special educational needs. The Roman Catholic network of high schools decide to give particular attention to the needs of learners with disabilities and there is a programme planed to make structural changes to their buildings. The policy on changes is actually discussed by a committee which has representatives from the schools and higher education (including the University of Leuven). All aspects of inclusion are considered not only physical access to facilities.   Thus, consideration is given to access to the curriculum and to teaching and learning materials for students with sensory impairments. The first planned programme of this kind began in 1995.

Turning now to look at the universities, they have received funding from the government for over 30 years to cover a number of aspects of student support: refectories, halls of residence, guidance and counselling services, etc. However, there has been no money allocated specifically for measures to support students with disabilities. The only additional funding which is available can be used by some individual students. This is provided by the Flanders Fund for the Social Integration of Disabled People. The finance available is restricted to students with sensory impairments. However, the scheme is not really set up in relation to higher education and so very few students make applications to it.   Much depends on the goodwill of the individual universities. At the time of writing (1997) three universities have developed a service for students with disabilities: the Free University of Brussels, the Catholic University of Leuven, and the University of Ghent. At these institutions, there is some kind of financial support from the student services section. Sometimes, there is a member of staff whose role and responsibilities includes working with students with disabilities; usually this is only on a part-time basis. The member of staff might be from the Faculty (academic) or from the central services. Over time, those who are involved in this work have built up a network of contacts including colleagues working in social services, housing departments, medical services, etc.

This lack of a centrally organised structure and financial system means that, in effect, those universities which do try to organise some support, are punishing themselves financially. The situation becomes even more serious since students with disabilities begin to apply only to those institutions where they know that some services exist. This puts additional pressures on the available services - meanwhile the other institutions continue to take no action to develop their provision. In this respect, some kind of national policy is needed desperately.

Provision and financial support

Like all other students, those with disabilities can apply for a grant to support their studies. When a grant is awarded, it is possible to apply for subsidised living accommodation in the halls of residence of a university. In addition, all students can apply for a range of other beneficial financial arrangements including additional family allowances and refunds of medical prescription charges. Students with disabilities can obtain information about assistive technology free of charge from VLICHT (the Information and Communication Centre of Flanders for Disability and Technology - which itself receives funds from the Flanders Fund for the Social Integration of Disabled People mentioned already). VLICHT has created a data base about technical aids and special equipment and provides information about costs, dealers, etc.

Students with disabilities can also have any costs of help with study repaid by the Ministry of Education. This covers the costs of transcription of learning materials into Braille format, the use of readers to record materials on to cassettes, and the costs of transport from home to the university. The Flanders Fund can be used to pay for the costs of adapting living accommodation although these are only covered if the alterations are made at the home address. If similar changes have to be made to the living accommodation at the university, the costs are never reimbursed. Students with sensory impairments can obtain "pedagogical support" up to a maximum of 30 hours per week. However, there are difficulties with this. Payments are rather low; there are also questions about the knowledge and expertise of the individual providing the support since this has to be in the same field of study as that of the student. Most students with disabilities prefer to try to get support from their tutors rather than looking outside the university since they feel that the tutors have more up-to-date knowledge of their subject.

Students with disabilities are unable to secure finances to pay for personal assistance, especially if they need care on a continuous 24 hour basis. Deaf students cannot be reimbursed for the costs of interpreters. Where alterations to buildings have to be made to allow access for a particular students, the costs cannot be reclaimed. Incidentally, in connection with this, a national law was passed in 1975 which promoted improved access to public buildings although no sanctions are applied for non-compliance. It is not really clear whether the universities are classed as public buildings. Recently, cases have come to court and legal actions taken about inaccessible buildings. However, resorting to law is not the answer. It would be more preferable if the community would face up to its responsibilities and accept that without the allocation of additional financial resources, problems associated with physical access to buildings will not be solved.

Supporting students with disabilities: a case study of the Catholic University of Leuven

The most celebrated development at the University of Leuven is the Working Group for Disabled Students (to be referred to as the Working Group from here on). The aim of the Working Group is to ensure that students with disabilities are included in all activities, not just those associated with studying. The origins of the Working Group go back to 1973 and from the beginning, support has been organised around co-ordination and the involvement of a range of different services working together co-operatively. The Working Group is a part of the university's student services/study advice service. In 1997 the Working Group comprised an interdisciplinary team of nine members of staff: two part-time members of the university staff (a psychologist who gives advice about study skills and who is also the Director of the university student services section, and a social worker) plus seven other members representing a range of services and sections who are delegated to participate according to the needs of the students at a particular time. They provide advice about courses and study skills, and about technical aids to study. The Working Group is responsible also for the organisation of living accommodation and the system for continuous personal assistance required by some students with disabilities. Students can obtain information about finances, career opportunities, and also - and very importantly - about student social life outside the classroom. The co-ordinator of the Working Group is the person with official responsibility for issues concerning examinations. There are two important regulations in the university's overall examination regulations which apply to students with disabilities. The first states that the form of the examination (e.g. oral, written) must always be adapted to meet the physical needs of students with disabilities. The second makes provision for special time allowances for students with disabilities.

More than 100 students each year make contact with the Working Group seeking some kind of support. Contact is voluntary - students with disabilities do not have to make themselves known to the Working Group. Once contact has been made, support is available for the entire period of the course. Of those who do identify themselves, around 40 per cent have impaired mobility, 30 per cent have sensory impairments, 20 per cent some kind of serious health problems, and 10 per cent have specific learning difficulties (e.g. dyslexia). The last-mentioned are supported (for example by identifying the condition and recommending the action needed) by the Department of Pedagogical Sciences.

In 1981, due in part to the initiative taken by the Working Group, a survey was undertaken within the University of all aspects of the University community which could be of benefit to disabled people. The inventory which resulted from the survey was presented at a two-day symposium. Given that the University of Leuven has 5,000 staff and 27,000 students, this exercise and the public presentation were very useful in raising awareness and allowing people to come together to establish links. Since 1981, the inventory has been updated on a regular basis. One development was the creation of a permanent inter-faculty research group which is concerned with problems faced by people with disabilities. The Working Group is represented in this forum.

In summary the Working Group is founded upon three principles. Firstly, the team of people involved is interdisciplinary and comprises staff from existing services who have acquired knowledge and expertise in supporting students with disabilities. Secondly, the team works with a cross-section of the university which is as broad as possible to ensure that as many people as possible are aware of disability. Thirdly, all tasks which do require to be undertaken by trained professional staff are carried out by them. However, there are some tasks which can be performed by others and this is encouraged and supported by the Working Group. Some of these tasks are associated with daily living in a community. This is the focus of the next section.

Providing personal assistance for students with disabilities

Fellow students comprise an exceptionally important group of people who have been stimulated to take on greater involvement with their disabled peers. It was because of a lack of personal assistants for students with disabilities that the Working Group started to recruit other students to work as volunteers. Today, with the development of adapted residential facilities (60 accessible rooms) in the Romero-huis near to the town centre and the university, there are groups of around 15 students who live together for the full academic year with a disabled student and who provide assistance without payment on a rota basis for 24 hours every day of the week. In early 1997 there were 220 volunteers participating in these support groups and their numbers continue to grow. Being a member of a support group brings priority when applying for accommodation in university halls of residence.

From the point of view of the Working Group, this form of living is very important. Students with disabilities are living in the company of their peers. They learn how to make their needs known (sometimes with the help of some assertiveness training). They view the support group as a form of personal assistance lent to them by a number of individuals. From the perspective of the non-disabled students, they are confronted in a realistic manner with a person with a disability and they can then rid themselves of any pre-conceived notions. The assistants are recruited through appeals, always in different faculties, in order to achieve the maximum impact and raising of awareness. Sometimes, students join the scheme having heard about it from their friends. The assistance provided involves the performing of a limited number of tasks since having 15 people available means that the work can be spread out and shared. The atmosphere within the groups is congenial and co-operative. This seems to be very attractive for some students. Where the individual student with a disability requires some kind of medical assistance (for example with personal hygiene) this is provided by a team of trained nurses. Where the assistance is with travel to and from classes, this is provided by classmates.

Some continuing concerns

On its own initiative, within the confines of its own specific context, and with a combination of external sponsorship and its own financial resources, the University of Leuven has managed to develop a support and advice system which has functioned to the satisfaction of the many students with disabilities who have completed their studies already. However, the programme described above is not the answer to all the problems. A volunteer system like the one at Leuven cannot be used everywhere. Other institutions will have to devise their own solutions to meet their own particular needs.

A major issue which remains is the choice of study programme open to students with disabilities. Specialists in the field of working with disabled people in general do not seem to have grasped a good understanding of the specific demands of higher education. Careers advisers, who have much to offer students, do seem to lack knowledge and experience of the opportunities and obstacles encountered by students with disabilities both in relation to access to university and then later after graduation when the students with disabilities are searching for further training or jobs. Staff working in careers advisory services might need a programme of awareness raising to eliminate some of their own prejudices and pre-conceptions; they might also need to find out more about the technology available to support people with disabilities. At the stage before students enter university, the careers advisers might need to find out more about the courses themselves - the content of the syllabus, the style of learning and teaching, the formal requirements for assessment and examinations.   On the other hand, perhaps this is the responsibility of a member of the university staff, ideally the person with whom the students with disabilities have first contact. If this task is carried out by a member of the generic service, some additional training might be needed.

Another issue of concern is related to access to learning and teaching for students with visual impairments. Transcribing material into Braille is still too time-consuming. Even where a battery of scanners is available, the demands are difficult to meet on time. The result of this is that by the time the material is ready for the student to use, the course has moved on. Perhaps this problem needs to be tackled in a more fundamental way since the ability to use a library with its catalogues, etc., independently is a key skill associated with life in a university. If some students have to rely on the intervention of a third party (and perhaps pre-selection of materials) the question remains as to whether this group of students are missing an essential part of a university education. Research commissioned by the European Community is being carried out at the University of Leuven relating to the process of making printed sources accessible more quickly in electronic form. For example, a legal reference book containing more than 1,000 pages was made accessible to a blind student using a portable personal computer within three hours. Sadly this was only an experiment and has not yet become the norm.

Students who are deaf or hard of hearing are the subject of our most serious concern. The massive flow of important verbal communication within the higher education context constitutes a permanent difficulty for these students. Whilst some staff might empathise easily with this difficulty, their responsibility for teaching large groups means that often they do not have the time available to give it their full consideration. Discussions about the use of interpreters continue although there are some fundamental questions such as where are the interpreters with the skills necessary for this work to be found? This has become the first priority for the Working Group.

Older difficulties remain. Attention has been given always to making buildings physically accessible. This is a major problem for older universities. The

University of Leuven was founded in 1475; its present facilities reflect 500 years of building history. Recent developments (for example science laboratories) are designed to be fully accessible. The older buildings near to the town centre still present problems of access - although there is sometimes a side entrance which can be used or, with good advance notice, classes can be relocated to more accessible rooms. There is plenty to be done still.

Conclusions

It is becoming ever more apparent that the provision of adequate facilities and services for students with disabilities is based on supplemental funding and additional training. Given the range of issue which meeting the needs of this group of students embraces, the availability of a competent, multidisciplinary team of staff is essential. Once such a team has been assembled, for policy to progress, the work of the team must be co-ordinated. Attention needs to be given to their training needs. Their knowledge and skills cannot be developed entirely through experience "on the job". This is a matter which has yet to be tackled. Given that there are others working to support students with disabilities in the other universities, a programme to provide such training on a regional basis (or even a national basis given the limited size of Flanders) would seems sensible. In terms of moving beyond adequate policy and provision and moving towards policy and provision which is of high quality, this might be the next stage in Belgium.

References

Van Acker, M. (1995), *Gehandicapte Studenten in het Hoger Onderwijs*, L.A.P.P. Tijdschrift van de Leuvense Afgestudeerden in de Psychologie en Pedagogiek: Leuven.

Van Acker, M. (1995), 'Hoger Onderwijs voor Gehandicapte' Studenten: niet verworven, wel in opmars, *Helioscope* (March), Brussels.

Van Acker, M. (1995), *Gehandicpate Studenten aan de Katholik*, Univeristeit Leuven, Leuvense Perspectieve, Leuven.

4 Policy and provision of support services in Canadian universities

Joan Wolforth

Over the past 15 years a significant increase has occurred in the number of students with disabilities attending post-secondary educational institutions in Canada. A parallel increase in services which support this group has also occurred. Students with disabilities are now likely to be found studying in both academic and professional programmes at all universities in Canada. This development, which at this point has been the subject of very little research, is probably the result of a number of factors. The manner in which support services are delivered has also evolved over the years. Originally service tended to be provided on an essentially ad hoc basis to an individual student. There is now a movement towards a more systematic approach, with an emphasis on student rights, the development of professional standards of service provision, and the passage of institutional policies which encourage complete inclusion within the university community.

There has been, as yet, no systematic attempt to gather statistics on the number of students who attend Canadian universities and who have a disability. Hill (1992) reported the results of a survey of 27 Canadian universities and found that during the 1989-90 academic year there were 2,223 students registered as receiving support services because of a disability. This survey included all large universities, but only 39 per cent of degree granting institutions. Therefore the actual number receiving service may have been significantly higher. Tousignant (1989) pointed out in a survey of Quebec universities, that it was difficult to obtain accurate enrolment figures because there was no common definition of disability being used to classify students, and no uniform method of identifying them. However in 1988-89, there were 537 post-secondary students receiving financial assistance from the Quebec Ministry of Education, of which 224 were studying at the university level. Many of the remaining 313 were likely to have been in university preparatory programmes at the college level, and would therefore have moved into the university sector within a few years. As an example of one university, Tousignant (1989) reported that in 1988-9 McGill

University was serving 78 students with identified disabilities. By May 1997 there were 245 students registered with the Office for Students with Disabilities, a 214 per cent increase in nine years. At the western end of the country, the University of British Columbia (D.R.C. 1995), reported an increase in students using their service from 122 students in Fall 1994 to 187 in Spring 1995. In Ontario, the province with the largest number of universities, Wilchesky (1986) had earlier described similar trends.

The impact of legislation

The increase in numbers of students is probably the result of several factors though there is no doubt that the general movement to a system of inclusive education at the school level has resulted in students graduating from high school, not only better prepared to continue to move the next level of education, but also with the expectation that they will do so. Education policy is a provincial responsibility in Canada and this movement away from the notion of special schooling for children with disabilities has been supported by provincial legislation such as the 1989 "Education Act" (Law 107) in Quebec, and the similar 1980 "Act to Amend the Education Act" (Law 82) in Ontario (see Smith and Foster (1996) for an excellent summary of Canadian provincial educational legislation for children with special educational needs).

These acts reflect a more general movement in society towards recognising the existence of minority groups and the protection of their human rights. In Canada, Section 15 of the "Constitution Act" passed in 1982 as the Canadian Charter for Rights and Freedoms, proclaimed the equality of all people under the law and protected individuals against discrimination on the basis of disability. Stainton (1994) pointed out that Canada is the only western country to offer this specific protection in a constitutional document. Human rights legislation at the provincial level across the country offers equivalent protection for institutions that come under the jurisdiction of provincial governments, and it is the provincial charters of rights and freedoms which generally apply to the university sector.

This legislative action should be seen within the context of a growth in awareness of human rights in general, and much of the impetus for Canadian changes probably came from events surrounding the Civil Rights movement in the United States in the 1960s and the United Nations Declaration of Human Rights in the 1970s. The United Nations Declaration on the Rights of Disabled Persons (1975), and the 1981 United Nations sponsored "Year of the Disabled" specifically encouraged societies to look at the situation of people with disabilities. These events also supported the development of a disability rights movement which began to demand support of all kinds for the inclusion of people with disabilities into mainstream society. (Hahn, 1985; Oliver, 1990; Shapiro, 1993; Nagler, 1993; Hahn, 1993; Barnes and Oliver, 1995.)

The movement from a traditional medical model of disability to the social model proposed by the disability rights movement, profoundly affects how disability is perceived. This perspective views the environment and institutions created by society as disabling and moves the focus from the functional limitations of the individual onto the responsibility of society to accommodate the individual. In the United States, the Americans with Disabilities Act (1990) enshrined in law many of the principles of this perspective. Though Canadian legislation addresses the issue in the broader context of equal rights for all, many of the specific changes demanded in the United States especially in the area of adaptations to manufactured goods, the provision of physical access criteria, and in the university sector (paralleling U.S. legislation, Section 504 of the Rehabilitation Act), accommodations for students with disabilities, have begun to be established in Canada as well.

In some ways, general human rights legislation may be preferable to legislation designed to target a specific group in society because, in the long run, it is harder to repeal the legislation which covers all groups than it is one that targets only one group. The ADA, while it has for the most part had positive effects on the process of inclusion, has not been universally seen as positive even by the disability movement itself (Pfeiffer, 1996) and may have created a potential for backlash. This may have been the cause of recent action taken by a major U.S. university against students with disabilities which decimated a highly respected service department (Shaw, 1997). Many Canadian service providers feel that under a general framework of equal rights they can act in a more creative and professional manner in the way they provide service for their students. They are not restricted by heavily prescriptive legislation with such distinctions as mandated and non-mandated services and are not as hindered by constant concern about the latest court ruling (Shaw, 1997). In fact the institution's legal obligation is to ensure the student receives "reasonable accommodation" a general term which has taken on a more specific connotation in the university sector in terms of providing services the student requires to succeed. In Quebec two phrases developed by the Ministry of Education have proved particularly useful, in defining parameters of inclusion, "neither discrimination nor privilege" and "a student has the right to admission without discrimination and the student also has the right to fail" (DGEC, Quebec, 1987).

Seeing equal rights legislation as preferable to legislation which defines specific rights for a specific group is not a universally accepted viewpoint of course, and the disability movement particularly in Ontario has been lobbying for an Ontarians with Disabilities Act, and ultimately federal legislation which would apply to the entire country. However, provincial human rights legislation has been used successfully by students to create change at the university level, and universities are generally aware that they risk a human rights complaint if they are seen to discriminate in any way against students who have a disability. This is a contrast to the situation in the United Kingdom where educational institutions are excluded from the already rather weak Disability Discrimination Act (1995) and where students can be refused entry to an institution on the grounds of, for example, inaccessible premises or lack of appropriate service (Parker and Myers, 1997). Such actions in Canada would result in a successful human rights complaint against the institution. It is also in contrast to Australia where, according to Jenny Shaw (1997) discriminatory actions on the part of universities have received little challenge from students using their Disability Discrimination Act (1993). In Canada access to post-secondary education for qualified students with disabilities seems to have become an accepted principle without significant numbers of court challenges and with legislation based on basic principles of human rights.

The growth in student numbers

Wilchesky (1986) hypothesised that one factor behind the increase in the number of students with disabilities entering universities was a drop in student numbers and a consequent push to recruit students from non-traditional groups. Some institutions such as York University, do have differential admission policies for students with disabilities but others do not. In Quebec, for example, students who have a hearing impairment are permitted to enter Francophone universities (universities where the language of instruction is French) with a lower grade on the compulsory French language entrance exam. This is in response to research which shows that these students consistently score lower on measures of French language proficiency. At McGill, however, a Quebec Anglophone university (language of instruction is mainly English), there are no special admission standards for applicants with disabilities and no affirmative action policy to attract these students. All students are considered for admission on the basis of their academic record, and since admission standards are highly competitive, especially in faculties such as Medicine and Law, students registered with the Office for Students with Disabilities are, without doubt, academically competitive with their peers.

The provision of service may itself account for some of the apparent increase in identified students, since before special services were established, institutions may have been unaware of the presence of, in particular, students with invisible disabilities such as learning disabilities and chronic medical conditions. Even so, there seems to be a consensus that a real increase of students with all disabilities has occurred, and while there are few concrete statistics available for the country as a whole, there is considerable anecdotal evidence to support this fact. This trend in Canada is paralleled by similar trends in the United States, Europe and Australia (Aune, 1993; Hartman, 1994).

Funding strategies

Adequate funding mechanisms have been of critical importance in encouraging the increase in numbers. Following recommendations suggested by Wesley (1988), the Government of Ontario led the way nationally when in 1990 it began to ensure that its universities received sufficient targeted funding to provide adequate service to students with disabilities. These grants were based, not on the number of students using the service, but on the total full-time students enrolment of the university. This resulted in large universities such as the University of Toronto receiving significant sums of money specifically earmarked for the provision of service. The service provision at the university level built on an already well established system at the college level, and the end result has been a rapid expansion in the number of services available to Ontario students and in the number of professionals providing those services.

In other provinces, such as British Columbia, the provincial governments include funding provisions for students with disabilities in global university budgets, always a vulnerable way to ensure students and services receive the intended support. In Quebec each university receives targeted funding from the provincial government based loosely on the number of students with disabilities it serves.

In a framework reminiscent of the British model of funding through Local Education Authorities, eligible students in Quebec can also receive individual funding to cover the cost of services such as notetaking and sign language interpretation, together with grants to purchase specialised equipment. This funding is available to qualified applicants (those with a verified disability) without the restriction of being a recipient of financial aid and whether the student is studying full or part-time, a not an insignificant provision since many students must study part-time for reasons relating to their disability. Financial assistance to cover living costs is also available to eligible students irrespective of their course load. Quebec students are also supported when they move on to postgraduate study. This is frequently not the case for students from other provinces. The Quebec system is the most generous in the country for eligible students. However eligibility requirements are strictly defined in terms of degree of functional limitation, and students with learning disabilities are, at this time, completely excluded from the programme. These students are however served, particularly by the Anglophone universities, from the institutions' own resources. A project is under way, funded by the Quebec Ministry of Education, to set up criteria so that these students can be funded. One major stumbling block is the absence of adequate testing instruments in French with which to diagnose such students. Lack of support for these students is in contravention of the Quebec Charter of Human Rights but so far the government's stand has gone unchallenged.

In provinces other than Quebec eligible students at the undergraduate level are frequently funded through the Vocational Rehabilitation Service for payment of direct services. This support is only available at the undergraduate level. In 1996, in provinces other than Quebec, the Federal Government made funds available to the provinces through transfer payments to the Canada Student Loan system for students with disabilities. Students at both the graduate and undergraduate levels who receive provincial financial assistance can apply for up to Can$3000 from Special Opportunities Grants to cover the cost of special services and equipment. This programme is of mixed usefulness because only those students eligible for financial aid may apply, and in some jurisdictions such services are already provided by the institution through other funding. However, in a province such as Alberta, where little targeted funding seems to be available, these grants may be the only way for a student to defray some of the costs of a service such as attendant care. Ontario and Saskatchewan add an additional Can$2000 per eligible student to the Can$3000 of available federal funds. No matter which Canadian university they study at, students remain residents of their home province for the purposes of funding service provision. Funding differences between provinces have implications for the inter-provincial mobility of students with disabilities and they may have less opportunity than others to study outside their home province (Wolforth, 1995).

Identifying students with disabilities

No university in Canada is able, under human rights provisions, to demand that students identify themselves as having a disability before admission. Some universities, such as the University of British Columbia and Memorial University in Newfoundland, have a voluntary declaration of disability on their application forms. Others include information on special services in acceptance packages and in university publications such as calendars and liaison information. For example, at McGill each accepted student receives a "Welcome Book" which, among general information about the university, includes information on the Office for Students with Disabilities and encourages students to identify themselves to the Director as soon as they accept a place at the university. This allows the student and the Office to plan for the transition into university and to set up special service provision such as sign language interpreters and notetakers. Formalised transition planning is widespread in the United States where it is covered under legislative requirements and there is a large literature on transition programmes. At this point, this is less systematically developed in Canada though all institutions provide support and information for new students.

It would appear that there is probably universal acceptance in Canada that students are responsible for self-identification if they wish to receive service. Normally, students meet with a service provider who determines with them the types of service they will require based on their knowledge of their own condition and the provider's knowledge of the university environment. Increasingly students are arriving from high school or college with an Individual Educational Plan (IEP) which sets out accommodations provided at previous levels of education and the service providers develop an IEP at the university level though not all providers may find it useful to follow this framework. There is no system comparable to the British "Access Centres". Assessment of student need is completed as part of the intake process with the service provider. The student is generally responsible for providing appropriate documentation to support the declaration of disability, though some universities do provide assessment for learning disabilities.

Providing services

Most Canadian universities now have in place a person designated to oversee support for students with disabilities, though not all these positions are full-time and some service providers fill several roles in the university. Hill (1992) found that 100 per cent of large institutions which responded to her survey (n = 15) and 66 per cent of smaller institutions (n = 12) had a service provider in place. However, service providers across the country were numerous enough by June 1997 to bring to fruition informal liaisons of earlier years to form the Canadian Association of Disability Service Providers in Post-Secondary Education. At the time of writing, the association is still gathering enrolment forms from across the country, so final membership numbers are not available. It is estimated that around 500 people are likely to be interested in this group. A list-serve for post-secondary service providers (CSNNET) established in 1996 had over 100 subscribers a year later, and has been the forum for much lively discussion. Canadian membership in the Association for Higher Education and Disability, an American organisation of service providers, rose from around 25 in 1985 to 85 in 1997. This is certainly not representative of the total number of Canadian service providers since membership is voluntary. In Quebec, for example, only 25 per cent are members of this organisation.

As discussed earlier, in Canada there is no formal legislative framework which directs how service should be delivered to students or what those services should consist of. Yet, contacts with colleagues across the country, together with the perusal of numerous manuals, handbooks and other materials developed by services at many universities, show a remarkable uniformity of level and organisation of service provision. Actual services promised to students would appear to be fairly consistently classified into one of five categories of disability: those who have various degrees of visual impairment; those who have various degrees of hearing impairment; those who have various degrees of orthopaedic impairment; those who have a learning disability (dyslexia etc.); and those who have a chronic medical condition (including those with mental health conditions). The types of services provided to students with disabilities are naturally determined by the nature of the disability itself. The accommodations are designed to ensure that institutional barriers, both architectural and institutional, do not prevent students from attaining their academic potential. They are therefore not designed to give privilege or advantage, but to ensure that the student can complete academic requirements under conditions which are equivalent to those provided for all students.

Once appropriate accommodations have been agreed to by both the provider and the student, different courses of action take place depending on the institution. Some institutions send letters directly to students' tutors detailing the accommodations required; others leave the student to do this alone and provide no documentation; others provide detailed documentation but give it to the student to pass to the tutor. For example, at McGill, students receive a letter addressed to each tutor confirming their registration with the service and giving general information on what is provided for students, and more specific information on the category of disability in which this student is included. The students then deliver these letters to their tutors and arrange to meet in private to discuss their specific needs. With this method, the tutor is provided with information on a type of disability but the student remains in control of how much personal information the tutor receives. This approach seem to satisfy the suggestion by Fitchen et al (1988), based on their research into the interactions between students and teachers that, "students should take the initiative to establish contact and dialogue with their tutors" (p.17). The tutor is invited in the letter to call the Director of the service for further clarification of any information. Few actually do, which seems to imply that students and tutors are doing well at sharing information. The majority of students seem to receive the co-operation they require from their tutors without further intervention by the Director.

Most universities attempt to accommodate to all situations presented by students with disabilities including students with temporary disabilities, within the academic and financial constraints of the institution. There is usually no blanket determination of service provision on the basis of stereotypical characteristics of a particular disability. The main purpose of an office for students with disabilities is to ensure that students who are eligible to do so, receive appropriate accommodations so that they can fulfil the academic objectives of their courses. In terms of evaluation of academic work, students are judged by the same standards as their peers but may achieve the objectives under alternative conditions. For example they may need to write their exams in a separate room and they may need to use a computer and extended time. (See Appendix 4.1 for a typical list of services offered by universities). An exciting recent development has been the beginning of work by, in the United States, the Association on Higher Education and Disability (Shaw, McGuire, and Madaus, 1997), and in Canada, the National Educational Association of Disabled Students, to begin the address the issue of national standards of service provision. Provided these standards aim at "best practice" objectives and do not attempt to be so inclusive that, in effect, they become minimum standards of practice, they should be helpful in judging which institutions are really committed to the inclusion of students who have a disability.

Strategies of service provision

Normally universities began by providing service to all disability categories from one service area, a pan-disability approach. As numbers and funding have improved, some institutions have moved to establish separate departments for students with a particular disability. For instance York University has separate departments for students who have a learning disability, those with a psychiatric disability, and those with a physical disability. The University of Toronto, and the University of Alberta have large, distinct departments which offer comprehensive service provision for students who have a learning disability. Carleton University in Ottawa has established an excellent service for students with orthopaedic problems who require attendant care. This includes a well supported residency programme. York University and University of Waterloo in Ontario also have excellent attendant care service which reach out to students in the community beyond the university. In another model, the Atlantic Centre at St Mary's University in Halifax, Nova Scotia, has a mandate to act as a centre of expertise and provide service and support to other universities in the region. However this arrangement of disseminating service from a central institution has not prevented neighbouring universities such as Dalhousie from developing a complementary level of service provision for its own students.

A number of writers (McLoughlin, 1982; Albert and Fairweather, 1990; Schuh and Veltman, 1991: Van Meter, 1993; O'Connor and Watson, 1994), have addressed the issue of how best to deliver service to students with disabilities. Early rehabilitation models of service delivery often emphasised the expertise of the service provider, which forced the student into the role of passive, grateful recipient of expertise. A more acceptable model should be one which emphasises and encourages independent action and growth of self-esteem. Current procedures in Canada encourage the student and the service provider to become partners in the service provision process. They are not yet at a point where Van Meter's (1993) proposed model of service delivery the "Integrated Access Model" could be achieved. She proposed a step beyond current models and suggested that the whole institution should be involved in service provision, so that the student interacts with each appropriate part of the enterprise, leaving the service provider to play the role of advisor to all parties. In fact, O'Connor et al. (1994) argued that specialist offices, unlike generic service provision, tend to highlight difference among students and discourage notions of inclusion. Such a model of service provision would seem to be a laudable goal to aim for, and there is no doubt that it is to the advantage of both the student and the service provider that service provision should be de-centralised throughout the university. However it is doubtful at this point that sufficient expertise is available at most institutions to provide for this generic approach. The educational expertise, and potential consequent levels of attitudinal change towards students with disabilities which would be necessary throughout entire institutions, may not yet have been achieved. Albert and Fairweather (1990) give some fairly straight forward examples of what can happen to students if decentralisation of service provision occurs before suitable structures are in place. Jarrow (1997) infers that the field has developed a specific body of knowledge and skills that will continue to be indispensable to post-secondary institutions. This is certainly the case in most Canadian universities.

Policy statement

Hill (1994), after surveying Canadian students, recommended that universities develop written policies to safeguard the rights of students with disabilities. Fichten (1995), in stressing the important role of such policies, pointed out the systemic and individual *hidden* barriers that can exist in institutions and which can prevent the success of students who have disabilities. "These reflect attitudes, values, thoughts, feelings, and actions of various groups of people:

administrators, tutors, service providers, decision makers in government, publicly funded organisations and private industry, family members, and the medical community - and, of course non-disabled students and students with disabilities" (Fitchen, 1995, p. 16).

She described how institutions can discourage students from applying by defining insurmountable admissions criteria. Even if admitted, students have received limited access to needed equipment and other accommodations. The appointment of a low status service provider who has no expertise or multiple responsibilities, can inhibit the access to, or the development of a service, as can a service centre in an inaccessible location. Unco-operative tutors can prevent access to information and damage self-esteem, and a system which functions by determining accommodations on a case-by-case basis rather than on the basis of institutional policy can also prevent students from receiving the assistance that they require.

Over the past three years a trend has emerged as universities have begun to do this. Walsh and Hardy (1997) in co-operation with colleagues across the country have collected and analysed policies which are currently in place. They reported this year that 45 universities (60 per cent) currently have such policies, 25 of these being Senate policies, that is, passed by the highest academic body in the institution. These policies range in form from general statements of support to those which guarantee specific student rights, and define lines of responsibility for their implementation. Such policies not only serve the purpose of a public commitment towards these students, they also ensure that the institution as a whole is accountable for that commitment, not just the designated service provider. Students seem to feel both welcomed and empowered by the implementation of such policies. Superficially, some Canadian policies resemble the Disability Statements recently produced in the United Kingdom and filed with the Higher Education Funding Council. However their objective goes beyond merely stating what is available in each institution, since the thorough ones, at least, are designed to be operationalised. Once they are passed by university Senates, frequently an arduous task rife with political negotiation, they are also not easily rescinded as can be the case with British Disability Statements.

The role of disabled students in developing policy and provision

Students themselves have also been active in ensuring the development of support within institutions. The National Educational Association of Disabled Students (NEADS) was founded in 1986 and holds a biannual conference attended by both students and service providers. They have initiated a number of useful projects in support of students and work closely with government agencies representing the views of their constituency. Student groups have also developed at the local level, Able York, and Access McGill being examples of this, and at the provincial level with groups such as the British Columbia Educational Association of Disabled Students (BCEADS) and the Association Québecoise des Etudiants Handicapés au Postsecondaire (AQEHPS). The Canadian Federation of Students also has a students with disabilities constituency group.

Conclusion

Despite the general increase in numbers of persons with disabilities attending university, and despite increased levels of service provision for them, this population would still seem to be proportionately under-represented in the university population. In a 1991 survey, Statistics Canada reported a discrepancy between the percentage of persons without disabilities who have a university degree (13 per cent) and the percentage with a disability who have such a degree (6 per cent). Yet as Fichten (1995) pointed out, higher education for people with disabilities seems to be directly related to higher levels of employment, greater job satisfaction, and more job security than is experienced by those without such an education. There is also a dearth of information on the success rates of students with disabilities, either in terms of statistics on the numbers of students who successfully complete university programmes, or on their rates of admission into graduate programmes, or their integration into the work force. As Jarrow forthrightly asserted, "we must take time, now, to document the success of our programs and our students. Only then are our students with disabilities assured that their immediate opportunities will translate into long term gains!" (Jarrow, 1992, p. 7). Let us hope that we have the time, the will, and the institutional and financial support to do so.

References

Albert, J. and Fairweather, J. (1990), 'Effective organisation of post-secondary services for students with disabilities', *Journal of College Student Development*, 31, pp. 445-453.

Aune, B. (1993), 'Report on an international conference on disability in higher education', *Journal of Post-secondary Education and Disability*, 10, pp. 27-35.

Barnes, C. and Oliver, M. (1995), 'Disability rights: rhetoric and reality in the U.K.', *Disability and Society*, 10, pp. 111-116.

DGEC (Direction générale l'enseignement collegial), (1987), *L'intégration à l'enseignement collégial des élèves handicapés: Problématique et mesures,* Quebec.

Disability Resource Centre, U.B.C. (1995), 'Newsletter', 4, (2), p. 7.

Fichten, C., Amsel, R., Bourdon, C. and Creti, L. (1988), 'Interaction between college students with physical disabilities and their professors', *Journal of Applied Rehabilitation Counselling,* 19, pp. 13-20.

Fichten, C. (1995), 'Success in post-secondary education', *Rehabilitation Digest,* 25, pp. 16-21.

Hahn, H. (1985), 'Towards a politics of disability: definition, disciplines and policies', *Social Science Journal,* 22, pp. 87-105.

Hahn, H, (1993), 'The politics of physical differences: disability and discrimination', in Nagler, M. (ed.), *Perspectives on Disability,* pp. 37-42. Palo Alto: Health Markets Research.

Hartman, R. (1994), 'Disability on campus: ADA reaffirms section 504', *Recruitment Admission, and Students with Disabilities,* pp. iv-v. HEATH Resource Centre, Washington, D.C.

Hill, J.L. (1992), 'Accessibility: students with disabilities at universities in Canada', *The Canadian Journal of Higher Education,* XXII, pp. 48-83.

Hill, J.L. (1994), 'Speaking out: perceptions of students with disabilities at Canadian universities regarding institutional policies', *Journal of Post-secondary Education and Disability,* 11, pp. 1-14.

Jarrow, J. (1992), 'Research: Persons with disabilities in post-secondary education', *Access to Post-secondary Education for Persons with Disabilities. Research Forum Proceedings,* pp. 3-7. U.B.C. Disability Resource Centre.

Jarrow, J. (1997), 'Why do we need professional standards?', *Journal of Post-secondary Education and Disability,* 12, pp. 5-7.

Nagler, M. (1993), 'What it means to be disabled', in Nagler, M. (ed.) *Perspectives on Disability,* pp. 1-3, Palo Alto: Health Markets Research.

McLoughlin, W. (1982), 'Helping the physically handicapped in higher education', *Journal of College Student Personnel,* pp. 240-246.

O'Connor, B. and Watson, R. (1994), 'Students with Disabilities in Post-Secondary Education: An Australian Perspective on Policies and Practices', paper presented at the International Conference on Excellence and Equity in Education, Toronto.

Oliver, M. (1990), *The Politics of Disablement,* London: MacMillan.

Parker, V. and Myers, L. (1997), 'Exploring Best Practice: The Legislative Context of Access to Higher Education for Students with Disabilities', paper presented at the Association of Higher Education and Disability, annual conference, Boston, Mass.

Pfeiffer, D. (1996), '"We won't go back": the ADA on the grass roots level', *Disability and Society,* 11, pp. 271-284.

Schuh, J. and Veltman, G. (9191), 'Application of an ecosystem model to an office of handicapped services', *Journal of College Student Development,* 32, pp. 236-240.

Shapiro, J. (1993), *No Pity,* New York: Random House.

Shaw, J. (1997), 'Indirect Discrimination: Habit or Design?', paper presented at the Association of Higher Education and Disability, annual conference. Boston, Mass.

Shaw, S. (1997), 'Professional standards and a code of ethics for post-secondary disability personnel', *Journal of Higher Education and Disability,* 12, pp. 3-4.

Shaw, S,. McGuire, J. and Madaus, J. (1997), 'Standards of professional practice', *Journal of Post-secondary Education and Disability,* 12, pp. 26-35.

Smith, W. and Foster, W. (1992), *Equal Educational Opportunity for Students with Disabilities,* Montreal: McGill University, Office of Research on Educational Policy.

Stainton, T. (1994), *Autonomy and Social Policy,* Aldershot: Avebury.

Statistics Canada (1991), *Health and Activity Limitation Survey,* Ottawa.

Tousignant, J. (1989), *Les personnes handicapées inscrites dans les universités québecoises,* Quebec: Direction générale de l'enseignement et de la recherche universitaire.

Van Meter, L. (1993), 'A new model for access', *Journal of Post-secondary Education and Disability,* 10, pp. 11-14.

Walsh, R. and Hardy, Donna (1997), 'Research Project on Disability Policies at Canadian Universities', paper presented at the Canadian Association of College and University Student Services, annual conference, Halifax, Nova Scotia.

Wesley, P. (1988), *Access For Disabled Persons to Ontario Universities.* A Report for the Ontario Council on University Affairs.

Wilchesky, M. (1986), *Post-secondary Programmes and Services for Exceptional Persons: North American Trends,* Canadian Symposium on Special Education Issues, Toronto. (ERIC No. ED 294 389).

Wolforth, J. (1995), 'Provincial borders: do they act as an element of systemic discrimination for students with disabilities?', *Canadian Program News,* Spring/Summer, pp. 2-3. Association On Higher Education and Disability.

Appendix 4.1

1.   Students who have a hearing impairment

FM "Phonic Ear" systems on loan.
T.V. Decoder for closed caption videos.
TTY/TDD telephone and answering service.
Amplified phones.
American sign language interpreters.
Oral interpreters.
Notetakers, including computerised C-note system.

2.   Students who have a visual impairment

Books on tape and four-track tape recorders.
Portable "artic" voice synthesisers.
"Visualtek" and "Optelec" CCTVs for enlarged print.
Braille printer.
Braille display keyboard.
"Oscar system" scanner - large print software and screen reader (artic).
"Iris" system scanners and JAWS screen readers ("Dectalk" voice), English and
    French, and JAWS for Windows.
Zoom text large print computers.
Large print and voice access to library data bases.
Talking calculators.
Talking dictionaries.
Braille materials for classroom use etc.
Recorder or "e-text" books, journals articles, course outlines, exams, etc. Liaison
    with R. F.B.
Enlarged printed material/exams.
Extra time for exams.
Library assistance.
Use of campus bus.

3.   Students who have a mobility and/or co-ordination impairment

Scribes for exams.
Use of computers for exams.
"Dragon Dictate" voice recognition software.
Alternative keyboards and input devices.
Use of campus bus.

Preferential parking spaces and rates.
Planning access routes.
Attendant care.
Adapted residence rooms.
Extended time for exams.
Orthopaedic chairs.

4.   Students who have chronic medical conditions

Assistance with time planning for courses.
Special exam arrangements.
Problem solving to accommodate the condition.
Use of campus bus.
Preferential parking places and rates.

5.   Students who have a learning disability

Taped reading material and exams.
Computers with spell checkers and voice.
Talking dictionaries.
Talking calculators.
Proofreading essays.
Proofreading exams.
Extended time for exams.
Exams on tape.
Notetakers in classroom.
Low contrast printing.

General services available to all students who have a disability

Computer laboratory, adaptive technology.
Student resource room and lounge.
Computer room at centre.
Adapted computers and scanners in 10 main libraries.
Tutoring.
Liaison with academic and administrative staff.
Financial aid and scholarship information.
Loan of portable computers.
"Access McGill" student group.
Senate-board Sub-committee on Persons with Disabilities.

5 Canadian universities: the status of persons with disabilities

David A. Leitch

Introduction

The perception of many people working in the field of disabilities is that there have been tremendous gains made recently by persons with disabilities with respect to accessing higher education in Canada. Based on my experiences over the past decade an intuition grew that the gains may not be as great as some people think. The literature was clear that there were few studies in this area and indeed as Jennifer Hill (1992) reported, no Canadian studies existed that looked at the numbers of persons with disabilities in relation to total enrolment figures at Canadian universities. Thus, there seems to be merit in this enquiry. A literature search confirmed Hill's views that studies outside of Statistics Canada do not exist. It is necessary to add here that it is common to find reports of individual organisations speculating on the numbers of persons with disabilities in higher education. Regrettably these organisations do not present any hard data or studies to support their assumptions. It is in part this casual speculation that has prompted this study.

Method

In the spring of 1995, a university graduate was hired to conduct a telephone survey with 47 Canadian universities. His task was to obtain data on the number of persons with disabilities attending their institutions along with total enrolment figures on full and part-time students. The selection of universities was based on the criteria used by the now famous Maclean's magazine survey: *Ranking the Universities: A Measure of Excellence* (see Lewis and Benedict, 1991). Their study included 46 universities. In this study a decision was made to add one additional university, namely a military college, the Royal Military College.

The Maclean's study includes only those universities that grant BA and BSc degrees, offer broadly based programs in the liberal arts and sciences, are independent of affiliation with a larger university and are not restrictive for reasons of religion or profession. Those criteria eliminated many reputable post secondary religious, military, technical, and agricultural institutions (Lewis and Benedict, 1991, p. 12). With the decision made on which universities would be included, the survey proceeded. The following is the exact description of how the survey was conducted and is in the form of a self report by the researcher. The numbers for most of the universities were obtained through the Saint Mary's University telephone directory. The numbers for all of the campuses of the Université de Québec were obtained through their calendars and local area telephone directories.

The researcher said upon reaching the switchboard: "Hi, I am calling from Saint Mary's University in Halifax, Nova Scotia and I would like to speak with the person or department on campus who co-ordinates the services for the physically disabled students."

After being connected to another party, he said, "Hello, my name is ... and I am calling from the Atlantic Centre of Support for Disabled Students at Saint Mary's University in Halifax, Nova Scotia. I am calling on behalf of the Centre's Director, Dr. David Leitch, who is currently doing a paper on access to higher education for physically disabled students. I am conducting a survey on universities across Canada to get a better idea of the number of physically disabled students who attended university in the past year. I have several different categories of physical disabilities and hope that you can give me the number of students who fit each category."

Usually after identifying myself and my purpose the person responding would inform me that they were not the people I want to speak with, "so and so" is and this is their number, or I would be told that I have reached the right person and they would be more than happy to help.

Since the accurateness of the data is pivotal to this study, an appendix is attached, which notes the response of the respective institutions (see Appendix One). The focus of this chapter is on the qualitative data obtained from the telephone contact.

Responses and discussion

Extrapolating from Jennifer Hill's (1991) studies of 27 universities in Canada we could estimate that there were about 3,869 persons with disabilities at Canadian universities in 1992. Our survey indicates approximately 6,890 persons with disabilities at Canadian universities. This represents an estimated increase of 3,021 or 78.03 per cent which appears to be a significant increase.

However, based on a qualitative review of the researcher's experiences and an examination of the sorts of disabilities included in the various categories in this study, I suggest that there are problems with the numbers in use today. I fear that without a critical and candid analysis of the problems, we risk trivialising the concept of persons having disabilities and render as problematic the study of the participation of disabled persons in Canadian universities.

It is also clear and regrettable that when some main offices or departments in a university were contacted they were sometimes uncertain about who was responsible for disabled persons on their campus. This again suggests problems and perhaps even a lack of commitment of the full integration of disabled persons into university.

Secondly, it frequently happened that those responsible for persons with disabilities were providing "off the cuff and/or rough" estimates. They often responded to the researcher with "I think we are not really set up to accommodate persons with disabilities", "here are very rough estimates", "here is my own list", "statistics included everything from wheelchairs to walkers but that I do not know the names of any of the students", etc. When one combines these sorts of responses together with this same respondent's inclination to include somebody with anxiety as a disabled statistic I become less than confident about the data and I suspect that the numbers of persons with legitimate and significant impairments may be lower than we were led to believe. Table 5.1 lists examples of vague responses.

Table 5.1: Examples of responses that indicate a degree of vagueness or lack of cxactness

1. She was unable to break the numbers down or be more specific regarding some of the categories.

2. The numbers that he gave were "very rough estimates ... going by my memory alone as we do not have a central registry".

3. She informed me that they do not have "too many disabled students", but did not elaborate. She did say that there is no way of knowing how many students are registered and that the university is trying to get a policy in place.

4. When asked about student's mobility impairments, he remarked that there were 4 students in this group and when pressed for details, said that they included "everything from wheelchairs to walkers", but that he did

not know any of the students by name.

5.   She did say that the numbers were not up to date and did remark that they categorise disabilities under cognitive, organic, etc.

6.   She was unable to break down the number of mobility impairments or hearing impairments.

7.   She proved extremely hard to get hold of and returned my numerous messages after 3 weeks. She informed me that the Special Needs Association is presently preparing a letter to the university to upgrade all of the services that it provides to students.

8.   However, he was able to give me a "very rough idea" as the University does not keep statistics on the categories we were after.

9.   When she returned my call, I was told that the Registrar's office does not keep these statistics, as the students are not asked to identify any physical disabilities on their applications. She also told me that the Counselling Centre does not keep these statistics.

10.   The Sister was very curt in answering the questions, first insisting that she had already answered these questions and then saying "that the University does not have enough disabled students for us to care about". The answers that she finally gave were from her memory alone. When asked about mobility impaired students, she replied, "Three, I think, or that's all I can recall", and when questioned about deaf students, she replied, "No-no, nothing like that here".

Appendix One lists replies from all universities contacted.

What's in a word?

The greatest concern emanating from this study is the excessive liberty taken with the categorising by nature of disability. Let me elaborate some of the difficulties in point form:

1.   Some co-ordinators and respondents make no distinction between deaf, hearing impaired or hard of hearing.

2.   Some co-ordinators and respondents make no distinction between blind and visually impaired.

3. Some co-ordinators and respondents include a person who walks with a cane as mobility impaired.

4. Under the category "Other" some universities include medical, learning disabled, psychological, psychiatric and temporarily disabled - broken arm.

5. Under the category "Medical", contact persons often included persons with AIDS, persons with chronic fatigue, persons with hand injury, persons with kidney disease, persons with environmental disorders, persons with addiction, persons with disease unknown, persons with allergy, persons with blood dyscrasia, persons needing study skills report and persons organically challenged.

6. In the area of learning disability there is still no uniform or standard set of criteria for inclusion. As James Yesseldyke indicated in 1982 there are currently 57 different definitions in use in educational settings.

7. Sometimes under the category "Other", learning disabled is included and sometimes not.

8. Sometimes under the category "Other", medical problems are included, sometimes they are not.

9. Sometimes under the category "Other", temporarily disabled is included and sometimes not.

10. Universities have not collaborated to standardise the definitions.

The above ten points indicate a dramatic lack of standardisation and contribute to the flawed pictures we currently have of persons with disabilities on university campuses. Essentially one must push for the commitment of government and universities to effect structural changes that will see participation levels of persons with disabilities increase in universities. The first step in effecting this change would be ensuring the availability of more accurate data and standardised recording practices. As far back as 1987 a National Forum on Accessibility to Education in Canada sponsored by the Council of Ministers of Education in Canada talked about this with respect to achieving greater access for disenfranchised groups into higher education. If this august body is sincere then there is much to be done.

A final word or two

Currently there are around 2,300,000 persons with disabilities between the ages 15-64 with disabilities in Canada. An extremely small percentage of these persons are part of the university system. As determined from the present survey in the spring of 1995 there is a mere 0.25 per cent of the present population of persons with disabilities aged 15-64 participating in the 47 Canadian universities surveyed. A comparative figure for the total enrolment of non-persons with disabilities for the same age cohort would be approximately 5.08 per cent or twenty times as many.

At this juncture three responses might be in order. Firstly, we in the field must be more exact. Other disciplines would not tolerate such a lack of refinement of the facts. Secondly, we must recognise that substantial tokenism persists relative to improving accessibility for persons with disabilities. Major structures within society continue to sustain existing inequities. Thirdly, there must be immediate recognition of serious consequences associated with universities independently determining categories, definitions of disabilities, and the criteria which satisfy their constructs of disabilities. We are already moving in a direction that may unwittingly trivialise legitimate disabling conditions. It is time to take stock of the response of institutions of higher education to persons with disabilities. Resources are needed to ensure that there is somebody with the background and experience in the area of disabilities who will be responsible for services and record keeping. Universities in conjunction with government must collaborate in establishing standardisation for the categorisations and criteria for inclusion in these categories. A starting point would be for universities to agree on World Health Organisation's definitions or some variation of the same. It is my feeling that if there were greater representation from disabled groups on the boards of governors of universities then we would see improvement in accessibility for the population of persons with disabilities.

If universities and government are serious about enhancing the participation of persons with disabilities in higher education, then work must commence on creating a Canadian committee of involved persons who would in turn expedite funding for such activities as the creation of a database for tracking the participation of persons with disabilities in higher education.

References

Disabled Persons Commission (1994), *Persons with Disabilities in Nova Scotia: An Overview of 1991 Statistics.*

Hill, J. L. (1992), 'Accessibility: Students with Disabilities in Universities in Canada', *The Canadian Journal of Higher Education,* Vol. xxii - 1.

Leitch, D. (1988), 'Higher Education and the Disabled Person', A paper presented for the Prince Edward Island Council of Disabilities, Charlottetown, P.E.I., Canada.

Lewis, R. & Benedict, M. (1991), 'Ranking the Universities: A Measure of Excellence', *Maclean's Magazine,* October 21, 1995.

Statistics Canada (1991), *Healthy and Activity Limitation Survey.*

Yesseldyke, J. & Algozzine, B. (1982), *Critical Issues in Special and Remedial Education,* Houghton Mifflin Co., New York.

Appendix One

Alberta

1. *Athabasca University*: (i) Switchboard (ii) Registrar (iii) I spoke with Ms ..., Supervisor of Registration at the university. She informed me that their campus is a long distance campus and that all courses are conducted through the mail. Thus, since their applications do not require students to self-identify any physical disabilities, the university does not have any records or information for the survey.

2. *Camrose Lutheran University*: (i) Switchboard (ii) I spoke with Ms ..., Director of Vocational Counselling. She informed me that the university is not really set up to accommodate physically disabled students, i.e. there is only one building on campus that even has an elevator. She identified three mobility impaired students, two permanently disabled, but all three make use of crutches and/or braces; no wheelchairs.

3. *University of Alberta*: (i) Switchboard (ii) Offices of Services for Students with Disabilities (iii) I spoke with Ms ... of the Office of Services. Claiming that she would need to compile the information requested, she faxed a pre-prepared sheet of disabilities and services that the office has done up. The sheet shows how many students in each of their categories as well as the services that were provided for these students.

4. *University of Calgary*: (i) Switchboard (ii) Student Resource Centre (iii) Services for Students with Disabilities. I spoke with Ms ... of the Services for ... She was able to give me the numbers requested from a sheet of their year-end statistics. She was unable to break the numbers down or be more

specific regarding some of the categories. All numbers were of persons making use of the Services office.

5.   *University of Lethbridge*: (i) Switchboard (ii) Student Affairs (iii) Mr ... is the Co-ordinator of the Student Counselling Centre on campus. The numbers that he gave were "very rough estimates ... going by my memory alone as we do not have a central registry".

British Columbia

1.   *Simon Fraser University*: (i) Switchboard (ii) Student Society (iii) Co-ordinator: Student with Disabilities. The numbers that Ms ... gave me were from her own list of clients for the past year. She informed me that they do not have "too many disabled students", but did not elaborate. She did say that there is no way of knowing how many students are registered and that the university is trying to get a policy in place.

2.   *Trinity Western University*: (i) Switchboard (ii) Student Affairs (iii) Counsellor: Student Affairs. The first thing Mr ... mentioned was that the numbers for the past year are low and do not reflect how it usually is. He told me that there were less than 10 students with disabilities in any of their programs. When asked about students with mobility impairments, he remarked that there were four students in this group and when pressed for details, said that they included "everything from wheelchairs to walkers", but that he did not know any of the students by name.

3.   *University of British Columbia*: (i) Switchboard (ii) Disability Resource Centre (iii) Liaison Officer Ms ... was very helpful, but not very talkative. She answered all of the questions on the survey, but did not offer any personal asides or notes. She did say that the numbers were not up to date and did remark that they categorise disabilities under cognitive, organic, etc.

4.   *University of Northern British Columbia*: (i) Switchboard (ii) ... (iii) Career Access Co-ordinator (iv) Co-ordinator of Counselling. Mr ... told me that the university is only a few years old and that the counselling centre has only been in operation for one year. He did tell me that as a new university, the planners had access for the disabled in mind when designing the buildings and that the university is 100 per cent accessible for persons with disabilities.

5. *University of Victoria*: (i) Switchboard (ii) Student Services (iii) Co-ordinator of Special Student Program. The statistics given to me were from December 1994. She was unable to break down the number of mobility impairments or for hard of hearing/deaf.

Manitoba

1. *Brandon University*: (i) Switchboard (ii) Student Services (iii) Counsellor. Ms ... explained to me that the counselling office has only recently started a new policy. She also remarked that the numbers only reflected self-declared students and that she knows of several other students who would fit into our categories, but they do not make use of the services provided.

2. *University of Manitoba*: (i) Switchboard (ii) Disability Services. The numbers that Mr ... gave me for each category were high and he was sorry but he was unable to break down the numbers any further change. For example, he told me that there are 97 students who fit into the mobility impairment category and that "this number reflects the overall numbers at the university. These students may range from wheelchair bound to back injuries to broken arms". The same was true for the 30 students classified as visually impaired, he was unable to break this number down into specifics as they do not differentiate in their statistics.

3. *University of Winnipeg*: (i) Switchboard (ii) Services for Students with Special Needs. When giving the number for visually impaired, Ms ... remarked that all of the 15 students were "legally blind". When giving me the number for mobility impaired, the total was of students who "use a chair or otherwise need assistance in evacuation procedures".

New Brunswick

1. *Mount Allison University*: (i) Switchboard (ii) Dean of Students (iii) Administrative Services (iv) Registrar (v) Meighen Centre (vi) Administrator. Ms ... is the Administrator of the Meighen Centre for Learning Assistance and Research. She mentioned that there are not very many disabled students on campus as "the University is not at all set up for disabled access". In fact, she does make note of one student in a wheelchair that "has his friends carry him in and out of classes". She makes note that the Meighen Centre is more set up for the learning disabled student. She

did recall one deaf student who graduated "a few years back, but I have no idea how they did it".

2. *University of Moncton*: (i) Switchboard (ii) Housing Services (iii) Student Services (iv) Special Needs Association (v) Liaison. Ms ... proved extremely difficult to get hold of and returned my numerous messages after three weeks. She informed me that the Special Needs Association is presently preparing a letter to the University to upgrade all of the services that it provides to students.

3. *University of New Brunswick*: (i) Switchboard (ii) Learning Centre (iii) Dean of Student Services. Mr ... was very sorry, but the University had only recently appointed a co-ordinator for disabled students and the position had not yet started. However, he was able to give me a "very rough idea" as the University does not keep statistics on the categories we were after. He did not have any idea of the number of mobility impaired students, he did recall one deaf student on the St. John's campus, but was able to point out four or five other physical disorders, but only going by the medical certificates on his desk. It should be noted that St. Thomas University is affiliated with University of New Brunswick.

Newfoundland

1. *Memorial University*: (i) Switchboard (ii) Glenn Roy Blundon Centre. This was the first university contacted. They were very helpful and requested that the survey be faxed to them. Ms ... pointed out that the numbers are only for those students who have identified themselves to the Centre.

Nova Scotia

1. *Acadia University*: (i) Switchboard (ii) Admissions (iii) Student Affairs. When first contacting the university, the switchboard operator had to put me on hold as she was "looking ... I'm not sure". After leaving messages for Mr ... over a period of two weeks, I was finally able to contact him. Basically, he told me, the University has no physically disabled students who have required the services that his office offers. He did mention that they were expecting a severely visually impaired person next year and that

he does see the odd person in a wheelchair, but that no one has required his attention.

2. *Dalhousie University*: (i) Switchboard (ii) Advisor for Student with Disabilities (iii) Director of Student Resources. After explaining the survey to Ms ..., she requested that the survey be faxed to her. When it was returned, it was from Ms ..., Advisor for Students with Disabilities. There was no telephone contact between Ms ... and myself, only the returned fax.

3. *Mount Saint Vincent University*: (i) Switchboard (ii) Student Affairs (iii) Counsellor - Special Needs Office. When I first spoke with Ms ..., she informed me that she would have to speak with the Registrar's office to get the information. When she returned my call, I was told that the Registrar's office does not keep these statistics, as the students are not asked to identify any physical disabilities on their applications. She also told me that the Counselling Centre does not keep these statistics. She does know of one visually impaired student that she counsels, but does not recall seeing any mobility impaired students as the campus "can be difficult to get around for anyone in a wheelchair".

4. *Saint Francis Xavier University*: (i) Switchboard (ii) Counselling Centre. I originally spoke with Ms ...'s secretary/assistant. She listened to the purpose of the survey and promised that she would give the message to Ms ... Several days later, I received a hand written note from Dr. Leitch who had taken a message over the telephone, regarding the number of students. She did note that these were only the students who had self identified.

5. *Universite de Sainte-Anne*: (i) Switchboard (ii) Registrar. Mr ... was away on vacation while the survey was being conducted. However, Ms ..., Registrar, was able to tell me of one student that she knows attending university in a wheelchair.

6. *Technical University of N.S. (T.U.N.S.)*: (i) Switchboard, (ii) Residence Co-ordinator (iii) Student Services (iv) Dean of Students (v) Registrar. I spoke with Mr ..., Registrar, who informed me that he knew of only one person in a wheelchair who was attending the University. Due to the nature of its programs, he told me that the University has never had a need to have a specific program and/or department to meet the needs of the physically impaired.

7.   *University College of Cape Breton*: (i) Switchboard (ii) Student Affairs (iii) Counsellor. I had originally spoken with Ms ... on my first attempt. After explaining the survey to her, she promised to fax down the numbers that were required. After waiting one week, I made another telephone call and reached her assistant who promised to have the information faxed. After another week, I tried to reach Ms ... once more, but only reached her voice-mail. After leaving a message, I have since tried, unsuccessfully, to reach her and she has not returned any of my calls.

Ontario

1.   *Brock University*: (i) Switchboard (ii) Department for Special Needs. When I first reached Ms ..., she told me that she would have to retrieve the fact sheet and could she get back to me. She returned my call within two days and gave me the information. She did point out that the number of mobility impaired ranged from quadrapalegics to back injuries and that the large majority of clients were learning disabled.

2.   *Carleton University*: (i) Switchboard (ii) Paul Menton Centre (iii) Co-ordinator for Physical Disabilities. When I first contacted Mr ..., the numbers he gave were "approximate, remembering these figures off of the top of my head". However, after discussing the numbers with Dr. Leitch, I placed another telephone call to him to get a few more specifics. This time, he was able to give much more accurate numbers, as the year end statistics had just been submitted. He pointed out that of the following numbers, the first is a single count and the second number is a multiple, that is students who have two or more disabilities. While the single total number is 727, the multiple number is 844, but he told me that the actual real number of students using the services provided was 791. Upon further questioning, Mr ... pointed out that the high number of students may be accounted for by some or all of the following reasons: (a) the University has a tunnel system connecting all 27 buildings on the campus, making the university 100 per cent accessible; (b) the University offers a year round attendant care system to students in residence. The residence offers 40 rooms that are specially constructed for wheelchair users. Other students are hired as personal care workers for physically impaired students. The program has been running for seven years and can handle up to 20 students per term. Although the students must pay for the service, it is mostly funded through grants from the provincial government. Also, he points out, that Ontario has a bursary

program for impaired students with a matching fund through the Federal government.

3. *Lakehead University*: (i) Switchboard (ii) Department of Kinseology (iii) Registrar (iv) Learning Assistance Centre. I spoke with Ms ..., Co-ordinator of the Learning Assistance Centre. She did not have the figures on hand, but asked that I leave the questions with her and she would get the answers for me. She also pointed out that the numbers were only of students who were self declared.

4. *Laurentian University*: (i) Switchboard (ii) Special Needs Services. I spoke with Ms ..., a counsellor at the Special Needs Services. She did not have the figures on hand, but was able to fax me a sheet of statistics. Please note that the Jesuit Fathers University of Sudbury is affiliated with Laurentian University.

5. *McMaster University*: (i) Switchboard (ii) Office of Ability and Access. I spoke with Mr ... of the Office of ... and he was able to answer the survey using the numbers from the 1993-94 fact sheet and adding to them from his memory. When he was contacted again regarding the large number of disabled students attending his university, he informed me that (a) the William Ross MacDonald School for the Blind was located only 30 miles from the campus and (b) he personally serves on the board for the school. This combined with the fact that Ontario schools have Itinerant Teachers for the Blind in the school system as well as several different types of resource workers in schools may explain the high number of visually impaired students at the university. The University has no special grants or hardware, other than the usual, for visually impaired students.

6. *Osgoode Hall - Law School of York University*: (i) Switchboard (ii) Student Services (iii). Ms ... is the Records Co-ordinator for the school. The numbers she provided me with were "strictly from memory" and applied to the 1994-95 school year.

7. *Queens University*: (i) Switchboard (ii) Special Needs Office. I spoke with Ms ... of the Special Needs Office. Some of the numbers she gave were rather vague and she had to be asked again to narrow it down. For example, she told me they had 77 mobility impaired. When questioned further, she was able to narrow this number down to 53.

8. *Saint Paul University*: (i) Switchboard (ii) Student Services. I spoke with Sister ..., the Co-ordinator of Student Services. The sister was very curt in answering the questions, first insisting that she had already answered these questions and then saying "that the University does not have enough disabled students for us to care about". The answers that she finally gave were from her memory alone. When asked about mobility impaired students she replied "three, I think, or that's all I can recall", and when questioned about deaf students, she replied "no-no, ... nothing like that here".

9. *Trent University*: (i) Switchboard (ii) Special Needs Office. I spoke with Ms ... of the Special Needs Office. The numbers that she supplied were a "rough idea for 1994-95". The category of mobility impairment in her statistics include "difficulty in either limb, repetitive strain, shoulder and neck injuries and arthritis".

10. *University of Guelph*: (i) Switchboard (ii) Centre for Students with Disabilities. I spoke with Ms ... of the Centre. The numbers that she supplied were for over the course of the last year and she was "going by a list of students and their disabilities" that she had to add together to get the numbers requested.

11. *University of Ottawa*: (i) Switchboard (ii) Student Life (iii) Centre for Special Needs. I originally had spoken with Mr ... of the Centre, but it was Yves Lahaie who returned my call. The numbers that he supplied were from the 1994-95 year end statistics. All universities in Ontario, he informed me, use the same six classifications; Mobility Impaired, Visually Impaired, Hearing Impaired, Learning Disabled, Psychiatric, and Medical.

12. *University of Toronto*: (i) Switchboard (ii) Special Services. From almost the first day of the survey, I had tried unsuccessfully to reach Ms ... of the Special Services. No matter who I contacted at the University, they all told me that she was the only person who could supply me with the statistics. After leaving numerous messages for her, all unreturned, Dr. Leitch was able to give me a sheet of statistics that he had from the university from the year before, 1993-94. Please note that Victoria University is affiliated with the University of Toronto.

13. *University of Waterloo*: (i) Switchboard (ii) Services for Persons with Disabilities. I spoke with Ms ..., Co-ordinator for the Services ... office. Of the numbers that she gave me, she was unable to break down the number of

blind and visually impaired students, as they do not differentiate in their statistics. As well, the number that she gave for mobility impaired were for "physically impaired, including broken legs, braces etc.". Their category for medical ranged from "AIDS, blood disorders, chronic pain, environmental allergies, asthma, anything not impeding mobility".

14. *University of Western Ontario*: (i) Switchboard (ii) Services for Persons with Disabilities. I spoke with Ms ... of the Services office. All numbers that she supplied were for the 1994-95 year. Of the 25 persons she classified as mobility impaired, "approximately 10-15 are in wheelchairs, the others have mobility impairment of some sort".

15. *University of Windsor*: (i) Switchboard (ii) Special Needs Office. I spoke with Ms ..., the Co-ordinator for the Special Needs office. She also pointed out that the numbers reflect only those students who have self identified. Of the 45 students she classified as mobility impaired, she said "the number includes back injuries and other physical ailments that impair mobility".

16. *Wilfred Laurier University*: (i) Switchboard (ii) Special Needs Office. I spoke with Ms ..., the Co-ordinator of the Special Needs office. She was able to answer the survey using the numbers from May 1994-April 1995. She categorises students "according to symptoms that are creating a difficulty and needing services". Of the 41 students she categorised as mobility impaired, she points out that it includes both temporary and permanent and that it also includes "any type of physical disorder, i.e. a broken leg or arm".

17. *York University*: (i) Switchboard (ii) Admissions (iii) Office for Persons with Disabilities. I spoke with Ms ..., Co-ordinator for the Office for ... She was able to give statistics for the 1993-94 year. All of the numbers supplied were for the three campuses of York University: York, Glendon and Atkinson. For mobility impaired, the number includes any students who make use of any assistive device or have any mobility difficulty. York also has an attendant care program which 12 students are currently using.

18. *Royal Military College of Canada*: (i) Switchboard (ii) Liaison Office. I spoke with Captain ..., Liaison Officer for the Military College. He informed that although there are no students with disabilities at the College, there have been some court challenges regarding them not allowing physically challenged students. He also informed me that he, personally,

does not support the notion of physically disabled students at the College as "all students must be prepared to go into a war zone".

19. *Ryerson Institute*: (i) Switchboard (ii) Counselling Centre (iii) Director, Access Centre. Mr ... was able to give me the exact numbers for Ryerson, as they had just finished doing last year's statistics. He was unable to break down the number of deaf vs. hearing impaired or blind vs. visually impaired as they do not differentiate in their statistics.

Prince Edward Island

1. *University of Prince Edward Island*: (i) Switchboard (ii) Registrar (iii) Student Services. I spoke with Ms ..., a counsellor with the Department of Student Services. The numbers that she supplied were for the past school year and included only those students who had self identified. She added, "while I am certain that there are probably others, they are not registered with her office".

Quebec

1. *Bishop's University*: (i) Switchboard (ii) Counselling Office. I spoke with Mr ..., Dean of Student Affairs. The numbers that he gave to me were from his memory and from speaking with others in the office. He informed me that the campus is 85 per cent accessible, while noting that the Student Union Building was not. He also let me know that the Counselling Centre primarily deals with learning disabilities.

2. *Concordia University*: (i) Switchboard. I was given Ms's ... name from Mr ... of Bishop's University and she, in turn, passed me along to Mr ..., the Co-ordinator of Services for Disabled Students. The numbers that he was able to give me were "approximate, but pretty accurate". He also informed me that fully 50 per cent of the students making use of his office were learning disabled, but he was unable to put a number to this estimate.

3. *McGill University*: (i) Switchboard (ii) Student Services. I was given Ms's ....name from Mr ... of Bishop's University as the person to speak with. She was very helpful, but did not have much else to add to the information.

4. *Universite Laval*: This university was contacted by Claudine Herlihy of the Modern Languages & Classics department due to my inability to converse in French with the persons at the university. She wrote that she spoke with a person from the "Bureau d'Accueil Personnes" on campus and that this person points out that these numbers were only for students registered with the Bureau.

5. *Universite de Montreal*: (i) Switchboard (ii) Translator (iii) Student Services (iv). Mr ... is a counsellor with the Office for Disabled Students. He was very helpful with the survey and did point out that the number of mobility impaired students included all students who are impaired including students with Multiple Sclerosis, Muscular Dystrophy, back injuries, etc.

6. *Universite de Sherbrooke*: (i) Switchboard (ii) Student Centre (iii) Disabled Students Centre. I spoke with Ms ... of the Disabled Students Centre and found her to be very helpful and forthcoming with the information requested.

7. *Universite de Quebec à Montreal*: (i) Switchboard (ii) Education of Handicapped Persons. I spoke with Ms ..., who was able to give me numbers for the 1994-95 semesters. There were some numbers that I was unsure of due to her accent, but we were able to work around the language barrier. She did point out that the Provincial government has designated a category of "Organic" to cover several of the disabilities that her office deals with.

8. *Universite de Quebec à Trois-Riveres*: Ms Herlihy was able to contact Ms ... of the Accueil aux Personnes Handicapees. She wrote that Ms ... pointed out that there were a few people on campus who were mobility impaired, but none of them required her services.

9. *Universite de Quebec à Chicoutimi*: Ms Herlihy contacted M ... of Student Services to get the information.

10. *Universite de Quebec à Rimouski*: Ms Herlihy contacted Ms ... of Student Services to get the information.

11. *Universite de Quebec à Hull*: Ms Herlihy contacted Ms ... of Student Services to get the information and also recorded that Ms ... told her that there were more students around, but not registered with her office.

12. *Universite de Quebec à Abitibi-Temiscamingue*: Ms Herlihy contacted Ms ... of the Services aux Etudiants to get the information.

Saskatchewan

1. *University of Regina*: (i) Switchboard (ii). I spoke with Ms ... of Student Affairs who was able to supply me with the statistics for the 1995 winter semester.

2. *University of Saskatchewan*: (i) Switchboard (ii) Student Services (iii). I spoke with Ms ..., the Director of Services for Students with Disabilities. The first time I spoke with her, the numbers she supplied were "approximate, off the top of my head". I spoke with her a second time at the request of Dr. Leitch to narrow some of the numbers down. She was able to supply me with the correct numbers from her files, bringing some totals down substantially. She also pointed out that Ms ..., Administrative Assistant for Enrolment Services also speaks and counsels with students. She told me that last year they had "just over 100 students registered, including learning disabilities".

6 Students with disabilities in higher education in Finland

Liisa Laitinen

The system of higher education in Finland

Finland is the sixth largest country in Europe with just over five million residents. In 1994, the number of students enrolled in universities was 128,300. Of these, around 25 per cent were new students. In Finland, there are 20 universities in total. Ten of these represent the traditional university with its many different faculties. Three specialise in engineering and technology and three in economics and business administration. The remaining four are academies of art. In addition there is one military academy which is seen as being at the same educational level as the universities. A new system of polytechnics (in Finnish *ammattikorokeakoulu*) has been created in the 1990s. These institutions, based on existing vocational education centres, offer higher education in the non-university sector. The first permanent polytechnics were introduced in 1996.

All universities have entry restrictions. All students have to pass an entrance examination if they wish to go to university. Once there, it takes three years of full time study before they can be awarded a first degree and a further two years of study before being eligible for a higher degree (Bachelor's and Master's levels respectively). A doctoral degree can be completed in approximately four years.

In Finland, the universities have a dual role. They are places where research takes place and they also offer studies based on the research. After graduation, students try to enter the world of employment. In recent years, Finland has gone through a period of severe recession and the number of unemployed people has grown threefold. This has led to an increasing demand on adult and distance learning education (e.g. the open university) although this type of education does not seem to have had much effect in terms of finding employment. Whilst all universities are supporters of the principle of life-long learning, they have been forced to give more attention to the employment opportunities for their graduates.

Disability and higher education

There are no reliable statistics about the number of students with disabilities in universities. There appear to be two reasons for this. Firstly, there is a concern to preserve the privacy of the individual. Secondly, this information has not been seen to be necessary. One source of information which might be used is the National Pensions Institute. Figures deriving from this source suggest that there are around 700 students with disabilities in universities. This information is part of what is collected in relation to the national health and social security system which has a concern to find employment for people with disabilities. (In this way, attending university might be seen as a kind of vocational rehabilitation for some students.)

It appears that most academic departments are willing to enrol students with disabilities on to their programmes. The most popular choices are within social sciences, law, and humanities. The academies of art and the military academy have not enrolled any students with disabilities so far. However, the Theatre Academy has indicated that it would be willing to arrange a programme for a class of students who are deaf or hard-of-hearing but in such a small country as Finland, this remains a theoretical option since it is unlikely that there would be sufficient numbers to constitute a class.

Most institutions do have a contact person for students with disabilities. Many have considered physical access to buildings, adaptations to lavatories, and other alterations to meet the needs of students with mobility impairments. Some universities have buildings which are very old and because they are of important architectural interest, they have protected status. It is not easy to install lifts in these buildings.

In relation to policies, most universities do take into account the special needs of students with disabilities. For example, it is possible to arrange for additional time in examinations; a range of assistive technology is available; materials can be provided in formats to meet the needs of blind and visually-impaired students; deaf students can use interpreters. However, as far as academic performance is concerned, there are no differences in the standards required from disabled students in comparison with their non-disabled peers.

State financial support can be obtained since it avoids students with disabilities having to arrange loans to fund their studies. This state support covers not only living costs but will also pay for personal assistance if it is needed. It should be noted that in Finland a law about service for disabled people was passed in 1988. One aim of this was to create equal opportunities for people with disabilities to live and participate in all activities of society and to ensure that people with disabilities receive equal treatment. They should not meet discrimination on account of their disabilities. As with similar laws in other countries, there is perhaps more in the way of rhetoric than reality.

In earlier times, having a university degree was considered to guarantee a job for a student with a disability. The last two decades have seen the majority of those students with disabilities graduating finding jobs with organisations for disabled people. With the current high rate of unemployment, public administration and other organisations have been reducing their staff. This has led to a situation where finding a job after graduation has become much more difficult - even when employment authorities are willing to help.

Policy and provision for students with disabilities at the University of Helsinki

The oldest and largest of universities in Finland, the University of Helsinki offers the widest range of courses. For over a quarter of a century, the policy has been to promote access for students with disabilities. Fortunately this work began in a period of economic prosperity. Today it would be much harder to start.

The University has an adviser for students with disabilities who also has the responsibility for co-ordinating the involvement of students, teaching staff, and the administration. The adviser arranges individual examination conditions for students who need additional time or who need to use special equipment. Sometimes this involves negotiations between teaching staff and the student. The adviser also works with those responsible for the University's buildings and furnishings to ensure that any programme of redevelopment and refurbishment takes into account the needs of students with disabilities. Sometimes, the alterations can be completed successfully. However, some of the buildings are quite old. Also the University works on over 400 different locations (including a research centre some distance from the main site and which has a sauna). In principle there is an attempt made to modify any buildings that are inaccessible/unsuitable although this is done only when students with disabilities actually enrol on courses in that particular department. The policy is re-active rather than pro-active.

The adviser is in regular and frequent contact with the Ministry of Education, KELA (the national health and social security system), organisations for disabled people, and the national library for blind people. In a small country like Finland, such close working links are easy. In 1996 the Student Library moved to new premises on the city campus. Now, wheelchair users have access to the textbook loans office. The special needs of disabled users were considered in the interior design of the building and the location of equipment. For example there is an adjustable workstation and some terminals are available for wheelchair users.

Quite a number of students have specific learning difficulties (e.g. dyslexia). Some are identified and diagnosed only after coming to the university and starting their courses. Certain kinds of support are available, such as micro-computers with proof-reading/spell-check software. Additional time in examinations can be arranged. However, this group of students is giving cause for concern in some departments because on some courses, the use of software is regarded as undermining learning. There are also courses where the participation of students with dyslexia is seen as a potential hazard for other students. Students with specific learning difficulties constitute a real dilemma when considering the rights and duties of the individual and questions concerning equality.

Continuing with this theme of equality, it might seem that some students with disabilities are better supported than others. Blind and visually-impaired students have a long history of studying successfully at the University of Helsinki. The development of electronic aids and technology has been truly revolutionary. The learning opportunities for this group of students have expanded significantly. On the other hand, being deaf does seem to isolate students from the mainstream education system. The use of sign language presents a number of problems. It is difficult to find sign language interpreters competent for work at university level. Also, when students need to take notes, they cannot always watch the interpreter and so they also need a notetaker. Thirdly, when tutors and students are working in a class where there is a sign language interpreter, some might find this a distraction and a disturbance. It is difficult to understand why study aids for deaf people are not becoming available quickly. One possibility might be for deaf students to make use of a small micro-computer which can translate speech into text very easily.

Conclusion

As can be seen from this brief account, some progress has been made for students with disabilities and learning difficulties in higher education in Finland. Working in such a small country can sometimes lead to feelings that one is isolated from developments elsewhere in other parts of the world. With closer contact with colleagues working with disabled students in other countries through attendance at international conferences, and seminars, it is reassuring to know that the problems and difficulties faced in Finland are those encountered by our colleagues and that we are united in our efforts to find strategies and solutions to overcome them.

7 Students with disabilities in German higher education

Renate Langweg-Berhorster

The system of higher education in Germany

In Germany, there are more than 300 institutions of higher education. The system of higher education consists of universities, technical universities and colleges, Gesamthochschulen (comprehensive universities), theological colleges, teacher training colleges, art academies, Fachhochschulen and Fachhochschulen for Public Administration. In 1990 about 66 per cent of the students in the Federal Republik were enrolled in universities, about 21 per cent of the students were enrolled in a Fachhochschule. Generally, the admission requirement for the universities is the Abitur, the secondary school-leaving certificate. Admission to a Fachhochschule can be acquired with a vocational training qualification. For specially qualified employed persons, there is in most of the Länder (i.e. federal states) a possibility to study without having acquired the Abitur.

There are some fields of studies where the number of students is regulated by means of restricted admission (numerus clausus). Admission depends on a centralised selection or on allocation procedures through the Zentralstelle für die Vergabe von Studienplätzen (ZVS the central office for the allocation of places at universities). Three different procedures have been developed in order to select and allocate students to those courses of studies where the number of applicants vastly exceeds the capacities of the universities and colleges. Firstly, in the distribution procedure every applicant is admitted to the course of studies he or she has applied for, but not necessarily at the university or college of his or her choice. Secondly, the general selection procedure is applied to those fields of studies in which there are more applicants than can possibly be accommodated at the universities. The available places are allocated in part according to the average grade in the Abitur and in part according to time which the individual has waited for a place at a university since the Abitur. Subject to this procedure are, for example, courses in architecture, biology, psychology, economics and law. Thirdly, the special selection procedure for medicine introduces in addition a special test as a basis for the allocation of places and also reserves a certain number of places to be distributed by the institutions on the basis of interviews.

Social services for students like student residences and cafeterias or restaurants are run by local Studentenwerke, the Organisations for Student Affairs. These are non-profit making organisations which are subsidised by the government. In Germany no tuition fees have to be paid in order to enrol on a course of studies at a university or college. Moreover, those students who have no means of their own and whose parents or possibly spouse cannot pay for their living expenses are granted public assistance. According to the Bundesausbildungsförderungsge -setz BAföG (Federal Education Assistance Act), loans and subsidies are granted by the local Organisations for Student Affairs on behalf of the Federation. The Deutsches Studentenwerk DSW (German National Association for Student Affairs) is a national union of local Organisations for Student Affairs. It functions as an umbrella organisation of the local organisations, safeguards the socio-political interests of the students and co-operates with other national and international university organisations.

Politically, the Länder (federal states) not the federation, are responsible for the system of higher education, private education having never played a significant part in German higher education. Therefore, important issues in the higher education system are addressed by the Ständige Konferenz der Kultusminister der Länder, KMK (Standing Conference of the State Ministers of Education and Cultural Affairs). In 1982 the KMK issued its recommendations on the "Improvement of Education and Training for Disabled Students in Higher Education". In this document the obligation for universities and colleges to give due consideration to the special needs of disabled students was specified. The recommendation covered eight primary areas:

- advice for those preparing to commence their studies, for students during their studies, and for graduates or students preparing to enter into employment or a profession;
- amendments to the examination and study regulations which would compensate for disadvantages arising out of the disability;
- measures to make buildings and other facilities functionally suitable for and accessible to disabled persons;
- social integration measures;
- sports facilities for disabled students;
- the appointment of Co-ordinators for Disabled Student Affairs at universities and colleges;
- the involvement of disabled persons in the planning and execution of measures for disabled people; and
- the improvement of information facilities and services through the establishment of an advice centre for disabled students at the DSW.

At an institutional level the Hochschulrektorenkonferenz HRK (German Rectors Conference, vice-chancellors and principals) dealt with the responsibilities of universities and colleges regarding the integration of disabled students in its recommendations of 1986 and, amongst other areas, addressed especially the work of the Co-ordinators for Disabled Students Affairs.

Students with disabilities in higher education

In Germany, 12.7 per cent of all students are disabled or suffer from chronic illnesses: 2.3 per cent of the students are disabled, 10.4 per cent suffer from chronic illnesses. This was one of the findings of the DSW's 14th Social Survey. Accordingly, approximately 200,000 students are disabled or chronically ill and approximately 50,000 students stated in this survey that their disability or chronic illness causes serious or moderately serious problems in their studies. The Social Survey showed that university studies are far less straightforward for disabled or chronically ill students than for their fellow students who do not face serious health problems. For example, the proportion of students who choose to change their degree course (subject) midway through the programme is higher. Moreover, students with disabilities or chronic illnesses have a break from their studies once or twice during their degree course more often than the comparative group of students without a disability.

Admission to higher education

Admission to the institutions of higher education in Germany is the same for applicants with a disability or chronic illness as for other students. However, in the centralised selection and allocation procedures provisions have been made in order to secure equal opportunity for disabled students. For example, in the selection procedures a small percentage of places is reserved for those for whom it would be an undue hardship to wait for their entry to a university. Those students with disabilities or chronic illness who can be expected to wait for some time can apply for an improvement of their waiting time or their average grade in the Abitur if they can show that their being at a disadvantage compared with the other applicants is directly related to their disability. Moreover, it is possible for disabled and chronically ill students to apply for preferential treatment concerning their choice of university location.

Once enrolled for a course of study at a college or university, students with disabilities often need special amendments to study and examination regulations in order to ensure the same opportunities as other students. For most of the state examinations students with disabilities are entitled to amendments, even though regulations vary in the Länder. Students of medical courses however, are not entitled to such amendments. Students who study for a diploma or M.A. (Magister Artium) degree, can always plead that in the general regulations which have been issued for diploma and M.A. examination regulations a provision to compensate for disadvantages because of a disability is included. However, not every university has adopted a corresponding provision into its own examination regulations.

Living in universities

Accessibility of the college and university buildings in Germany for students who are wheelchair users is not provided everywhere. Nevertheless, a recent survey at the institutions of higher education, which was carried out by the Advice Centre for University Applicants and Students with Disabilities, shows that new buildings and renovations are generally carried out according to the standards set by the Deutsches Institut für Normung DIN (German standards institute). These standards consist of dimensions which are recommended by the institute as a planning basis for designing buildings without obstacles. However even though the newly built colleges and campus universities are generally accessible for wheelchair users, those colleges which are situated in older buildings, which sometimes are listed, and given protected status are sometimes still partly or completely inaccessible to students who use wheelchairs. The needs of students with sensory impairments often have not been taken into consideration, too. Only in the last few years awareness of the special needs of these students concerning such interior design aids such as improved lighting and acoustics in buildings and rooms or tactile, acoustic and topological orientation aids has been growing.

In some of the student hostels which are run by the local Studentenwerke there are rooms accessible for students who use wheelchairs. Students with disabilities also generally receive preferential treatment in the allocation of student hostel places. Nevertheless there is always a demand for more accessible accommodation for wheelchair users and adapted accommodation for students with sensory impairments, especially since rooms in student hostels are much cheaper on average than rented flats in private property.

Visually and hearing impaired students often need special technical equipment in order to compensate for their disability. This equipment is only sometimes provided by the university: for example some 30 colleges or universities provide special workplaces for blind and visually impaired students. Only very few universities provide portable transmitter/receiver equipment, induction loops or directional conference microphones for students with hearing impairments. If the necessary technical equipment is not placed at the disposal of the students with special needs by the university or college, students have to buy the equipment themselves. In order to finance the equipment students can apply for support under the Bundessozialhilfegesetz BSHG (Federal Social Security Act). Some kinds of equipment are paid for by the health insurance scheme in Germany.

Financial support

Difficulties for disabled and chronically ill students often result from the more time they need to organise their living conditions and their studies. Maintaining mobility, finding accommodation which is accessible for wheelchair users or students with mobility disorders, finding and paying for academic assistants and technical aids or organising personal care are some of the problems they face. In addition to the actual illness or disability these problems will have a direct influence on the general financial circumstances of the students. Students with disabilities often need to spend considerable time and energy on the effort to apply for financial support from various authorities. Because they often exceed the maximum period for which support is granted, students with disabilities or chronic illness lose their BAföG (Federal Education Assistance Act) support much more frequently than do students without a disability or chronic illness.

In addition to this, students with a disability or chronic illness also find themselves confronted with additional disability- or illness-related costs, for example costs towards special equipment or academic assistance or costs toward maintaining their mobility. Health insurance schemes do not always pay for needs related to the disability. Since BAföG has no instruments or provisions for taking these additional costs into consideration, students find themselves dependent upon social service assistance. According to BSHG funding is possible for example for personal assistance, technical equipment, academic assistants, additional costs toward a higher rent, purchase and maintenance of a car etc. The Federal Social Security Act provides funding under certain conditions only. Because of problems with financing their studies, disabled and chronically ill students will find themselves in a position in which they are forced to combine their studies with earning additional money through some form of gainful employment more frequently than other students.

Advice and information for students with disabilities

Advice services are offered by various institutions and facilities for students with disabilities and chronic illnesses.   Specialised careers counsellors at the employment offices, Study Advice Centres at the university or college, advice offices at the local Organisations for Student Affairs, student interest groups and the Allgemeiner Studentenausschuá (ASTA) (approx. student union) can serve as sources of information for disabled students and applicants.   Moreover, almost every university or college has appointed a Co-ordinator for Disabled Students Affairs who is familiar with the study conditions at the respective university or college and who will be able to support disabled applicants and students. However, one of the problems in the area of advice services for students with disabilities is a lack of possibilities for further qualification for the advisers of disabled students.

Information is also provided by the Advice Centre for University Applicants and Students with Disabilities, which was set up at the DSW in Bonn with financial support from the Federal Ministry of Education and Science (today the Federal Ministry of Education, Science, Research and Technology).   One of the main areas of responsibility of the Advice Centre is the nationwide provision of information to university applicants and students with disabilities. It maintains a list of contact persons and organisations and compiles its own information material which is then made available to interested students and organisations. For example, the Advice Centre issues a brochure, in which a survey of preparation of studies, academic assistance and advice facilities is provided. Furthermore, the Advice Centre regularly organises conferences and seminars for disabled and chronically ill persons who are considering studying, for students in their first semesters, as well as for graduates.   The Advice Centre also holds seminars for advisers of disabled students to enable them to extend their knowledge of different aspects of the disabled students' situation.   Information about various issues, e.g. new legislation or special efforts at individual universities, is distributed among advisers and student interest groups by the Advice Centre.

The Advice Centre also collects and documents information material of interest to disabled people who are considering studying, to students with disabilities and to organisations and institutions actively providing counselling services for disabled students and/or university applicants. For example, the Advice Centre collects information on mobility services which provide personal support and on legal advice centres in the towns where colleges and universities are located. During the last few years, further efforts have been made by the Advice Centre to collect information on the study situation in other countries in order to be able to inform German students with disabilities who want to study abroad about living and study conditions in the country they wish to go to.

Moreover, the Advice Centre represents the interests of disabled university applicants and students at a political, administrative and public level. It addresses the problems faced by disabled persons interested in studying and by actual disabled students, points out deficiencies in the study conditions which such students find and submits proposals on the improvement of these to the appropriate authorities and agencies for discussion. For example, some years ago the Advice Centre had a part in the improvement of the terms of grants and their repayment according to the Federal Education Assistance Act. At present the Advice Centre is involved in an initiative for the improvement of examination regulations for disabled and chronically ill students in state examinations.

The Advice Centre has an Advisory Committee from which it receives important stimulus for its work. The Advisory Committee is composed of representatives from various relevant areas:

- associations and interest groups for disabled persons;
- the universities and colleges;
- the local Studentenwerke;
- the Federal Ministry of Education, Science, Research and Technology;
- the German Rectors Conference; and
- the disabled students themselves.

Conclusions

Regarding the overall situation of disabled people in Germany, which forms the framework in which the situation of students with disabilities has to be reviewed, an improvement has been achieved on the legal level. Following years of efforts made for an antidiscrimination legislation in Germany, an additional clause was incorporated into the German Constitution in 1994, stating that no one may be discriminated against because of a disability. Due to this addition, a further improvement of the situation of disabled persons in Germany is expected. Perhaps this passage in the Constitution will enhance awareness of the still often discriminatory and difficult situation in life of disabled people in our country.

References

Budde, Hans-Günter und Leszcensky, Michael (1990), *Behinderte und chronisch Kranke im Studium.   Ergebnisse einer Sonderauswertung der 12. Sozialerhebung des Deutschen Studentenwerkes im Sommersemester 1988* Hannover, HIS Hochschul-Informations-System GmbH.

Peisert, Hansgert and Framhein, Gerlind (1994), *Higher Education in Germany* Bonn, Bundesministerium für Bildung und Wissenschaft (Federal Ministry of Education and Science).

Schnitzer, Klaus u.a. (1995), *Das soziale Bild der Studentenschaft in der Bundesrepublik Deutschland, 14,* Bonn, Bundesminister für Bildung, Wissenschaft, Forschung und Technologie.

Information leaflets/publications from Deutschen Studenten Werks:

- (1993), *Behinderte studieren: Praktische Tips und Informationen der Beratungsstelle für behinderte Studienbewerber und Studenten des Deutschen Studentenwerks,* Bonn, Deutsches Studentenwerk, Beratungsstelle für behinderte Studienbewerber und Studenten.

- (1993), *Studienbedingungen behinderter Studierender an den Hochschulen der Bundesrepublik Deutschland. Ergebnisse einer Umfrage des Deutschen Studentenwerks vom Februar 1993* Bonn, Deutsches Studentenwerk, Beratungsstelle für behinderte Studienbewerber und Studenten.

- (1993), *Studieren mit Behinderungen: Dokumentation der Fachtagung anläßlich des zehnjährigen Bestehens der Beratungsstelle für behinderte Studienbewerber und Studenten des Deutschen Studenten Werks* Bonn, Bundesministerium für Bildung und Wissenschaft.

8 Disabled university students in Greece

Despina Sidiropoulou-Dimakakou

Introduction

Higher education in Greece is offered in 17 publicly funded and monitored Universities (Higher Educational Institutes) and in 12 Technological Educational Institutes. Universities offer both undergraduate and postgraduate studies. Undergraduate studies lead to a first University Degree ("Ptychio") after a minimum of four years of studies. In some disciplines such as engineering and medicine, studies are one to two years longer respectively.

The academic year starts on the 1st of September each year and ends on the 31st of August of the following year. The teaching courses are separated into two semesters beginning in the middle of September and ending in the middle of June.

The Technological Education Institutes constitute the latest form of higher technological education in Greece. After the completion of three years of studies, a diploma is awarded and there is the opportunity for the graduates to enrol - after formal exams - in the first year of university and in any course equivalent to their studies.

Higher Education and degrees offered by non-state colleges or universities located in Greece are not validated as university degrees. According to State Law (No. 1351-83) students have to sit the university entrance exam which is called the General Examination and which is held every June. The number of the students who enter university is determined every March by the Minister of Education in accordance with the proposal of the Senate of each university and of the Council of Higher Education. For the Military Schools, this number is decided by both Ministers of Education and Military Forces, on the basis of the demands from the military sector.

The students who are entitled to sit the entrance exams are the holders of a lyceum (senior higher school) certificate or an equivalent secondary education school certificate or the European Baccalaureate. There are also some special categories of candidates who are accepted by the university. One of these categories consists of disabled students who are blind, deaf, or have a number of other medical conditions.

The students are enrolled at the university on the basis of:

1.　their declaration of preference of a specific department; and

2.　the grades they receive in the General Examinations.

The organisation and the monitoring of the universities are governed by State Law (No. 1268/82).　According to this law, the universities are fully self-administered. They are financed by the State and supervised by the Minister of Education and Religion.　Books and various facilities including medical insurance for the undergraduate students are provided by the State free of charge.

The undergraduate students are offered scholarships and loans, under specific conditions:

1.　scholarships of progress are offered to the students who have excellent academic records; and

2.　scholarships and loans are offered to those who face financial difficulties and have good records.

Both the undergraduate and postgraduate students are provided with free housing and food but this depends on the family's income.　All university students have a special reduction (5 per cent) for bus and train fare.

Greek universities are mainly responsible for the organisation and development of courses for postgraduate studies.　In these courses, Greek students or students from abroad are accepted after the completion of a "first university degree".　Two types of postgraduate studies can be distinguished:

1.　the Programmes for Postgraduate Studies which include research and taught courses and can lead to the award of a Doctorate.　After the successful completion of the first two years (four teaching semesters) students are awarded a diploma of postgraduate studies equivalent to a Masters degree. Usually this diploma is considered a necessary condition for the continuation and the completion of the Doctorate.

2.　the Doctorate which is an advanced academic degree equivalent to a PhD. Doctoral work entails research and writing a dissertation which will be supported in a final oral examination.　The duration of the research and the writing of a dissertation must take at least three years.

University students with disabilities

According to State Law (No. 1946/91) students with severe disabilities - those who are blind, deaf, the ones who have thalassaemia, hydrocephaly, and pernicious anaemia - enter the university without sitting any exams. For those who have some kind of special need resulting from a disability or medical condition - permanently or temporarily - the university entrance examination is adapted to meet their needs i.e. oral exams for dyslexic students as well as for those with physical disabilities (State Law No. 57/90). Students with disabilities are enrolled unless there is a particular prohibitory decision of the department i.e. blind students are not accepted in Medicine; deaf students are not accepted in Physical Education or in Theatre or Drama.

Table 8.1:   Students with disabilities at the University of Athens (1992-1993)

Disabilities	Males	Females	Total
Thalassaemia	108	181	289
Deafness	20	17	37
Blindness	20	17	37
Motor disabilities	8	2	10
Other cases	13	1	14

Source: The Counselling Centre of the University of Athens, "Activities Report", 1994.

Although the State Law facilitates their entry to university, in practice they cannot attend the courses due to their disabilities and consequently the acquisition of knowledge is extremely difficult for them.

The difficulties start with the fact that the Directorate of Higher Education of the Ministry of Education does not have a separate department organised to deal with the problems of disabled students. On the other hand, the Universities themselves do not have the infrastructure to provide the required services. As a result disabled university students face various serious problems such as the lack of:

• suitable study methods and study aids;
• interpreters for deaf students and adapted libraries for blind students;
• adequate careers counselling, study orientation and careers information;

- counselling to develop crucial life skills for successful living; and
- adapted buildings causing difficulties for students with impaired mobility when using university classrooms and contacting university staff and their fellow students.

All these difficulties can lead to a kind of "learning isolation" for students with disabilities since most of them are restricted to studying at home alone and also to a kind of "social isolation" since they can not participate in the social life of the university community.

To be more specific, blind or partially sighted students cannot read the syllabuses and reference books since most of them are not transcribed into Braille or recorded onto cassettes (the Faculty of Law is the only Faculty in the University of Athens where materials are transcribed into Braille). For the same reason they cannot use the university libraries. Therefore they are obliged to ask for volunteers or to pay some people - not always suitable - to record the books on to cassettes for them.

Deaf or hard of hearing students do not attend courses or seminars since there are no sign language interpreters at the universities. So they miss a significant part of the learning process and the related knowledge.

Students with physical disabilities - especially wheelchair users - have serious problems travelling round the campus and getting access to the faculty offices, libraries or the administrative services since there are no adapted buildings on the university campuses nor is there any adapted housing.

Things become even worse if we add to the previous list the complaints of the disabled students concerning their social isolation. Most of them are unable to take part in the social life of the university such as cultural events, sports, festivals, excursions and the like. This forced abstinence brings about a feeling of isolation and makes them feel marginalised and anxious about the future.

The disabled students are not offered any specialist careers guidance services or psychological counselling services before or during their university studies. As a result, most of them are concentrated into specific departments on the basis of the lack of problems in completing the work and/or to find a job after graduation or because there are a few other disabled students enrolled in the same department.

The state offers disabled university students a personal allowance which ranges from 17,000 to 102,640 drachmas per month depending on the kind of disabilities.

Issues for consideration

Pre-entry stage

In general, preparation for the transition from high school to university is poor in Greece. Of course, the high school students are provided with careers guidance and orientation services (grades 9-11) by their teachers. Unfortunately the vast majority of teachers are not well trained and skilled in careers guidance practice and techniques. As a result most of the students do not succeed in acquiring self-knowledge and careers information.

Disabled students face additional problems. Firstly, their teachers are unable to adjust the techniques and activities of careers guidance to the special needs of these students. Secondly, there are no research findings to show that jobs are suitable or not for disabled students - in relation to the labour market needs as well as to the specific disability.

The consequence is that disabled students miss the opportunity to discover their intellectual capacities, interests, and motives in order to explore the academic fields and make a wise choice of studies. As a result, the criteria on which disabled students academic choices are made include:

1. the nature and the severity of student's disability;

2. student's gender;

3. student's parents' attitude about specific academic fields;

4. the student's opinion about the study conditions, the job finding opportunities, and the social status of a specific specialisation (Tsinarelis, G. 1993).

Before the start of studies, disabled students can collect information about adapted study methods, transcription of study materials, and accessibility of the buildings from the Secretariat of each Department. Unfortunately there is no person solely responsible for informing and supporting disabled students. So each university implements support in existing services.

Academic issues

During their programme of studies, disabled university students face serious problems of access to the curriculum. The universities lack the necessary electronic equipment, transcribed study materials, accessible libraries, and specialist personnel (i.e. note-takers, sign language interpreters) to make the curriculum accessible to disabled students.

Most of the disabled students cannot cope with the study programmes which are planned on a full-time basis. A part-time programme on the basis of credits or on the basis of the number of courses could be more realistic for them.

Also disabled students face problems caused by the traditional assessment strategies which are not always suitable. An adaptation of the form and the period of the examination - depending on the kind of disability - is absolutely necessary.

Finally, the university community is not aware of the situation and the various problems which are faced by disabled students. As a consequence neither the teaching nor the administration staff are sufficiently aware to be in a position to offer them special help.

A case study: the University of Athens, the Counselling Centre and disabled students

The Counselling Centre of the Psychology Department was founded in 1990 and is the only university section which tries to provide services for disabled students. The main objective of the Centre is to help university students deal more effectively with educational, personal, and interpersonal issues. In this context the personnel of the Centre (some of them are volunteers) try to help the disabled students make their life better and their studies more straight forward and more effective.

The activities of the Counselling Centre concerning disabled students include the following. Firstly, there is the implementation of a project on the integration of the deaf students in the university. The project was partially financed by HORIZON (Project No. 91003E1) and its duration was for two years. The objective of the project was the training of 15 students of the department (all females) about issues relating to counselling deaf people. Part of the effort was the development of good social relationships among them and the group of 18 volunteer deaf students in order to facilitate the participation of the deaf students into the university social life. The trainees worked as study facilitators for the deaf students as well as counsellors, giving them psychological support and help in their every day life.

Secondly, the experience gained as a result of this project, has led to the formation of a network, supporting students with physical disabilities and another one, supporting students with visual impairments. There is also a network of fellow students under the guidance of two doctorate candidates.

Thirdly, disabled students are provided with psychological and careers guidance services.

Fourthly, one of the initiatives of the Centre is an awareness campaign to establish an identity for the special needs of disabled students in the university community. Part of this effort resulted in the adaptation of a few classrooms for disabled students with impaired mobility.

Fifthly, disabled students of the University of Athens have been included in a census every year since 1992 on the initiative of the Centre.

Finally, with the help of blind students the staff of the Centre have started the transcription of the books of the Psychology Department into Braille.

The Counselling Centre cannot offer much to disabled students without the necessary financial aid for hiring the professionals who provide the services needed. I have to stress that most of the collaborators who work for the disabled students are volunteers or postgraduate students. On the other hand technical support and administrative help is needed as well as the exchange of international experience and information on new guidance approaches.

My view is that the provision of services on study orientation, careers information, study methods, technical aids, medical care, scholarships, allowances, guidance in every day life and job readiness is of great importance for disabled students. In the meantime, to achieve these goals would require the co-operation of various professionals and thus the formation of an interdisciplinary group of experts to work on it. Emphasis must be given to occupational choices since those with disabilities may have difficulties that restrict their choice of occupations. This means that there is a need for continuous co-operation between the counselling services of secondary and higher education.

Since there are no other university agents for counselling or advising disabled students, it is absolutely necessary for the Counselling Centre to be financed and generally supported by the State, in order to achieve its goals. The provision of the required services is the only way for disabled students to experience life at university as a time of personal development and not as a traumatic experience.

Conclusions

It is no doubt true that many things have to be done for people with disabilities in order to have full access to learning and working. They face various barriers depending on the cultural and financial environment of the country where they live. Usually they are victims of social stereotypes, considerable prejudice by potential employers and possible bias by teachers and counsellors. Attitudes rooted in the concept of stigma affect behaviour towards disabled people, in the same way that sexism, ageism, and racism exist.

Disabled students in Greek universities need a supervisor or a co-ordinator of services as soon as the academic year begins. This person will be responsible for introducing disabled students to their fellow students and to the staff. Moreover he/she will be responsible for giving all available study information to disabled students such as syllabus, teaching approaches, study methods, accessibility of courses, methods of assessment as well as information on adapted accommodation, intensive day-to-day personal assistance, paramedical assistance and the like. He/she may also be responsible for the co-ordination of fellow student groups and ready to deal with any educational problems that may arise during the academic year.

In my view, it is important to change the regulations of the universities which might discriminate against students with disabilities; otherwise the opportunity to study for disabled people will continue to depend on the goodwill of staff and fellow students.

First of all, the universities must offer part-time study programmes at least for disabled students. Also, the disabled students usually encounter difficulties because of inappropriate forms of examinations. Depending on the kind and severity of the disability, students must be given the possibility of taking oral or written exams, using special equipment, having additional time, being assisted by a scriber/amanuensis or an interpreter and so on.

The universities must be given an extra budget for hiring specialist staff, (e.g. sign language interpreters), buying the electronic equipment needed for every kind of disability, and making building alternations which are necessary for wheelchair users.

The teaching staff must be aware of the special needs of disabled students, in order to give them some special help e.g. provide the students who have writing problems with photocopies of the overhead transparencies, the diagrams and the structure of the lectures, or give photocopies in large print to those who have problems with blackboard reading etc. Of course, this means that lecturers must be provided with photocopiers, photocopying paper, and other special equipment.

As Greece is not a wealthy country, and has also undergone a long period of recession, steps must be taken to ensure economic stability. Due to this fact, universities face financial difficulties and the authorities give priorities in giving money to the vast majority of the students, which means to the non disabled. This sounds logical to the technocrats, who are not interested in the minorities. That is why I think that the most important first step is for everybody in the university community to have a positive attitude towards disabled students and not be biased against them. Otherwise we will have no success, even if we have a big budget and the most modern equipment available.

References

Counselling Centre of the University of Athens, (1994), 'Activities Report', *Department of Psychology*, Athens.

Herr, E.L. & Cramer, S.H. (1992*), Career Guidance and Counselling Through the Life Span*, Harper Collins, New York.

Kalantzi-Azizi, A. (1994), *Students with Special Needs at the University of Athens*, proceedings of the European Interdisciplinary Congress on the Disabled, Rhodes-Greece, 8-10 May 1995 pp. 752-758, Ellinika Grammata, Athens (in Greek).

Ministry of Education and Religion, (1994a), *Special Education Information Bulletin*, Organisation of Educational Publications, Athens (in Greek).

Ministry of Education and Religion, (1994b), *Legislation for the Assessment of Students with Special Needs*, Organisation of Educational Publications, Athens (in Greek).

Ministry of Education and Religion (1994c), 'Guide of Studies after Finishing Secondary Education', *Organisation of Educational Publications*, Athens (in Greek).

Official Government Gazette of Greece, No. 71, 20 May 1994, Athens.

Sidiropoulou-Dimakakou, D. (1994a), 'Disabled Students at the University of Athens-Greece', *FEDORA Newsletter*, January 1994 p. 10.

Sidiropoulou-Dimakakou, D. (1994b), 'Disabled Students at the University of Athens-Greece: A Project for the Integration of the Deaf Students', presentation, *FEDORA 5th Congress*, Barcelona, 27-30 April 1994 (unpublished).

Sidiropoulou-Dimakakou, D. (1994c), 'Career Guidance and Counselling for the Disabled Women', *Proceedings of the European Interdisciplinary Congress on the Disabled*, Rhodes-Greece, 8-10 May 1995 pp. 197-205, Ellinika Grammata, Athens (in Greek).

Sidiropoulou-Dimakakou, D. (1995), 'Career Guidance and Counselling of the Disabled Students: A Non-Existent Matter', *Review of Counselling and Guidance*, No. 32-33, Athens (in Greek).

Zoniou-Sideris, A. (1988*), Occupational Training and Rehabilitation of the Disabled*, Nepheli, Athens (in Greek).

9 Disabled students and higher education in Ireland

Carmel O'Sullivan

Higher (Third Level Education) in Ireland

There are many similarities between the system in Ireland and the one in England. Entry to Third Level Education is based on a points system which is calculated on the results of the Leaving Certificate Examination. Entry to universities is competitive. High grades are required, particularly for courses offering a small number of places relative to the number of applicants. Applications are administered through the Central Applications Office. Applicants may state if they have any special needs resulting from a disability. If they do not wish to make this statement on the form they may communicate it to the relevant Admissions Officer at the institution to which they are applying.

The state pays course fees for all undergraduates. Maintenance grants are available but they are means tested. The National University of Ireland (NUI) offers a very small number of grants to students with disabilities, who are attending one of the NUI colleges. Students apply for these grants after registration.

The government through the Departments of Health and Social Welfare offers allowances/pensions to persons with disabilities. These are also means tested. The Department of Education administers a fund for students. A committee reviews each application.

Due to increased awareness and greater facilities at Second Level, more students are now aspiring to Third Level Education. This is welcomed by the universities despite the fact that they have not received any extra funding to provide the relevant facilities. Whilst there is a policy of equal opportunity for all, students with disabilities can be limited in their choice of courses e.g. a blind person could not pursue a course in Science involving laboratory work.

A case study: supporting students with disabilities at University College, Dublin

History and development

Students with disabilities have always been welcome at University College, Dublin (UCD). In the past they have taken their place in a very natural way within the student population. However, due to changes in Second Level Education and increased aspirations, students with disabilities are now looking beyond the traditional areas of employment. Therefore, there is a big increase in the numbers attending University. Also, students with more severe disabilities are applying for places in College. In 1989, UCD initiated the Access Programme to meet this demand. As there was virtually no experience in this area, the programme developed on an ad hoc basis and struggled to meet the needs of the students. Very soon it was obvious that greater funding would be necessary if the programme was to be organised professionally.

UCD applied for funds from the European Social Fund. Funding was granted through the Horizon Programme. This was the injection needed to get the Access Programme established within College and to achieve the aim of providing the academic and the support services necessary to equalise the educational opportunities for students with disabilities in UCD.

In more recent times the Higher Education Authority has reviewed the funding situation for Third Level colleges where programmes for students with disabilities are organised.

Objectives of the Access Programme

The objectives of the Access Programme are:

1.   To create an awareness among people with disabilities that Third Level Education is available to them.

2.   To encourage the disabled community to aspire towards Third Level Education, and to co-operate with other third level institutions developing similar programmes.

3.   To provide the facilities which will create equal opportunities for disabled students within College which will enable them to compete in the employment market on an equal basis with their non-disabled peers.

4.   To conduct an awareness/educational campaign for all staff of University College, Dublin.

5.   To provide personal and individual services for students ensuring continuing support within the larger university community.

6.   To provide special equipment for those students who need it, and ensure that teaching facilities are suitably adapted.

7.   To encourage departments to develop their services to meet the needs of students with disabilities.

8.   To promote the development of facilities for students with disabilities within the sports complex.

9.   To encourage development within the Careers and Appointments Office to cater for the needs of students with disabilities.

The Philosophy underpinning the policy

Integration is fundamental to the success of the Programme. Every effort has to be made to prevent marginalisation of these students. That is why the focus must always be on the person and never on the disability. This will ensure that all planning and programmes are based on the dignity of the person. Every disability demands personal inventiveness which adds to the wealth of human accomplishment. The presence of people with profound disabilities ultimately enriches life and elevates the spirit of all people.

Personnel

The Programme involved the following staff: co-ordinator, librarian, Brailling officer and part-time Braille operators, 2 personal assistants, note-takers, interpreters and readers service (voluntary).

Admissions

A committee has been set up by the Registrar to deal with particular applications from people with disabilities. The purpose of this committee is to make decisions about those who do not have the required points for entry but may be deemed eligible on the basis that it was the disability which prevented qualification. This is an example of what would be called "affirmative action" in the United States. They would be judged to be intellectually capable of pursing the course and therefore could be awarded a place.

The following provides some brief statistical information about the students in the Access Programme.

Student Profile

Mobility Impaired	41
Hearing Impaired	19
Visually Impaired	25
Other	38

In addition, approximately 20+ students with disabilities enter UCD without referring to the Access Office.

Facilities at University College

In relation to the major groups of students with disabilities, there are a number of points to note. With reference to students with impaired mobility Belfield is the largest and most accessible University Campus in Ireland. Major improvements are underway and the University has a commitment to improve access to all its buildings by installing ramps, signs, accessible toilets, lifts etc.

For students with visual impairments, a wide range of facilities are available: enlarged photocopying, exam questions transcribed to Braille, Brailling, tape recording, audio cassette facilities (libraries), taped lectures, orientation and mobility assistance, Braille and speak, reading service, computer software packages, close circuit televisions, voice synthesiser and 21" computer screens.

For students who are deaf or hard of hearing, the following are provided: radio aids, recording equipment, notetakers, interpreters (provided in certain situations) and taped lectures.

Campus residential accommodation

Students with disabilities apply for a place in residence in the normal way. However a small number of places are reserved for these students. The apartments are adapted and modified as required.

The Student Trust Fund

Several College Clubs and Societies make donations to this fund which is used for the personal needs of students with disabilities. For example, one student was helped with the purchase of a wheelchair. Some students were given financial help to enable them to go on Summer study trips. The real value of this initiative is that it heightens awareness of disability amongst the general student body.

Current issues/problems

At the time of writing there are a number of concerns. Firstly, while great progress is being made, the greatest problem is providing brailled material for blind students. It is a very costly and slow process. Efforts are continuing to develop and improve the service.

Secondly, there are questions about dyslexia. This is a condition which varies so much that it has been decided to study the situation more deeply. Hopefully this will enable College to develop a satisfactory policy with regard to admissions and examinations.

Thirdly, it has become recognised that there is a need to develop awareness amongst all staff in order to dispel the idea that disability is a welfare issue only. Responsibility for students with disabilities is shared by everyone if the institution is to be truly and fully inclusive.

Finally, as students are now getting increased opportunities to participate in Third Level Education, efforts must be made to convince employers that they too should provide equal opportunities in the work place for graduates with disabilities. It seems short-sighted to raise the hopes of people with disabilities within education only to find that this leads to frustration later on when those who are successful try to make use of their qualifications in the job market.

Conclusion

There has been a very significant development in Ireland in recent times. This was the creation of a national umbrella organisation. The Association for Higher Education Access and Disability (AHEAD) was set up to promote the full participation of students with disabilities in Higher Education. It is funded mainly by EU funds from the Horizon Programme. (Information is available from the Director, Newman House, 86 St Stephen's Green, Dublin 2).

Corporate membership is open to all Third Level Institutions. Individual membership is open to all Third Level students.

While still in its infancy AHEAD is doing an excellent job in promoting the needs of students with disabilities. Along with publications on Examination Guidelines, the Legislation on Disability and Higher Education, AHEAD recently held a seminar on Employment Issues for Graduates with Disabilities. Faculty networking and the sharing of good practice will lead to progress in developing policy and making provision for students with disabilities.

10 Including students with disabilities in higher education in Lithuania

Adolfus Juodraitis and Juozas Petrusevicius

Introduction

Having re-established independence on March 11th 1990, the task of the new Lithuanian Republic was not only to make use of the potential which had built up already within the higher education sector but also to expand it and introduce into it some of the innovations and changes which had been made in the Western countries

Today, Lithuania's higher education system is able to train highly qualified specialists and then offer them the opportunity to update and improve their qualifications and possibly even to retrain. There are 15 locations offering higher education. Six of them are universities: Vilnius University (founded in 1579), Vilnius Pedagogical University, Vilnius Gediminas Technical University, Kaunas Technological University, Kaunas Vytautas the Great University, and Klapeida University. There are also seven academies: the Lithuanian Music Academy, the State Art Academy, the Medical, Veterinary, and Agricultural Academies, the Lithuanian Military Academy, and the Police Academy. The remaining two are the Lithuanian Physical Training Institute and Siauliai Pedagogical Institute. (The latter is being reorganised into the Northern Lithuanian University.)

At some points in recent history, the population of students in higher education was decreasing. In 1989 there were 69,500 students whilst by 1993 this figure had fallen to 52,900. The peak occurred in 1980 when there were 71,000 students. It is difficult to identify causes of this phenomenon, although no doubt the general economic and financial situation had some influence. Also, the prestige of higher education had fallen. Despite being financed by the state, the higher education institutions are autonomous and are responsible for deciding their own curriculum, the number of students, the requirements for entry, etc. Admissions procedures vary; sometimes there are traditional written examinations, sometimes the examinations involve oral presentations. Some students gain entry on the basis of their performance in the secondary school leaving examinations which might be considered to be a more democratic approach. However this approach does not always mean that those who enter are the most suitable for the courses they join. Following experience in other countries, the system for assessing students' work has changed with three levels of achievement now in place (B - ordinary, A - higher, and S - with special emphasis on certain subjects). The state is concerned that the diplomas and qualifications obtained in Lithuania are recognised in other countries. In order to achieve this, curricula are moving towards patterns found in other countries - for example modular structures with credit accumulation systems. There are also efforts being made to increase the numbers of students and staff participating in foreign exchanges. New specialities are being developed - estate management, business management, information management, environmental studies, political studies and so on. These new subjects could contribute to making higher education more attractive. A further example of Lithuania's striving to adopt good practice found in other countries is the appearance of private colleges where Christian social education, psychology, tourism, hospitality management, catering, etc. are taught. The qualifications available in these colleges do have validity and national recognition.

The new Lithuanian Republic tries to preserve national traditions and principles in its education system whilst at the same time introducing the changes based on the experiences of other countries. One issue which demonstrates this clearly is the issue of including children with special educational needs in mainstream schools. In order to tackle this successfully, it is necessary to consider pedagogical, psychological, and legal strategies. Without this, the successful inclusion of learners with disabilities into schools will not take place. Sometimes, the success is linked to factors such as the overall economic context over which the education system has no influence and whose role cannot be anticipated.

Education and learners with visual impairments

The Lithuanian Republic has rather an outdated system of education and rehabilitation for people with special educational needs, especially for those with visual impairments. It is evident also that, in comparison to other countries, the overall place of disabled people in Lithuanian society is poor. The present situation has not resulted from negative state policy or indifferent social attitudes towards people with disabilities Much more responsible is the political context of the country. During the long periods when the country depended heavily on Poland, Germany, and then Russia, there were radical changes but these related to social systems which had quite different values. There were signs of progress.

For example, during the second half of the last century, attempts were made to care for those who had become blind as a result of war. A special committee was established which in 1881 became the Tsarita Maria Alexandrovna's Shelter Committee of the Blind with departments in Vilnius and Kaunas. Sadly, the education of people in the provincial nations received little attention in Tsarist Russia.

It was in 1928, ten years after the declaration of independence following the First World War and the Russian Revolution, that education was first provided for children who were blind or visually impaired. The number of pupils attending the new Institute for the Blind grew only slowly. Because of a serious lack of finance, the school could not provide the six year curriculum which could lead on to higher education. The curriculum depended heavily on the attitudes and wishes of the school authorities and those supporting it financially. Blind and visually impaired people had little opportunity to obtain diplomas in higher education although a very small number who had both the finances and the necessary determination did complete their studies. In 1944, the Lithuanian Association of the Blind was founded and this became associated with giving closer attention to making suitable educational provision for blind children. Currently, those leaving the two residential special schools in Vilnius and Kaunas have much better opportunities to participate in higher education. A major step forward in facilitating this was the availability of specially trained staff. In 1971 part-time courses began at the Siauliai Pedagogical Institute to train teachers of the blind. Today, in some institutions, there can be up to 50 per cent of the staff who have been trained at Siauliai.

There are students with visual impairments studying in higher education on a number of different courses - history, literature, Russian, law, journalism, mathematics, and psychology. If previous patterns are followed, many will themselves become teachers or researchers. Whilst this indicates that some progress has been made, there is still some way to go before it can be said that people with visual impairments experience a fully inclusive society.

Education for deaf and hard-of-hearing learners

One of the most important factors contributing to successful inclusion in education originates in the psychology of society. This is best seen, perhaps, when exploring the process of adaptation and integration of people with other kinds of impairments (hearing, speaking, moving). The first school for deaf children was founded on a philanthropic basis in Vilnius in 1805. The authorities in that city paid considerable attention to the education of people who were deaf or hard-of-hearing. A draft plan for establishing an institute for people who in those days were called deaf and dumb was devised, financial support was planned, a curriculum designed. A similar school was established in Klapeida. It is interesting to note that the language of instruction was different in each of the two schools. In Vilnius, Polish was used whilst in Klapeida it was German. The most significant development came with the creation of the Society for the Deaf and Dumb in 1938. After this a more systematic approach to education began. A residential school was founded in Kaunas, and during the period of Soviet influence, two further schools started. Having realised the importance of early identification and early intervention, the provision of education for pre-school children with hearing and speech impairments began in Vilnius, Kaunas, and Siauliai. In 1964-65, there were 492 pupils in the major three schools for deaf children (in Vilnius, Kaunas, and Telsiai). In 1990 there were 462 pupils and in 1991, there were 375. This fall in numbers does not mean that the incidence of hearing and speech impairments is decreasing. What has happened is that there are special classes attached to two mainstream schools in Siauliai and Panevezys. The situation in Lithuania with regard to the education of children who are deaf or hard-of-hearing is one of transition. There remain many issues to be addressed.

Education for learners with mobility impairments

The situation for learners with mobility impairments is similar to that of deaf people. In terms of access to higher education some development has taken place but these have been on an ad-hoc individual basis. For example, in 1996 there were two students who were wheelchair users on courses at Siauliai. This prompted some adaptations to buildings. The entrance to the main building was improved by the provision of a ramp. In 1991 the Law of Social Integration of Disabled people was passed. This aimed to stimulate the process of inclusion into society and to create an effective rehabilitation system. An indication that this law is effective will be to see greater numbers of children with disabilities being educated in mainstream schools.

Developments at Siauliai Pedagogical Institute

Since 1992 the Faculty of Special Education at the Siauliai Pedagogical Institute has been taking part in a project funded by the European Community under the TEMPUS initiative. The two main tasks of the project have been to update the strategies for training teachers working in special education and also to promote inclusive education. The approach was collaborative, involving working with colleagues from the University of Grenoble in France, and the Manchester Metropolitan University, England. Students at the Pedagogical Institute can specialise in teaching of children with a range of disabilities and learning difficulties. More recently, the Faculty started to train social workers and educational psychologists who should also make an important contribution to the movement for more inclusive education. The 1991 Law mentioned above also envisages the reconstruction and adaptation of public buildings and changes to the physical environment. The alterations made at the Pedagogical Institute to facilitate access for wheelchair users is an indication that the law is starting to become effective. It is estimated that there are 50,000 people with mobility impairments in Lithuania.

In the future, another significant development will take place. This concerns the provision and training of interpreters to work with deaf and hard-of-hearing people. A consequence of this will be that there will be opportunities for deaf people to work as teachers. It can be argued that tacking the difficulties faced by deaf learners is the most difficult of all. Recently, at Vilnius University, six out of seven deaf students studying economics failed to complete the course.

Developments in other higher education institutions

Until now, there has been no co-ordinated programme to facilitate the inclusion of people with disabilities in higher education. In fact, many of the problems they encounter in other countries, have still to be recognised in Lithuania. Currently there are no statistics about the number of students with disabilities participating in higher education. The majority of the students will be on courses at the Vytautas the Great University, Kaunas and at Vilnius University. These are Lithuania's two most important cities. There, facilities are more advanced. For example there are opportunities to use public transport. There are plans to be implemented in the period ending in 1999 for students unable to use public transport to be provided with special transport. This programme will be funded from state sources. Also, at the Vytautas the Great University, there is a member of staff who has responsibility for students with disabilities. The responsibilities of the post are similar to those found in other countries and include aspects of academic life and also student social life and the activities of daily living. Some special arrangements are in place - for example free photocopying, and the loaning of special equipment. Every year, they can participate in a special summer camp. In 1996, there were 20 students with disabilities enrolled at the University studying on variety of courses.

In order to develop policy and provision, the University is collaborating with a group of colleagues from Germany to organise a symposium for staff who teach students with disabilities. This will lead to a better understanding of the different special needs of students with disabilities and so they can try to be more effective teachers.

Conclusions

Despite all these signs of progress, Lithuania continues to lack a coherent approach to policy and provision for students with disabilities in higher education. The government is trying to support all people with disabilities (including students in higher education) by giving them grants and additional financial allowances. The Council of Disabled People in Lithuania proclaimed 1996 as the Year of Disabled People which did stimulate further developments towards a more co-ordinated system. In moving towards this, educational psychologists are seen as playing a key role since through their interventions, they might minimise the chances that people with disabilities might fail to adjust to society and also they might work towards the elimination of negative attitudes and stereotypes held by non-disabled people.

What is really needed is the provision of services for disabled people to be made a part of the responsibilities of all government ministries and departments. With improved co-ordination, supported by the availability of additional funds and backed by laws, the social situation of people with disabilities in Lithuania would improve considerably. Society would develop more positive attitudes and in turn this would allow people with disabilities opportunities to develop their potential, secure appropriate employment, and make their contribution to society. Students with disabilities who are successful in higher education might be the leaders of this process.

References

Gudonis, V. (1985), *The History of Lithuanian Teachers of the Blind,* (in Lithuanian - no translation available).

Karvelis, V. (1969), *The Education of Handicapped Children in Soviet Lithuania,* (in Lithuanian - no translation available).

(not attributed) (1990), *Lithuania 1918-1938,* (in Lithuanian - no translation available).

(not attributed) (1990), *The First Decade of Independent Lithuania 1918-1928,* (in Lithuanian - no translation available).

Whiteman, M. and Lukoff, S.F. (1964), 'A factorial study of sighted people's attitudes towards blindness', *Journal of Social Psychology,* Vol. 64, pp. 339-353.

11 Students with disabilities in the Netherlands

Willem Temmink and Piet Vriens

Introduction

Respect for minorities is one of the core values of democracy. In order to ensure that this occurs many organisations ranging from the global such as the United Nations, the national such as governments, and institutions such as universities have formulated rules, regulations, and policies. Despite these efforts, their overall impact has been disappointing. A good example of this might be with regard to the employment of people with disabilities. The contemporary economic climate with its great emphasis on cost effectiveness and efficiency seems to work against recruiting staff who might be perceived to harm these characteristics. This is as true of the governments which enact the laws as much as it is for private enterprises which are expected to comply. In the prevailing conditions of high unemployment, employers prefer to take on staff who are young, fit, and healthy. This is the contemporary late 20th century context in which people with disabilities find themselves - in the Netherlands and also in many other parts of the world.

Higher education in the Netherlands

In 1996 there were approximately 400,000 students in higher education, studying in one of the 13 universities and 73 Hogescholen. Higher education in the Netherlands consists of two different parts. The first stage covers 42 credits and ends with a mid-degree examination (propedeuse examen). Only those, who pass this can continue with their studies. This is also the point at which some students choose to change institutions. There is very centralised control of studies. Thus, according to national legislation, one credit is the equivalent of 40 hours of study. Full time students have to study for 40 hours per week and the academic year is 42 weeks long. At least 168 credits are required in most advanced study programmes and some require more (e.g. medicine).

The system in the Netherlands has two distinct routes. There is academic higher education and there is vocational higher education, more closely linked to specific professions. Each is provided in different institutions, the former taking place in the universities and the latter in the Hogescholen. On completing courses in higher education, students can use the title "master". In universities, students can also refer to themselves by other titles: doctorandus, meester (in law) and ingenieur (in technology). On the vocational route, all students can use the title "bachelor" whilst in some fields of study there are special titles.

The system is based on the Higher Education and Scientific Research Act of September 1993.ᐟ Before the changes which this Act introduced, all the different kinds of vocations had their own schools. The changes brought about a more unified system. There is a central register (CROHO) of nationally recognised study programmes. These programmes have to have central approval before the institutions receive funds and for students to obtain financial support.

The aim of our universities is to develop the intellectual potential of the country. Having a disability does not necessarily affect an individual's capacity for thinking. If the country wants to make best use of its human resource potential, then it has to ensure that there is access to higher education. In the Netherlands, more and more pupils with disabilities and learning difficulties are entering higher education. This is partly as a result of the improved quality and availability of support in primary and secondary education. Many more pupils with disabilities and learning difficulties are taught in inclusive schools. The progress made in assistive technology has been important as have the political activities of disabled people themselves who have become more prominent in society as they demand the same rights as others.

The 1993 Act is especially important for students with disabilities since it ensured that the needs of this group were taken into account for the first time. For example, the Act requires that the various Faculties in universities have to draw up special examination regulations. Each Faculty in the different universities has done this differently. However, all seem to have tried to implement the law rather broadly so that it is sufficiently flexible to meet as many different individual needs as possible.

Even so, higher education still seems to be apprehensive about including students with disabilities. There is a clear lack of awareness and a shortage of staff with training, expertise and specialised knowledge. The situation has not been helped because of the problems that the higher education system itself has faced. There has been a significant increase in the number of students going to university and this has not been accompanied by a commensurate increase in the resources need to meet the increased demand. Academic staff have bigger classes and they are unable to spend as much time meeting the needs of individual students. Higher education, like the business world, has had to pay attention to improved cost effectiveness and more efficient use of resources. In order to ensure that costs are kept in check, there are fewer grants and scholarships for students. Many students have to take out loans and to work to pay for their higher education.

Higher education and students with disabilities

Given the circumstances outlined above, the situation of students with disabilities is a difficult one. Some might be hesitant about starting a higher education programme because of the costs involved. Others might feel that their chances of completing their studies successfully have declined.

If this is the case, then it is very sad. Certainly, it has not always been like this. In the past, many students with disabilities obtained good results. Their tutors were able to give them the level of support they needed - although the support was regarded as an extra, a "favour", a kind of philanthropic gesture more associated with 19th century charity rather than being a standard part of the service given to students. Universities have been reluctant to establish proper systems for students with disabilities including rights of appeal when they encountered difficulties. Perhaps the universities might be pushed to improve their services if more applicants with disabilities and their parents and friends complained when they met ignorance and hostile attitudes. The situation which many universities are in is self-perpetuating. The universities do not develop policy and provision, for example for students who are blind or deaf, and so they do not receive any applications. They can then claim that because they do not have applications, there is no need to develop facilities and services

A major sign of progress is the appointment of a member of staff who has responsibility for welcoming students with disabilities and co-ordinating their support when they start their programmes of study. A fundamental principle underpinning all of the work is to develop the independence of the student and to put the student in control of decision-making about her/his own future. Staff working in the office for students with disabilities ideally should have knowledge and experience although such people are not easy to find. In some places, medical staff have been closely involved but this is not always useful since they do not know about the kinds of issue faced in the academic context of a university. As an example of this, there was one student with a visual impairment who could not read texts in normal lighting. When she met her eye specialist, he suggested that she completed all her course reading at home where the lighting conditions could be manipulated. During the day she could simply attend the lectures. This strategy meant that the student lost a lot of time. Perhaps the eye-specialist was unaware that the student could use cassette recordings of the books or that reading might be possible using assistive technology such as an adapted computer and video screen. It is only through working alongside students like this one that staff can develop their knowledge and thus be in a position to offer sound advice.

Students with disabilities at the University of Amsterdam

An institution was founded in Amsterdam in 1632 to train students in philosophy and commerce. The actual tuition took place in the homes of the teachers and it was only in 1877 that something akin to the university of today emerged. However, there remain some similarities in that teaching in 1997 is still spread throughout the city although most faculties are located near to the centre of the city. By 1900 there were 900 students, by 1935 there were 2,500, and by 1960 there were 7,500. In 1997, 26,000 students were enrolled on courses at the University.

At the formal level, there is a committee for disabled people which considers a wide range of issues including those which apply to staff with disabilities employed at the University. In terms of day-to-day matters and students, the University has a student counsellor who has responsibility for students with disabilities and the co-ordination of services to support them. The task is not easy, partly because of the nature of the university's infrastructure and its location in the city. In fact some students might decide to study in other places because of difficulties associated with architecture and location. Many of the buildings are old and so access for wheelchair users is sometimes a problem. In some of them, access to the upper floors is possible using the special stair lifts which have been installed. Moving between buildings can be difficult because of the cobbled streets, the narrow uneven pavements, and the steep slopes of bridges crossing the many canals. Sometimes the best way to travel between buildings is by taxi but then this raises the question of cost. The physical environment can also create difficulties for students who are blind or have visual impairments. On the positive side, students who are deaf and need to use interpreters have this support provided free of charge with costs paid for by the social security system.

One aspect of provision where students with disabilities can be seen to experience inclusiveness is the system of study advisers. It is the responsibility of study advisers in each faculty to contact all students (including those with disabilities) at the start of their first year of the course. They can give advice on all matters including life outside the classroom; they are there not simply to advise about problems related to studying. Because of the pressure on the time of the tutors, the role of the study advisers has become more important. This is true for all students although it might be of greater significance for students with disabilities.

The work of "Handicap and Studie"

"Handicap and Studie" is an organisation established to give assistance to students with disabilities in secondary and higher education in overcoming difficulties in education, employment, and social life. It is based in Utrecht where there is a small information centre which can be visited. The organisation publishes "Binding", a quarterly magazine containing topical articles and information useful to anyone with an interest in policies and provision for students with disabilities.

Contact is established with students with disabilities during their last term in secondary education. The students and their parents can apply for advice and help on many matters: information about courses and about the universities, technical equipment, living accommodation, transport, welfare facilities, and - often the most important questions - finance. In the Netherlands students who complete their courses successfully within four years do not have to repay their student loan. However, because of their impairment, many students with disabilities can take much longer to finish. A key to retaining their participation and involvement in tertiary education is the availability of finance. Whenever any information is provided in response to a request, efforts are made to make it directly relevant to the person who made the enquiry. It cannot be assumed that because people share the same impairment, their needs will be the same. This applies also to the courses and the institutions; differences between the universities have to be taken into account. Sometimes, students with disabilities meet with staff from "Handicap and Studie" who are also in touch with the higher education specialist advisers.

The organisation tries to influence national policy. It has promoted inclusive education for students with physical and sensory impairment and it has developed a critical attitude towards national government policy. When legislation seems not to be in the best interests of people with disabilities, efforts are made to force changes. For example, some of the regulations about matriculation can be unfair to students with disabilities, (e.g. the length of time in which courses are to be completed). Working with staff from the universities, "Handicap and Studie" has tried to persuade the government to recognise this and sometimes there has been supplementary legislation or exceptions to rules accepted.

Conclusion

In the Netherlands, we are still learning much about working to develop policy and provision for students with disabilities. Our experience is growing and in the absence of literature, this continues to be our main source of knowledge and expertise. Further advances will be made if the students with disabilities passing through the system start to claim their rights. Not only will this lead to changes in wider society, there will be an impact on the education system so that those who follow them into our universities can be assured of a much less problem-centred experience.

12 Supporting students with disabilities in the Slovak Republic

Elena Mendelova

Background

Whilst the Slovak Republic is relatively young, its origins go back many years and it has some very old cultural and educational traditions. The capital, Bratislava, is rich in history dating as far back as the Early Stone Age. In 1536 it became the capital of the Hungarian part of the Habsburg Empire. It was the seat of the Hungarian Parliament and government offices; the kings and queens of Hungary held their coronation ceremonies in the city. Between 1563 and 1830 eleven kings and eight royal wives were crowned there.

Moving to more modern times which saw the decline and disappearance of the Habsburg Austro-Hungarian Empire, the first university within what is now the Slovak Republic was founded in 1919. This was the Comenius University in Bratislava. It can trace its development back to the establishment of the Academia Istropolitana in 1467.

Today, there are 5,000 members of staff working with around 18,000 students. The University has 12 faculties which attract students from all parts of the Slovak Republic as well as from other countries.

In addition to the Comenius University, there are 12 other universities in the Slovak Republic. These consist of over 50 faculties, each of which has its own academic structures and systems (e.g. academic senate, research committees, deans, etc.). They are also independent in terms of their curricula and their strategies of teaching, learning, and assessment.

No official statistics are collected about the number of students with disabilities in universities in the Slovak Republic. An effort was made recently to gain some indication of numbers by contacting all faculties in all universities. Sadly, only around half of those contacted replied. Of these, there were 13 faculties which were working with students with disabilities. The total number of students was 38 and apart from those in Bratislava, all had been pursuing their courses without any special support. Most students had visual or mobility impairments. (It is only recently that dyslexia has been seen as a disability in the Slovak Republic.)

The situation of students with disabilities in the Slovak Republic

In the past, having a disability has been a major obstacle preventing participation in higher education. Having a disability was seen as having two dimensions - problems for the individual with the disability, and problems for the institutions and especially for the academic staff. Students with disabilities found it very difficult to get into universities. A very small number have progressed through the system and are working now as teachers, physicists and musicians. They were given lots of support by their families.

Today, the number of students with disabilities who are able to enter university and study independently is growing. Most of them who have obvious sensory and physical impairments are nor recognised as being different in any ways from other students since there is no special support available and so registering as a student with a disability is unnecessary. They undertake their programmes of study in the same way as all other students. Where they need specialist advice or information, this is given by the department responsible for student affairs. Occasionally, the responsibility for providing the service rests with the dean or vice-dean of academic or curricular affairs.

Developing the support centre for students with visual impairments

The support centre for students with visual impairments at the Comenius University, Bratislava, is the first and currently the only place of its kind which is geared towards supporting and guiding students with disabilities. It used as its model the system already established at the University of Karlsruhe but adapted to take into account the local context and environment. The centre was set up in November 1993. It was built in connection with a TEMPUS Project called 'New Study and Vocational Opportunities for Visually impaired Students'. The centre is located within the faculty of Mathematics and Physics but support is available for students in all faculties and on all courses. The main aim of the centre is to facilitate the inclusion of blind and visually impaired students into university life, both in its academic activities and also in social life outside the classroom. It is about full preparation for life and not just about helping to secure vocationally-oriented qualifications.

The activities of the support centre can be grouped into three areas. Firstly, there are educational and technical aspects. Blind and visually impaired students can obtain standard personal portable computers with additional specialist software which enables them to have access to information in the format which they prefer. This includes enlarging software, voice-activated software, and Braille. Students can have tuition on how the equipment can be used. Also they can be shown how to gain access to the Internet. Secondly, there are the services provided by the centre in relation to study materials. Staff in the centre transform the course literature into whatever format the students need. The main aim is to try to ensure that blind and visually impaired students have access to the texts at the same time as their sighted peers. The third aspect of the work is the provision of information and advice. Applicants from special schools, their parents, and their teachers are told about the special support facilities available to ensure that study takes place in an inclusive context. Advice is given about the kind of equipment which is needed to facilitate this inclusion. The centre also contacts relevant faculties and academic departments in advance to alert them to the needs of the students. Where there are entrance examinations and tests, the centre co-operates in whatever ways are appropriate. The centre takes responsibility for introducing blind and visually impaired students to their fellow-students. They try to promote the creation of a group of students who can offer assistance to the blind and visually impaired students on a daily basis if the latter encounter problems with their courses. The availability of this kind of support seems to be necessary at the start of the course. When the blind and visually impaired students are settled, they find their own friends and relations with others on the course develop in a natural way as with other students.

Admissions and entry to the university

During the past few years, good working relationships have been established between the support centre and the faculties where students with disabilities have taken courses. In some cases, there was some reluctance on the part of the academic department and the academic staff since they envisaged many serious difficulties. However, suitable solutions have been devised and the initial anxieties have been allayed.

Applicants with disabilities are encouraged to contact the support centre before they apply for a place. The response to this initial contact is to send information to the applicant (for example about special equipment) and to get in touch with the faculty/department. Criteria for entry to courses are based on results obtained in secondary education and also in an entrance exam. Students with disabilities do not have prioritised entry at the Comenius University or indeed at any other university on the Slovak Republic. As the number of applications is greater than the number of places available, some selection has to take place. Sometimes the competition is substantial. For example, for the 40 places available to study Psychology at the Comenius University, there are around 4,000 applicants. Clearly, it is important for the students to get good results in the schools and in the entrance examination if they are to have a good chance of being offered a place. Students with disabilities are treated no differently although perhaps the chances of securing a place are strengthened if the faculty/department has had previous successful experience of working with students with similar needs.

On-course support

Students who are blind or who have visual impairments work closely with the support centre throughout the entire period of their courses. Each student has her/his own individual programme. Often it is possible to make some modifications to the curriculum or to the content of courses. More difficulties occur when students are taking combinations of subjects or are taking specialised courses/options.

Because the approach adopted by the University and the study centre is one of inclusion and student independence, personal assistance is not provided. Students are offered training to make them more independent. Each programme is devised to meet the specific needs of the individual student. The training does assume that the students do have a certain level of skills already, for example in using equipment. Clearly every student is different and it is dangerous to generalise. However, the students who appear to present the more serious difficulties are those who come from the specialist, segregated educational institutions. This group of students do not seem to be prepared well enough for living independently and studying in an inclusive environment. They do not seem to have skills associated with independent personal mobility, communication skills, interpersonal skills, and self advocacy skills.

Having said that, it is also fair to say that there is a matching lack of awareness of disability within the wider society. There have been many discussions about the concept of 'equal opportunities' and what this means. In order to make progress, the argument have to be very convincing. In the past, there have been indifferent and even hostile, and negative attitudes shown by staff and fellow students towards those with disabilities.

Staff from the support centre have organised some disability awareness raising seminars for teachers in schools and also for university staff in faculties and departments where students with disabilities have been enrolled on courses. These, together with involvement of the support centre in open days should contribute to heightened levels of awareness. There also seems to be more awareness in the mass media and so this should also help.

Conclusions

Staff at the Comenius University have been active now for four years and have devised strategies and solutions to overcome many difficulties. Students who are blind or who have visual impairments are beginning to graduate in more significant numbers. As news of this spreads, more students who have visual impairments are applying for places. There is still much to do. Without doubt, staff in the support centre will have plenty of work so that the progress already made will continue. To reach a position with which everyone feels satisfied will take a long time. Meanwhile, everyone who is involved will do their best to ensure that students with disabilities do have opportunities to participate in higher education.

13 Students with disabilities in higher education in Spain

Maria Pilar Sarto Martin

Introduction

The question of meeting the needs of people with disabilities is the focus of detailed debate in contemporary Spain. Some progress has been made and with this in mind, it is important to mention some recent legal measures affecting policy and provision of special education. Within the current Spanish political democracy, it is important to look at Articles 27 and 49 of the Constitution of 27 December 1978 which state that all citizens have the right to education and that the purpose of education is the full development of the individual, according to the principles of co-existence and fundamental human rights and liberties (Article 27). The Constitution states also that the public authorities must undertake policies to support, integrate and rehabilitate people with physical, sensory or mental disabilities. Special measures will be taken so that this group of people can enjoy the rights guaranteed to all citizens by the Constitution (Article 49).

It is clear from reading the Constitution that people with disabilities in general have the right to participate in the education system at any level. The central or regional governments are responsible for providing whatever resources are needed for people, irrespective of the nature of the disability, to participate fully in their immediate surroundings and social context. On 7 April 1982 the Disabled Persons' Social and Work Integration Act was passed, providing for the first time, a framework which promoted the full inclusion of people with disabilities in education, work, and social life. According to the provisions of the third section of the Act (especially Articles 23, 26, 30 and 31) the individual with a disability will be integrated into mainstream education and, where necessary, will receive support and resources (Article 23). Article 26 states that special education is an integral, flexible and dynamic process which has to be adapted and applied to meet the needs of individuals. This includes the various stages and gradations of the education system, particularly those which are compulsory and free. The aim of this to secure the full social integration of the disabled individual. This means full participation in employment and social life so that people with disabilities can live independently and feel that their lives are satisfying. Article 30 provides for the free education of people with disabilities in mainstream schools and colleges, and in special schools where appropriate. The final Article which must be considered is Article 31. This makes it clear that people with disabilities who attend universities and whose disability hinders quite seriously their ability to take examinations in the same way as their non-disabled peers can request additional opportunities to sit the examination. This law also requires universities to change the format of the examinations if requested in order to meet the needs of the disabled student. In all cases, whilst meeting these requirements, the academic levels and standards must not be lowered.

Since the passing of this Act, there was an increase in the number of small units providing care and support for specialist groups.   There were also more rehabilitation centres and more sheltered employment schemes.   Recently the focus has shifted towards making people with disabilities more independent. For example there is now a National Centre for Personal Independence and Technological Aids (Centro Estatal de Auotonomia Personal y Ayudas Tecnicas - CEAPAT). Despite developments such as these, the overall situation is that both the availability and quality of provision differs between areas.

Education before university

In order to have a better understanding of the position of students with disabilities in higher education, it is necessary to know a little more about changes which have taken place in the education system as a whole in Spain. In recent times the system has changed completely. Changes came first in 1970 with the General Education Act which could be seen as a move away from education for a privileged minority to a system of mass education. The intention was for pupils to remain in school until the age of 16 and to allocate more money to education especially for building more schools. In reality, the Act was ineffective and many students continued to leave school at age 14. Today, the number of students who began their studies under the old system has fallen and most are now embraced by the new system established in 1990 (the General Organic Law of the Education System - LOGSE). It is envisaged that the old system will have disappeared entirely by 1999. The new model was implemented in the academic year which started in 1992 and applied to the first year of primary schooling.

Following the implementation of the LOGSE, the primary stage of education starts with children at age six and ends when they are 12. The old secondary system was marked by a number of divisions. In order to progress to secondary education of an academic type, pupils had to obtain a qualification similar to the French Baccalaureate (the Bachillerato Unificado Polivalente - BUP). Those who failed were directed towards vocational education.   To enter higher education, learners had to take a pre-university course (Curso de Orientacion Universitaria - COU). The BUP and the COU were classed as secondary education and were not available without payment. The introduction of LOGSE has brought important changes. All pupils now experience a free, common secondary education (educacion secundaria obligatoria) to age 16. At this point, the former division between vocational and academic reappears. For the latter, there is a shorter Bachillerato which replaces the COU. Pupils can choose between four routes: natural and health sciences, humanities and social sciences, technology, and the arts. However, to continue into university, passing an entrance examination remains a requirement. This assumes greater significance where the number of places available is limited; the marks obtained (notas) become crucial.

At all stages, learners with disabilities and learning difficulties are dealt with in terms of their individual needs. The methods of teaching are adapted so that the individual can reach the objectives set. Special attention has been given to the identification of needs, the involvement of parents, and regular monitoring of progress. In accordance with principles of inclusion and independence, placing a child in a segregated school is limited. Following the 1982 Act (see opening section) the Royal Decree on Special Education Planning (R.D. 6/3/85) set in motion a programme of including pupils with disabilities and learning difficulties into mainstream schools. The changes which have occurred since the 1990 Act have continued this policy. A later government order in 1990 established an experimental programme for including learners with disabilities where the second stage of compulsory secondary education was being taught and this has been renewed at least once since then. The government has permitted changes to the 'Bachillerato' curriculum to meet the needs of learners with sensory or mobility impairments, including partial or total exemption from certain subjects where appropriate.

The university system in Spain

In Spain there are 27 universities founded before 1975, 16 founded since 1975, five universities run by the Roman Catholic Church and five private universities. Within the country there are several autonomous regions where the universities are administered by the regional education authorities, and some enjoy a greater or lesser degree of independence in matters related to their curricula and their teaching. The legal basis for the independence of the universities is the Organic Law of University Reform 1983 (Ley de Reforma Universitaria -LRU).

Higher education has seen enormous growth in the last 30 years or so. In the early 1960s, there were around 60,000 students enrolled whilst the number had risen to over one million by the start of the 1990s. The huge increase in numbers and the speed with which the growth occurred created many difficulties both for staff and students. It was no surprise that serious attention was given by the government to higher education and that the 1983 Act has been seen as so important. The Act tackled some of the traditional problems of the sector and attempted to give it more freedom to operate efficiently and effectively to meet the new demands. There were accompanying changes in the framework too. New universities were established in areas where they were needed - in some case to provide additional places in locations which had already established institutions; in others the setting up of a higher education institution filled a gap in provision.

A number of other changes have resulted in mixed success. Efforts to resolve the issue of the number of tenured staff have not been fully worked out since it has not been easy to redeploy staff between old established departments where staffing is plentiful and new departments in which staff are needed. The improved availability of financial support for students has improved overall access to higher education but the resources directed towards the institutions have not kept pace with the expansion and so problems have been created. The level of autonomy which the universities now possess is debatable since there remain many powerful influences outside the institutions, for example the Council of Universities which is linked to the Ministry of Education and which has to be involved in many decisions. The Council has had the responsibility for drawing up a list of subjects in which degrees can be awarded to update the rather restricted list which was in operation for many years. A greater element of competition is present in the sector and this is manifest in several ways. The government has allowed the creation of many new institutions, notably the private universities.   Competition also occurs through recruitment as the universities develop new courses and as students have greater freedom to choose to study away from home.

The 1983 Act also brought new qualifications (titulos) and new courses (carreras). However the typical pattern remains rooted in academic study within a traditional faculty structure. Undergraduate studies (cursos) take four years and consist of two stages (ciclos). Each takes two years, the first stage being a foundation and the second allowing for specialisation. Students can exit with a diploma at the end of two years; after four years, successful students are awarded a degree (licenciatura) There are also postgraduate qualifications.

The Royal Decree of September 1992 requires universities with a limited number of first year places available to set aside three per cent of these places for students who are recognised officially as having disabilities or who have no hearing or speech.

The University of Salamanca

There are records dated 1218 referring to an old school in Salamanca. In the old library of the present university, there is a charter issued in 1243 by King Alfonso IX of Leon which includes the founding of a university in Salamanca. By the early 16th century, this had become one of the most important centres of learning in Europe. Many distinguished scholars have visited and taught in Salamanca. During the period of colonial expansion, universities were founded in Lima and in Mexico which made use of the Statutes of the University of Salamanca.

Today, there are almost 31,000 students registered with the university. This places it in 18th position in ranking of state universities based on the number of students. There are just under 12,000 taking Diploma courses (i.e. first stage qualifications) and just over 19,000 studying for first degrees (second stage qualifications). There are over 1,500 postgraduate students. Compared to other institutions, there are more students taking courses in humanities. In recent times, numbers on courses related to health care and socio-legal studies have grown. The number of students taking courses in the natural sciences is below the national average. A wide range of facilities and services are available for students (e.g. halls of residence, advisory counselling and health services, sports, etc.). The University has 1,860 academic staff of which under half are permanent. Teaching is associated with 72 different qualifications and takes place at 23 different centres.

Students with disabilities at the University of Salamanca

In 1992 the United Nations General Assembly declared 3 December to be the International Day of Disabled People. This had two aims: to achieve the full and equal enjoyment of human rights and to ensure full participation in society. Two years later, students in the Faculty of Education Science, Special Education and Educational Psychology organised a debate on integration/inclusion in the University. People with disabilities, professional organisations, tutors, students and also the Vice Chancellor took part. One result of this was to find out how many students with disabilities were studying in Salamanca and what difficulties they were meeting in order to pursue their courses. No precise numbers emerged although it appeared that there were 24 students with disabilities on courses at that time. From the point of view of these students, there had to be a major focus on the attitudes of society towards disability. Overall, the event was judged to be successful and certainly there was a greater level of awareness afterwards. This was assisted too by the event being reported in the local press.

At the same time as the debate was taking place, an investigation was underway to find out more about the experiences of students with disabilities at the university. Efforts were made to discover which courses had enrolled students with disabilities and then to contact the students to ask them about what kinds of difficulties they encountered. It was evident from the debate mentioned in the preceding paragraph that a major problem is collecting statistical data about the number of students and the kinds of impairments they have. Not all students with disabilities provide the information when they enrol. Only those who apply for the three per cent of reserved places declare that they have a disability. It was a priority that students with disabilities could be identified. Those involved in the investigation used official records kept by the faculties, personal contacts with some of the students with disabilities, and information taken from the Spanish national organisation for blind people (O.N.C.E. which was able to give information mainly about students who were blind or have visual impairments) and the government department responsible for education (which provided information about students who were deaf or hard-of-hearing). The Ministry of Education and Science (Further Education Section) has devised guidelines for examination boards when considering the university entrance examinations and the participation of students with disabilities. Students who are deaf or hard-of-hearing can be allowed up to 25 per cent additional time. Instructions about the examination have to be provided in written form. Interpreters have to be available if there is an oral examination. Students who are blind can have up to 50 per cent additional time. Materials have to be transcribed into Braille if appropriate. The examination should take place in a suitable room. This is also a consideration when arranging examinations for students with impaired mobility. This group of students can have access to a range of assistive technology if they need it.

Contacts with the Faculties tried to discover the number of students, the kinds of impairments they had, the courses they were following, and the stage at which the students were on courses. Administrative staff in the 12 Faculties appeared to be very interested in the investigation and were very helpful. However, the picture which emerged was confused since some students had declared their disability at enrolment whilst others were known only through personal observations and contacts. The next phase was to contact the students - including those who did not have disabilities since they were sometimes able to put the investigators in touch with friends who had disabilities. A semi-structured questionnaire was devised to be used in interviews with students with disabilities. The questions covered personal and academic matters, strategies used by particular faculties to meet the needs of the students, and the availability of support, both human and technical. From this it was hoped to identify the facilities and services which the students used most. In the final questions, students were asked for their views on inclusion and integration into the life of the university.

As a result of the efforts of the team carrying out the investigation, it became possible to provide information about several aspects of policy and provision for students with disabilities. The findings are set briefly below:

Students with disabilities - type of impairment

Mobility impairment:	20
Visual impairment:	16
Hearing impairment:	8

Students with disabilities: gender

Male:	23
Female:	21

Students with disabilities: level of studies

Diploma:	13
First degree:	29
Masters:	1
Doctoral:	1

Students with disabilities: Faculty (note that some students are on courses which involve more than one subject)

Law:	9
Psychology:	6
Economics:	5
Teacher Training (Primary):	4
Librarianship:	2
Translation and Interpreting:	2
Pharmacy:	2
Medicine:	3
Physiotherapy:	1
History:	1
Business management:	2
Business studies:	3
Spanish studies:	1
Chemistry:	1

Physics: 3
Mathematics: 1
Journalism: 1
Social Science: 1

From the investigation, it appeared that the difficulties encountered by the students differed according to the nature of the impairment. Blind students and those with visual impairments said that the main barrier for them was access to information. Students with impaired mobility drew attention to physical access to buildings and to how this was made worse by roadworks and also by road traffic. They suggested that there should be traffic lights and zebra crossings near to entrances to Faculties whose buildings are located on busy roads, for example the Faculty of Psychology. Many of the new buildings have been constructed with the needs of people with disabilities in mind. However, as has been said earlier, the University of Salamanca is very old and many of its buildings were erected a long time ago. They present considerable difficulties for students with impaired mobility. Because of the historic nature of these buildings, it is not always possible to make alterations and modifications. There also many steep hills and cobbled streets with narrow pavements and high kerbs. These make very difficult for some students to lead independent lives. Deaf students indicated that the main barriers for them are gaining access to the curriculum through employing suitable communication strategies. They suggested that many of the rooms used for teaching are too large and have poor acoustics. The deaf students felt that they were missing lots of information being transmitted in classrooms. In their view, the University should make some financial contribution towards the provision of communication support, both human and technical (e.g. hearing aids, radio microphones, induction loops).

One service which was of crucial importance to all students is the library. All students were concerned about access in various forms. There was concern that some students with disabilities take longer to read and use books and so they might benefit from having an extension to the standard loan period. Students with disabilities also mentioned social life, leisure activities and opportunities to participate in sports. Perhaps the latter should be developed as a matter of priority given that the Disabled Persons Social and Work Integration Act gives people with disabilities the right to participate in cultural, sporting, and leisure activities. Alongside this there is the requirement for those responsible for these to make them accessible.

When asked about the attitudes of teaching staff, students with disabilities reported that in all but a few exceptional instances, there was a willingness to make provision as long as this did not lead to any unfair advantages. As examples of co-operation there were staff who loaned their own personal copies of relevant books to students with disabilities; others adapted their usual classroom teaching style to meet the needs of students who were deaf or hard of hearing by standing still and facing the class all of the time; many teachers were willing to arrange additional, individual tutorials outside of normal hours. There is scope to build on this goodwill. Tutors could be asked to provide learning materials, especially lecture notes, reading lists etc. - in advance to that they could be adapted to meet the needs of blind and visually-impaired students. This would mean that they would gain access to the materials at the same time as their sighted colleagues. All of the students felt that tutors do need to know more about disability.

Turning now to consider what might be done to develop and improve policy and provision, the students with disabilities made several important points. Some specific suggestions were made. For example within the Faculty of History and Geography, the lift to the first floor should be altered to improve access to the facilities on that floor. More rooms could be fitted with induction loops. Furniture could be purchased which meets the needs of some students with disabilities - allowing wheelchair users to position themselves at desks and work benches. In general terms, there is a need to bring together the university authorities and the city council to consider the architectural and environmental barriers. The outcome of this should be a co-ordinated approach to remove the barriers in a planned way with set targets to be reached by pre-determined dates. One immediate change which would benefit some students with disabilities would be permission to drive their cars through the pedestrianised zones. In starting to undertake any improvements, it was suggested that organisations of disabled people should be consulted. Further co-operation could bring changes to making adapted living accommodation available and also the provision of adapted transport to be used for journeys to and from the university.

A significant move forward occurred in May 1995 when the University organised the first seminar on the integration of students with disabilities. Subsequently, a document entitled 'Ten Ways to Integrate' was published. This was based on the work of the student association (A.S.P.E.R.) which had been responsible for the seminar. The document contained recommendations to the University about issues to which attention was needed: provision of information, collection of data, training of staff, availability of personal assistance, access to buildings, improved living accommodation, accessible transport, and networking with other organisations and institutions. The document was passed first to the Student Advisory Service. Throughout the academic year 1995-96, one of the most important objectives of the Student Advisory Service was to ensure that students with disabilities were integrated fully into all aspects of university life. A plan was devised and implemented, based on three underlying principles. Firstly, students with disabilities should be able to participate in the academic, cultural, and social life of the university. Secondly, the university should collect statistics about students with disabilities on an annual basis. Thirdly, it should guarantee its commitment to improving access and removing barriers.

Already action has been taken. There are questions on the enrolment form which ask students about their impairment and the ways in which it impinges on all aspects of their life as a student (e.g. study patterns, living accommodation, transport). There has also been an access survey of the university which has been carried out by a team with expertise and experience of such tasks. Other changes are less tangible. However, there is more information available now about financial support, adapted housing, access in the city, and careers. These changes appear to be having effects quickly since the number of students who declared that they have an impairment rose to 148 in the academic year 1996-97.

Conclusion

Until recently, the difficulties encountered by students with disabilities have been ignored by the higher education system in Spain. Measures are being taken now to overcome this neglect. As can be seen from this account of the situation at the University of Salamanca, there is much to be done. The hope is that by taking measures such as those described above, the University of Salamanca and all other universities will move to a position where people with disabilities are offered opportunities to participate which are fully inclusive.

Note

I am grateful to Cathy Doyle for translating this chapter from the original, Spanish text.

References

Brown, P.M. and Foster, S. (1991), *Integrating Hearing and Deaf Students on a College Campus: Successes and Barriers as Perceived by Hearing Students.* American Annals of the Deaf; Vol. 136, No. 1, pp. 21-27.

Boxer, M. (1990), *Learners with Special Needs. Tutor Awareness.* Adults-Learning-(England); Vol. 1, No. 10, pp. 274-77.

Craft, D. H. (ed.) (1994), *Inclusion: Physical Education for All, Journal of Physical Education Recreation and Dance;* Vol. 65, No. 1, pp. 23-55.

Lazarus, B.D. (1993), *Guided Notes: Effects with Secondary and Post Secondary Students with Mild Disabilities*, Education and Treatment of Children; Vol. 16, No. 3, pp. 272-89.

Ley de Integracion Social Del Minusvalido (1982), Boletín Oficial del Estado, 7 de abril, Madrid.

Ministerio de Educacion y Ciencia (1986 y 1990), *Guía de la Integración*, Dirección General de Renovación Pedagógica, Madrid.

Ministerio de Educacion y Ciencia (1989), *Libro Blanco para la Reforma del Sistema Educativo*, Madrid, M.E.C.

Nelson, J.R. et al. (1990), *Faculty Willingness to Accommodate Students with Learning Disabilities: A Comparison among Academic Divisions*, Journal of Learning Disabilities; Vol. 23, No. 3, pp. 185-89.

Ross, C.J. (1997), *Contemporary Spain: A Handbook*, Edward Arnold: London.

Sevilla, J., Ortega, J., Blanco, F., Sanchez, B. and Sanchez, C. (1991), *Física general para estudiantes ciegos y deficientes visuales: diseño, construcción, experimentación y evaluación de material didáctico.*, Escuela Universitaria de Fisioterapia de la ONCE, *Revista sobre ceguera y deficiencia visual, nº 6,* Madrid.

Universidad de Salamanca (1995), *Guía para estudiantes universitarios,* Gráficas Varona, Salamanca.

14 Students with disabilities and learning difficulties in higher education in Sweden

Majken Wahlstrom

Introduction

Before discussing policy and provision for students with disabilities and learning difficulties, it will be useful to say something about the overall system. Within Sweden there are 33 universities and university colleges run by the state. There are also 26 university colleges for students of heath sciences or who wish to become paramedics. The Stockholm School of Economics is a semi-private institution. In 1994-5, there were almost 218,000 higher education students. The award of a degree in Sweden is defined according to credit points (poang). A Higher Education Diploma requires at least 80 credit points and can be obtained after two years study, a Bachelor's degree requires 120 credit points and takes three years. The system continues and embraces higher degrees. As in some other countries (for example the Netherlands) there is a national system of credit points. One credit point is associated with a weekly workload of 40 hours and corresponds to one week of full time study.

Swedish post-secondary education has always had as one of its characteristic features an element of national planning and regulation. The aims, duration, location and financial support for most programmes of study have been set down by the Swedish Parliament. Until 1989, the government was also responsible for devising the curriculum for some of the longer programmes of study. In July 1993, a new Higher Education Act was implemented. In the new system which this legislation introduced the numbers enrolled and the allocation of financial support are influenced by student demand and also the achievements of the various university departments in terms of quality of courses and success rates of students. The reforms have given greater autonomy to the universities with regard to admissions, organisation of study programmes, and use of resources. New features such as diversity of provision and competition between providers have emerged. Certainly, many students now have a much wider choice of what to study and where. Despite these changes, the National Agency for Higher

Education still has a role in monitoring quality and advising on the accreditation of professional degrees.

Admissions to university and students with disabilities

From the perspective of students with disabilities, there are some worrying aspects of the changes particularly those which relate to admissions and to resource allocation. An earlier Higher Education Ordinance does state that applications from students with disabilities must be given consideration both by the centralised admissions organisation and by the admissions staff in the universities. In some ways, this means that there is a system of priority at the entry stage. Applicants can indicate on their application form that s/he has a disability. Competition is quite fierce since for many courses there are limits on the numbers.

All students are selected using the results they obtain in secondary school and/or the Swedish Scholastic Aptitude Test (SweSAT). The latter is very similar to the American Scholastic Aptitude Test. It is really a general test of study skills and is used to provide some kind of estimate of the prospective student's ability to complete higher education successfully. The usual form of the SweSAT comprises six subtests in Vocabulary, Reading Comprehension, Interpretation of Diagrams, Tables, and Maps, English Reading Comprehension, Computational/Mathematical Skills and General Knowledge. Using this combination, the test can indicate which type of courses applicants might be best suited to. The system operates in such a way that the situation of applicants is viewed in terms of whichever results give them the best position; they do not have to decide whether to use the school record or the SweSAT results. In reality, most applicants choose to take the test. For many students with disabilities, this too is their preference. However for some students with disabilities there are some issues to be addressed. For example, students who are blind or visually impaired, who in earlier times felt that the tests did disadvantage them, since 1995 have the right to use Braille or cassette recorders. There are other modifications for this group too. The Reading Comprehension is shorter and the Interpretation of Diagrams, Tables, and Maps is omitted. (A trial involving six blind students occurred at the University of Stockholm in 1993 which suggested that the latter is too complex at this stage.)

University policy for students with disabilities

The Higher Education Ordinance requires every university to consider the needs of students with disabilities. Every year, all universities must set aside at least 0.15 per cent of their funding for undergraduate studies to support provision for students with disabilities. The most up-to-date figures at the time of writing indicate that there were 528 students studying at 20 universities in the academic year 1993-94. Nine of the 20 were incurring very significant extra costs and so the government allocated additional money which the University of Stockholm was given responsibility for distributing. Most universities do have policies and provision for students with disabilities which means that they share similar approaches - for example in arranging special examinations which might be oral or written or which might be the availability of extra time, or hiring readers for blind students and interpreters for deaf students.

At the University of Stockholm, there is a stock of special equipment which can be loaned to support students with a range of impairments (e.g. text scanners, Braille writers, personal computers, etc.). The demand for these items seems very great during the period of university examinations. At the University of Orebro, there is a special office in which special equipment such as a scanner, a Brailling machine, and some adapted computers are located for students' use. The universities in Gothenburg and Lund have also started to develop their reserves of special equipment. Blind and visually-impaired students in all universities can make use of the Swedish National Library of Talking Books without charge. Students who need personal assistance can obtain special funds from the Swedish National Board for Attendants Service to pay for human support, which for some has to be provided on a round-the-clock basis.

Access and transport

Access to buildings at Swedish universities is generally good. The statutory requirements imposed by the National Board of Occupational Safety and Health ensure that at least one entrance to all official buildings must be accessible for wheelchair-users, for example by having ramps as well a stairs and by having a hinged door as well as a revolving door. One lift must be accessible with an entrance measuring at least 0.80m in width and with low-level controls. There must also be accessible lavatories in all public buildings. Despite all of these adaptations, a pilot survey undertaken in late 1994 suggested that some students continue to encounter difficulties. In particular, many could not open doors from their wheelchairs without assistance because the doors were too heavy.

Public transport also has to be accessible according to the law. However, developments have moved forward only slowly. In the urban areas, there is a transport service which allows people with disabilities to travel free of charge either by taxi or in specially-adapted vehicles. There are restrictions placed on this sometimes, for instance in relation to length of journey or frequency of use.

Financial support

Like most other students, students with disabilities finance their studies through loans and grants. The Swedish system of loans contains a proportion (25 per cent) which is non-repayable. The normal pattern is for students to receive financial support for 12 semesters (six years) although exceptions can be made for postgraduates. These loans are not available to students from overseas. In order to obtain a loan, the National Board of Student Aid checks the student's results to ascertain that they are satisfactory. The system can be used by part-time students but they can only receive a maximum of half the sum awarded to full-time students. As in other countries, many students with disabilities do pursue their studies on a part-time basis as a result of their impairment. Also, some students with disabilities might be unable to progress through the system as quickly and their impairment could have a negative influence on their performance. To prove this, they must have a certificate from a doctor. At the time of writing, the government has announced its intention to look again at the system for providing assistance to students in post-secondary education.

Students with disabilities: a national survey

In March 1994 a questionnaire was sent to all students with disabilities in Sweden who were known to be having support from their universities. There was a good response with 77 per cent returning the questionnaire. The questions were about opportunities for studying, the availability and nature of support available, and the attitudes of teaching staff and other students.

The survey indicated that students with disabilities were older than their peers. There was almost an equal balance of males and females. The students said that their main purpose in studying was to gain qualifications and find employment after graduation. The extent to which they are success in this is not clear. The rise in the number of unemployed people in recent years has restricted the chances for those with disabilities to obtain work. This is despite the financial support provided by the government to employers who recruit disabled staff.

The largest group of students were deaf (53) or hard-of-hearing (64). Policy and provision for this group of students seems to have been a feature of the recent past. The students were taking a variety of courses including teacher training, psychology, architecture, law, physiotherapy, drama, and engineering. To be able to take advantage of these opportunities, the students need sign language interpreters but there is a shortage of interpreters in Sweden. Some universities employ their own sign language staff, others hire them when they are required. Sign language has been recognised as the first language of deaf people by the Swedish government. For many years, there has been a debate about whether deaf students should be directed towards particular universities to study specific subjects or whether they should be allowed to enter any institution. In the case of the latter, sometimes they have to delay joining a course for one or two terms since there are no interpreters available. This debate is a very delicate issue and no easy solutions have emerged. Since 1995, all universities have been asked to inform the National Co-ordinator for Students with Disabilities when they have interpreters who are not working with their own students. Also, students who are deaf and need interpreters are asked to contact the National Co-ordinator when they are applying for places. In this way, some attempt is being made to match students to available human resources. If more than one individual deaf student choose to study on the same course in the same place, this leads to even better use of scarce human support. All of the above is very much concerned with academic life. One should not forget life outside the classroom. The 1994 survey suggested that most deaf students experienced feelings of loneliness and isolation.

Students with dyslexia

As late as 1990, dyslexia was acknowledged to be a medical/neurological disability in Sweden. The number of students claiming to have dyslexia has grown and the demand for study support has followed. Examples of the kind of support given include additional time in examinations, using oral instead of written examinations, special tutorial support with reading and writing, and assistance with notetaking. Students with dyslexia can also use the facilities and services provided by the National Library of Talking Books. However, there is still much prejudice against dyslexia. Some people see students with dyslexia as being lazy, troublesome, or uneducable.

In Spring 1995 the government asked the University of Stockholm to work on a pilot project to adapt the SweSAT for use with students who have reading and writing difficulties. Progress with this project was described in a paper delivered at an international conference (Altonen and Malmdahl 1997) and this short account is based on the conference report. The purpose of changes to the tests was to give the best possible assistance to prospective students when competing for places in universities. The National Agency for Higher Education conducted a trial with 18 students with dyslexia which was successful. The involvement of the University of Stockholm builds upon this initial experience.

The adapted test was first used in 1996. The modification is to the Reading Comprehension section which is shortened. The conduct of the test is different and makes use of multimedia presentation. The text appears on a screen and at the same time it is read aloud. This allows the words on the screen to be followed by listening to the spoken version. The colour coding of words and phrases is also intended to help with following the text. The student retains control of the scrolling of the screen and the speed of the spoken version by using the mouse. Students are also given printed versions of the test.

The number of students taking part was limited to 70, all of whom had to provide evidence of their dyslexia which was acceptable to the National Agency for Higher Education. A list of those judged competent to issue certification was included with the application forms when they were distributed. Also, those on the list had to conduct their diagnostic assessment using a standard template. Prospective students intending to take the test were given a diskette which gave them the chance to practice. This was especially important for students living in isolated parts of the country.

The project is to be evaluated by the National Agency for Higher Education in 1998 and the findings presented to the Ministry of Education and Science. There is much interest in the results, both in Sweden and in other countries since meeting the needs of the large numbers of students with dyslexia is a problem shared by all.

Conclusions

In the 1994 survey many students mentioned the barriers resulting from the attitudes of others and their resistance to change. There are several strategies which might be used to overcome these. The first concerns the availability of information. There are some developments to note on this. For example in 1996 a paper was published which explored the situation of students with disabilities in the job market (Holmlid 1996) whilst more recently, in connection with a project called "Extended Local Support for Disabled Students at Universities and Colleges", a detailed report has been published about students with disabilities on courses at the University of Stockholm (Kim 1997).

A second issue raised in the 1994 investigation was the need for improved training for staff. This has two dimensions: training for teaching staff and also training for the growing number of specialist support staff. Certainly there is progress to record relating to the latter. In June 1996, as part of a European Community funded Horizon project, a seminar was organised for all advisers for students with disabilities working in Swedish universities. The sessions covered many important dimensions: admissions, finance, assistive technology, and the provision of information. A number of colleagues from other countries contributed their expertise. Building upon this, plans have been made for many of the advisers to undertake further professional development by participating in a specially designed seminar programme in England in 1998. If this programme is effective, the staff can return to their universities and they themselves can work to raise awareness and develop more positive attitude amongst their colleagues in the academic structure. Perhaps this is the crucial measure in the efforts being made to ensure that students with disabilities in Sweden do have the same opportunities as everyone else to participate in higher education.

References

Altonen, T. and Malmdahl, N. (1997), 'The Swedish Scholastic Aptitude Test for Dyslexics: their second chance for higher education and lifelong learning' in Van Esbroek, R. et al. (eds), *Decision-making for Lifelong Learning*, VUB Press: Brussels.

Hildebrand, M. (1994), *A Guide to Higher Education Systems in the European Community and EFTA Countries,* National Agency for Higher Education (VHS): Stockholm.

Holmlid, A.S. (1996), *Disabled University Graduates in the Job Market, Division of Student Affairs*, University of Stockholm.

Kim, Hi-Young (1997), 'The Goal is for Everybody to Take Part: A Report on the Situation of Disabled Students at Stockholm University', unpublished text.

National Agency for Higher Education (1995), 'Swedish Scholastic Aptitude Test', National Agency for Higher Education: Stockholm.

Wahsltrom, M. (1994), 'The Situation of Disabled Students in Sweden: A Pilot Survey', University of Stockholm.

Wahlstrom, M. et al. (1996), 'Integration of disabled university students in Sweden' in Van Esbroek, R. et al. (eds), *A Successful Adjustment to University and Progression Beyond: A European Context*, FEDORA: Louvain-la-Neuve.

Wedman, I. (1992), 'Selection to Higher Education in Sweden, Division of Educational Measurement', University of Umea.

Addendum

Set out below is the full text of the policy document "Disabilities and Higher Education" published by the Vice Chancellor's Office of the University of Stockholm in March 1993 (Dossier No. 462 Reg. No. 1466/93).

The objective of Stockholm University

The number of people with disabilities enrolling in higher education has increased in the past few years.   The term disability is used to refer to a permanent or long term impairment of a somatic function. Documented reading and writing difficulties are equated with a disability.

It is our public responsibility to offer students with disabilities the support they need in their studies. The overall objective is to offer the individual students such forms of support as will enable them as closely as possible to conduct their studies under the same conditions as students with disabilities.

Pre-requisites for students with disabilities to accomplish their higher education

1.   Students with disabilities must like all other students be assured of high quality teaching and a favourable environment for their studies.

2.   Stockholm University must set aside extra resources in order to be able to meet the need of students with disabilities for special support. A counsellor with specific responsibility for disability issues must be available at the University.

Essential features are :

- the accessibility of the physical surroundings,
- the psychological climate,
- the possibility to plan the total study environment individually,
- the possibility to modify the course of study, and
- the availability of special information on the conditions of students with disabilities in relation to finance, accommodation, travel, technical and practical support, health care, insurance, leisure, the co-operation and information exchange between different providers of education, handicap organisations, and other public authorities.

Forms of support

Students with disabilities who have enrolled for higher education at undergraduate or postgraduate level shall according to need receive such forms of support as are directly related to their education.

Among the forms of support which may be considered for students with disabilities, the costs of which shall be charged against the grants for extraordinary educational expenses, may be mentioned notetaking help, reading help, sign language interpreting, transport help within the university campus, extra teaching and tuition, sponsoring by a fellow student, extended time for examinations, technical aids and other important equipment.

Decisions on the granting of costs for extraordinary educational expenses are made after consultation between the disabled student and the university's counsellor for students with disabilities on the need and extent of support. Decisions concerning the continuation of existing support shall take into account whether the results achieved by the student are acceptable, considering the student's special situation.

General advice

The special counsellor at the university shall continue to monitor the student during the entire period of education.

Modification of the curriculum (or equivalent)

If a course or part of a course contains elements such that the student with disabilities is judged not to be able to follow or assimilate the course or part of the course because of his disability, then this fact should be made clear to the student by the director of studies in a meeting when the student is starting his studies. Based on this meeting, the director of studies (or the equivalent) should in consultation with the counsellor decide if the curriculum should be modified for the student.

Such modifications may mean that a certain course or part of course is omitted or that its contents are changed. If a part of a course is omitted then it should be stated whether the time allotted for the omitted part is to be used for further studies of one or more other parts or if a new part, not present in the curriculum, should be added.

Modification of the contents of course/examination certificate

If the modification of the curriculum (or the equivalent) has meant the omission of something that is seen as an essential and obvious part of the education, then the modification and the date when it was decided should be stated in the course or examination certificate.

Individual examination

If the disability prevents the student from being examined in the manner stated in the curriculum (or the equivalent), then the student should be given the opportunity to be individually examined in some other form.   In a case of examination involving sign language interpretation, two interpreters should be present.

Individual modification of the course of study

In some cases the disability requires a slower rate of study than the norm.   It is assumed that the director of studies, the student counsellor, and, if necessary, the special counsellor for students with disabilities will, together with the student create an individually modified course of study to enable the student to complete the education.   The individual course of study should be monitored on a regular basis.

In its published information on available courses and how to apply for them, Stockholm University shall recommend applicants with disabilities to make contact with the university in order to discuss their possible need for support as early as possible and no later than the time of application.

15 Students with disabilities and learning difficulties in higher education in the United Kingdom

Alan Hurst

Educational policies and provision have undergone radical changes since the start of the sequence of Conservative governments since 1979. These have had a major impact on all sectors from pre-school through to higher education. The policies are based around a number of fundamental principles which the Conservatives have tried to introduce into all aspects of life in the United Kingdom. These include competition and the effects of market forces, wider choices, cost-effectiveness, efficiency, and the transfer of funding away from central government to other sources. All can be seen in the changes to higher education including those affecting students with disabilities and learning difficulties.

At this point, perhaps it is appropriate to comment on the changes in terminology which have occurred. With the concern for more politically-correct language, and encouraged by the activities of disabled people themselves, the issue of terminology has become more important. It is also one which colleagues in other countries should recognise. In this connection, for example, the use of the definite article 'the' prefacing a descriptor such as 'disabled' is no longer acceptable; it is preferable to use 'disabled people'. Within education, until around 1980, the term 'handicapped' was the one most often employed. Following the report of the Warnock Committee in 1978 (DES 1978), this group of learners within the school sector were referred to as having 'special educational needs' and this label spread to the higher education sector. However, this could be interpreted very broadly to encompass a wide range of learners and so there has been a move back towards a clear focus on disability. This has been modified somewhat following changes in terminology from within the further education sector where reference began to be made to 'students with learning difficulties and disabilities'. Certainly, in 1996 this is the term used by the Higher Education Funding Council. It will be interesting to see whether a recent report on policy and provision in further education (the Tomlinson Report) also has an influence and references appear to 'inclusive learning' and to distinctions between 'learner support' and 'learning support', ideas which stem directly from Tomlinson (FEFC 1996).

Having outlined the wider context, it is appropriate now to consider, in brief, the structure of higher education in the United Kingdom so that it is possible to understand more clearly issues associated with the development of policy and provision for students with disabilities and learning difficulties.

The system of higher education in the United Kingdom

Prior to 1992, the higher education system comprised three main types of institution: universities, ranging from the old-established and famous through to the large Victorian city and the more modern green-field 1960s locations, polytechnics which had been designated in the late 1960s and whose origins were in science, engineering, and technology but which diversified into most areas of the curriculum, and colleges of higher education whose main focus was on teacher education but which also diversified especially when the numbers entering teacher training were cut by the government. In 1992 the Further and Higher Education Act brought greater unity to the system. Most polytechnics chose to change their names and to call themselves universities whilst the colleges of higher education described themselves as being 'university sector' colleges. Despite the changes, there is still a recognised status ranking of institutions and courses. The 1996 Research Assessment Exercise added more weight to the notion of a hierarchy. A major effect of this is that students have to compete for places, especially on the more popular courses at the high status institutions.

When looking at the undergraduate student population in 1996, there is a balance between students over 21 years of age and students who enter higher education around age 18 as a continuation of their formal education. The basic entry/matriculation requirement is two passes in the General Certificate of Education Advanced level examinations (GCE 'A' levels) which are held annually in May/June. Since entry is competitive, students must secure the best grades possible and usually in more than two subjects. Admission to universities is by a central system using a single application form. (There is an opportunity on this form to indicate that the individual has a disability and, by using a coding system, the nature of the disability.) Applicants list six courses/universities on the form and universities choose who they want. Sometimes applicants are interviewed but today, most offers are based on the information given in the application and on the GCE 'A' level grades. Entry qualifications vary depending on subject choice etc. Many mature students do not use this route to enter higher education; instead, they might continue their studies following successful completion of special access or foundation courses devised by the institutions themselves. The undergraduate first-degree courses are usually three years long. A recent trend has been to organise these on a modular basis within a credit accumulation structure.

A major concern for both students and institutions is funding. Looking first at students, the course tuition fees are paid directly to the institutions by the students' local education authority in the case of full-time courses. However, with the large growth in student numbers, the government feels that the country can afford this no longer and it is discussing a number of schemes whereby the students themselves will have to make a significant contribution (for example, via a graduate tax). Also, in the United Kingdom, it is common for the younger students to use entry to higher education as the opportunity to move away from home. To cover their daily living costs, students can apply to their local education authorities for a grant. This is subject to a means test which relates to the income of their parents. The government has also been concerned about this expenditure and in 1990, it introduced a system of top-up loans. These were not taken up in the numbers expected and over time, the government has frozen the level of the maintenance award so that more students are forced to take out a loan, repayable once they are in full-time employment and earning a particular salary. Part-time students do not have access to any of these sources of money and so they have to fund themselves.

Income from student fees is a major source of income for the institutions and until recently, they tried to admit as many students as they could to maximise this. However, entry to the different subjects is now controlled more tightly and there are penalties both for over- and under-recruiting. The money for higher education comes from the government. Prior to the Further and Higher Education Act 1992, it was distributed to the institutions via two different routes. The universities were the responsibility of the University Grants Committee (UGC) and this tried to allow the members as much freedom and autonomy as possible. The polytechnics and colleges of higher education received their funds first via local education authorities and later via the Polytechnics and Colleges Funding Council, both of whom were much more directive and interventionist than the UGC. The 1992 Act brought a single funding body via the establishment of the Higher Education Funding Council for England (HEFCE) - note that there were also similar councils in Scotland and Wales whilst the arrangements in Northern Ireland were different again, given the very small number of higher education institutions located there.

Making progress for disabled students has been hindered by the lack of information, both quantitative (about the number of disabled students - see O'Hanlon and Manning 1995) and qualitative (about the experiences of disabled students - see Hurst 1993). In the future, the information collected by the Higher Education Statistics Agency (HESA) should be useful. In the meantime, possibly the best figures are those provided by the organisation responsible for applications (UCAS).

Table 14.1:   Applications for Places 1995

	Applicants No.	Applicants %	Accepted No.	Accepted %
no disability	403,445	96.19	279,506	96.18
dyslexia	3,446	0.82	2,433	0.84
blind/p.sighted	418	0.10.	279	0.10
deaf/p.hearing	646	0.15	450	0.15
mobility diffs.	443	0.11	298	0.10
personal care	73	0.02	28	0.01
mental health	183	0.04	101	0.03
unseen disabs.	9,062	2.16	6,348	2.18
multiple disabs.	580	0.14	376	0.13
other disabs.	1,146	0.27	777	0.27
total with dis.	15,997	3.81	11,090	3.82
overall total	419,442	100.00	290,596	100.00

Source: UCAS Statistics 1995

Whilst an indication of the success of any efforts to widen participation might be an increase in numbers, this does ignore the quality of the experience. In recent years there has been an increasing concern with 'quality' and this should include the quality of what disabled students encounter.   The 1992 Act introduced quality monitoring strategies although the extent to which these take into account disabled students is still not clear even now four years after their introduction.

A final point to note and one which forms a link with the remainder of this chapter is that within the United Kingdom, there is national charity whose main purpose is to develop opportunities for students with disabilities and to support those who work with them. This is called Skill: National Bureau for Students with Disabilities. It is a small organisation which came into being in 1974 and has its offices in London. It has around 1,200 members. Policy is decided by a Governing Council of around 80 members who represent a range of constituencies. The implementation of the policy is the responsibility of the salaried staff whose activities are monitored by a small elected Executive Committee on behalf of the Governing Council. Skill publishes a range of information which is useful to staff and students. It also organises conferences, special interest groups/working parties, and a network of groups in the regions. These meet on a regular basis and offer a very valuable channel of communication between those working in the institutions and the Skill staff who are working at the more strategic, policy-oriented level. The crucial role played by Skill will become evident in almost all of what follows. (See Cooper and Corlett 1996 for a more detailed account of Skill and current provision.)

Policy and development: disabled students

The major development affecting most disabled students has been their improved financial situation relative to other students following changes made in 1990. When top-up loans were introduced in that year, the government also introduced modifications to the existing additional grants available to disabled students. These took the form of new allowances so that disabled students can apply now for:

(a) an additional general allowance to cover costs incurred directly as a result of participating in higher education and having a disability - for example more frequent use of telephones, photocopiers, etc. - in 1996-97 the maximum available was £1,245 which can be claimed for each year of the course;

(b) an allowance for the purchase of special equipment - for example a cassette recorder, a lap-top computer - in 1996-97 the maximum available was £3,745 which can be claimed only once, the assumption being that the equipment will be useful throughout the course, although it is sometimes possible to seek additional money to upgrade equipment; and

(c) an allowance to cover the costs of non-medical personal assistance - for example to buy the services of signers, notetakers, etc. - in 1996-97 the maximum available was £4,975 which can be claimed for each year of the course.

Despite the success of the Disabled Students Allowances (DSA) many issues remain and these are being drawn to the attention of the government Department for Education and Employment (DfEE) regularly. (For a full discussion of issues surrounding DSA see Patton 1990.) Thus, DSA are not available to part-time students. Many people might have to study on a part-time basis as a consequence of their disability. The attraction of part-time study for disabled people is demonstrated by the success of the Open University whose numbers are far in excess of any other institution. Changing the system to include part-time students would involve the approval of parliament and recent governments have been unwilling to allow time for this. Probably they fear the huge increase in demand which could follow and which would come at a time when there is a concern to cut government costs and to shift responsibility for funding to other sources. DSA is not available also to many postgraduates and so suitably qualified disabled researchers might be discouraged from taking opportunities for further, more advanced studies. DSA is also subject to a means test. Despite the apparent wealth of some parents, being excluded from DSA and then having themselves to bear the costs can create serious financial burdens for some families (see the account of Tim Roberts, a deaf student and his parents in the 'Times Educational Supplement' Feb. 16th 1996).

Whilst the funds for the DSA originate with central government, the system for allocation is administered by the local education authorities. Currently, there are around 100 of these and they operate in different ways. (This contrasts with the system in Scotland where application is made using a single, simple form which is processed at a central office at the Scottish Education Department.) Some of their practices are helpful to disabled students, others create additional difficulties (for example by insisting that students obtain a number of estimates prior to purchasing the goods or services, by insisting students pay for goods or services first and then reclaim costs, and so on). A particular feature to emerge is the large number of students claiming DSA on the grounds that they have a specific learning difficulty (usually dyslexia). In the early days, this came as a major surprise to both the local authorities and to the institutions. This aroused considerable concerns and anxieties for everybody although it is fair to say that the situation has not been helped by attempts to abuse the system.

In March 1995, the Department for Education announced its intention to review DSA. A letter was sent to a small number of organisations seeking views on many aspects including definitions, identification, and assessment of needs, and institutional and local education authority practices. The responses to the letter were interesting. Skill highlighted four key issues in its overall approach: the support needs which DSA should and should not cover, the responsibilities of the higher education institutions themselves, the inconsistencies amongst the local education authorities especially on assessments and on evidence required, and problems resulting from delayed payments. The body representing the local education authorities felt that more direction from central government would be helpful, as would improved liaison between the various parties involved. They saw no cause for concern about inconsistencies although the issues associated with dyslexia do receive particular attention. The group representing the universities (the Committee of Vice Chancellor and Principals - CVCP) suggested that most of the issues could be resolved by others rather than by anything which they might do themselves. The CVCP response concentrated heavily on what the local education authorities might do whilst matters which the institutions could address were ignored.

In late July 1995, information about DSA was included in an interim report on further and higher education and since then more consultations have taken place. The DfEE issued revised guidelines to the local education authorities which were intended to offer further clarification. At the time of writing (Autumn 1996) there is no evidence to indicate how effective this has been. The issue of finance for disabled students has become entangled in the wider debate about funding higher education and is an issue which is likely to be examined by the National Committee of Inquiry into Higher Education created in Summer 1996 and due to report in Summer 1997 (the Dearing Committee - see below for further discussion).

Policy and development: the higher education institutions

For many years, some institutions have been trying to develop high quality provision for disabled students. With a few notable exceptions amongst the traditional universities, greater progress was made in those institutions which were the former polytechnics. Much has been accomplished despite there being no financial incentive to do so. Funds had to be taken from current operating budgets. Many institutions did little or nothing, preferring to use their limited resources for more prestigious activities. Also, why should they bother when others were making provision? The issue here is the provision of funds to encourage those less committed to take action whilst at the same time sustaining those already involved so that they do not feel that by incurring expenditure they are imposing a self-inflicted penalty.

Following the Further and Higher Education Act 1992, the government required the higher education funding councils to pay attention to the needs of disabled students. Each country approached this directive differently. The following section looks in detail at the work of the English Funding Council and then in brief at the approaches of the Scottish, and Welsh groups and also at what has happened in Northern Ireland which does not have a funding council. This section will then be followed by an outline of one higher education institution in which reference will be made to the projects supported by money from the HEFCE.

England

The HEFCE established a small Advisory Group on Access and Widening Participation. Skill: National Bureau for Students with Disabilities was invited to represent disability interests. In early 1993, it was announced that £3 million was available to support the development of policies and provision for disabled students. Institutions were encouraged to devise projects and to bid for funds, their applications being judged against pre-determined, publicised criteria (HEFCE 1993a). This produced 103 bids and, had all been supported, the total cost would have been over £8 million. In deciding which bids to support, the Advisory Group tried to balance supporting those new to the work with giving recognition to those whose policy and provision was more advanced and who wished to make further progress. After much discussion, it was decided to support 38 projects (HEFCE 1993b). Skill was invited to play a key role in disseminating information deriving from the projects. This was done through the publication of a termly newsletter and by occasional meetings. Another dimension of dissemination was the final report produced by the HEFCE itself (HEFCE 1995a) and a national conference. An external consultant was employed to carry out a thorough evaluation of the projects and the special initiative.

Despite criticisms of both the funding methodology and also the time scale, the exercise was repeated in 1994-95. Again, £3 million was available and again institutions were invited to bid although it was made clear that institutions could not seek funding to continue work started under the auspices of the first initiative since an important criterion for the allocation of the original bid was that progress should be embedded in the institution. This time, 91 bids arrived whose total cost was in excess of £10 million. The Advisory Group tried to make effective use of the limited funds and many of the 49 bids selected for support did not receive all the money they asked for so that savings could be used to fund other projects (HEFCE 1994a & 1994b). The same system for monitoring, disseminating and evaluating projects was used and again the HEFCE published a final report incorporating a section based on the findings of the evaluator plus accounts from the individual projects (HEFCE 1996).

There is no opportunity in this account to discuss the two initiatives and the overall evaluation in detail but it would be useful to give a brief indication of some of the findings. On the positive side:

(a)   whilst many of those involved were already members of existing networks of practitioners, there was an increase in the number of events at which people were able to meet and to exchange ideas, information, and experiences;

(b)   the evaluation exercise was able to take into account the benefits of the formal events but what should not be forgotten is the value of informal contacts made during refreshment breaks and acted upon later in the form of telephone calls, e-mail links etc.;

(c)   there was an increase in the production of materials concerned with disability in higher education - pamphlets, guidebooks, reports, videos, etc.;

(d)   many institutions made brisk progress in developing their policies and provision and thereby the choices open to disabled students have been extended; and

(e)   some of those where progress was made devised strategies to ensure that any gains made continued beyond the life of the project.

Looking now at some of the more disappointing aspects and linking directly with the final point above:

(a)   some institutions did not continue the work despite the advice from the HEFCE that they should have regard for this when making the original bid;

(b)   dissemination appeared to be only partially successful especially in terms of its impact on institutions whose bids were not supported and also in terms of the sharing of information and the avoidance of duplication of activities - not all projects made regular contributions to the Skill newsletter nor were they represented at the national conferences;

(c)   in order to try to maximise the impact of the project, many institutions had to recruit new staff, many of whom lacked appropriate background and experience - hence the need for staff training and induction became more obvious; and

(d)   in producing regular reports, projects - perhaps understandably - seemed less willing to comment on their difficulties and failings although this was important if others were to benefit from the experiences and avoid the same problems.

Having paused to reflect on progress during 1995-96, the HEFCE announced a third special initiative to operate between 1996-99. The longer time scale does address some of the earlier criticism. However, only £6 million was available (effectively £2 million per year) and again the total required to support all 80 bids was far in excess of this. By another very thorough and detailed analysis of the bids, the Advisory Group was able to support 31 projects (see Circular 23/96 for details). It will be interesting to see if the longer time-scale has any significant effect. The Advisory Group is also discussing strategies to monitor and evaluate this new initiative and has set aside a proportion of the £6 million to fund this.

There are a number of other dimensions to the work of the HEFCE but it is perhaps better to discuss these in the closing section. It is appropriate now to look briefly at how the other funding councils discharged their responsibilities towards disabled students.

Scotland

Overall, the situation in Scotland was that few institutions had progressed to the extent that had occurred in England and so for 1993-4 the Scottish Higher Education Funding Council (SHEFC) undertook an audit. A key finding from this was the importance of the role of disability co-ordinators in the institutions. In response, in 1994-95 SHEFC provided partial funding to support the appointment of co-ordinators in all institutions, and to fund entirely the post of overall national co-ordinator. It also allocated £2 million for the purchase of equipment although a condition of this was that institutions had to work in partnership with each other on a regional basis. Also important was the publication of a book offering guidance and support (SHEFC 1994). The impact of all of this was striking. Institutions began to develop their own policies and provision in a more systematic way and to work together to share ideas and experiences. The progress was sustained by SHEFC's agreeing to continue funding the posts in 1995-96.

Wales

Given that only 14 institutions are involved, it was hardly surprising that the Higher Education Funding Council for Wales (HEFCW) started out on a different route. In 1993-94 £2 million was distributed to institutions on a pro rata basis to allow them to improve their infrastructure. In the guidance notes, the HEFCW indicated that some of the money might be used to improve access and facilities for disabled students. Sadly, only a small number followed this advice and so for 1994-95 the strategy adopted was similar to that in England. The sum of £120,000 was set aside and bids were invited. Seven projects were supported and a national dissemination conference was held in May 1995. In 1995-96 there HEFCW reverted back to the infrastructure approach although an additional

£1 million was made available to support work which would be of direct benefit to disabled students.

Northern Ireland

The situation in Northern Ireland really concerns only two universities. In 1994-95 and again in 1996, they were encouraged to submit bids for funds to support specific projects. The bids were considered by the HEFCE Advisory Group using the same criteria as for bids from English institutions, and since they were judged to be of some merit, the Department of Education for Northern Ireland agreed to fund them. As in the other countries, there has been some immediate progress.

Policy and development: a case study - the University of Central Lancashire

For many years, first as Preston Polytechnic and then later as Lancashire Polytechnic, the institution has tried to devise and implement effective policies and make high quality provision for disabled students. Its underlying policy is enshrined in the Mission Statement which states that the aim is "to provide the widest possible access to those individuals who seek to benefit from its educational activities and to remove barriers to those with special needs". Meeting the needs of disabled people is part of a wider concern with equal opportunities for which the University has gained a good reputation and for which it has been commended in a Higher Education Quality Council report.

The formal structure includes a Disability Advisory Group which meets at least three times per year and is chaired by a pro vice-chancellor. It represents a wide range of staff and students and has some responsibility for initiating, supporting, and monitoring policies. The day-to-day responsibilities for managing the services lie with the Head of Student Services. He ensures that the policies and practices are carried out as efficiently and effectively as possible and are in accordance with the Office for Disabled Students Directory of Procedures. This covers policies on admissions, assessment of support needs, the provision of assistive technology, examinations, liaison with tutors, use of specialist support workers, personal assistance, equipment loans, funding, and residential accommodation. Having this Directory of Procedures means that the team of staff involved in this work operate in a consistent fashion.

In 1996-97 there were approximately 550 students (out of 15,000) registered with the Office for Disabled Students. Most were undergraduates and included a wide range of disabilities and learning difficulties. To support them, there were five full time staff whose work is co-ordinated by a Senior Adviser. In addition, two members of the academic staff are seconded to this work for a part of each week and there is also a part-time specialist careers adviser. To give technical support, the University established a Specialised Learning Resources Unit which is based in the Library and Learning Resources Centre. This involves two further full-time members of staff and four who are part-time.

The major step forward in the development of policy and provision came in 1987 when the University appointed its first full-time adviser for disabled students. Since then, considerable progress has been made. Clearly, the University spends a considerable sum on the salary costs of staff. In addition a significant fund is made available for use by staff working with disabled students. If asked to attribute the cause for the scale of the operation and the progress made, reference would be made to the interest and commitment of very senior staff and the general culture of helpfulness and support which permeates the institution.

Having said that, without doubt the financial support of the HEFCE via the three special initiatives has been very valuable. The 1993-94 project aimed to fill gaps in existing provision. Thus, whilst the University had a strong tradition of giving support to blind students, services for deaf students were at a low level. The University applied for funds to appoint a full-time communicator. This was linked to the development of Deaf Studies as a subject on the Combined Honours Degree Programme which had proved an attraction for deaf students. A second group of students whose needs were not being met adequately were those with specific learning difficulties. The situation had become serious given the sharp rise in the numbers claiming to be dyslexic. Funds were sought to employ a psychologist on a part-time basis to carry out the necessary diagnostic assessment procedures and to make recommendations about the students' eligibility for DSA and what it might be used for. Money was needed also to employ a specialist dyslexia support tutor. Also, based on the University's Specialised Learning Resources Unit, funding was requested so that additional staff could be employed to meet the growing demand. Finally, a small sum was to be used as bursaries to support the needs of part-time students. The overall financial requirement was for £70,000 and this was approved in full by the HEFCE Advisory group.

In implementing the project, several issues emerged:

(a)   the number of students claiming to have a specific learning difficulty was such that the demand on the services of both the educational psychologist and the specialist tutor was excessive;

(b)   the growth in the number of deaf students, each following a different course, indicated that to employ a single full-time communicator was impractical; permission was obtained to use the services of a local organisation which could meet the demand when deaf students were timetabled in different classes at the same time; and

(c)   the number of requests from part-time students indicated that there was a need to consider the financial situation of this group.

At the end of the year, the University employed an experienced, external consultant to evaluate the project and to make recommendations for future action. The University also took steps to ensure that progress made during the project was not lost.

The 1994-95 bid tried to build on this prior experience. Firstly, funding was requested for staff cover to allow the senior adviser to create 'Registers' and to recruit suitably qualified and experienced people from the local community who would be able to offer support to students with a range of needs - readers for blind students, audio-typists for deaf students, specialist tutors for dyslexic students, and information technology trainers. Such a system offers a flexible resource to cope with an unpredictable demand and avoids the University itself employing staff who might become under-utilised later. Secondly, money was also sought to allow the technician from the Specialised Learning Resources Unit to initiate links with the National Federation of Access Centres (NFAC) with a view to the University's becoming a member. This would be useful when assessing the assistive technology needs of disabled students. Thirdly, the University also wanted to appoint a specialist careers adviser; having been successful in recruiting disabled students, it had become essential to give more consideration to their employment prospects after graduation. Fourthly, with a view to securing a more independent financial base for the work with disabled students, the University wanted to appoint a specialist fund-raiser. The final component of the bid was concerned with staff training and development. This recognised the need to offer a career structure and improved professional recognition for those working with disabled students in higher education. The University proposed to work in conjunction with staff from other institutions regionally and nationally to develop the first programme of courses and qualifications which would match what is available to staff working in careers guidance, counselling, etc. Whilst the bid was supported, the University was allocated only £70,000 of the £95,000 requested.

Progress was made with all dimensions of the project although with more problems than during the previous one. Recruiting a specialist careers adviser took longer than anticipated and this dimension of the project started late. However, once underway, the importance of having such a service available became evident very quickly and this should be recognised when the project ends. Appointing a specialist fund-raiser took even longer and so the financial security which had been hoped for was not achieved. Also, compared with the specialist careers work, this dimension of the project was less successful. There are many potential explanations for this including the locating of the post in a different section of the institution for line management purposes and the subsequent difficulties of communication. Progress with the other dimensions was good. The University was visited and audited by members of the NFAC and became a probationary member in Autumn 1996 and a full member in 1997. The development of a programme of courses and qualifications progressed through the appropriate academic routes and was validated successfully in Autumn 1995. The programme will be delivered using a balance of distance learning and residential sessions. A number of awards are available ranging from a basic certificate for those new to the work to the possibility of a higher degree for the more experienced and enthusiastic (see the following chapter for details).

When the HEFCE announced its third special initiative, the University again asked for financial support for two projects. The first considers the needs of deaf students in the classroom and will look at ways in which communicators etc. are used currently both in the University of Central Lancashire and elsewhere, and at ways in which their training and effectiveness might be improved. The second involves the devising and delivery of a systematic, developmental programme of awareness raising and training for all staff throughout the institution. The HEFCE Advisory Group allocated £166,000 with the University expected to make up the shortfall from the bid (£30,000).

The staff training programme accords with the University's philosophy underpinning all its work with disabled students. This sees disability as an issue for everyone and not something which is the concern of a small number of specialist staff. Over the years, the University has tried to develop high quality provision for all students, irrespective of the nature of their disabilities. It has rejected what has been described as the 'centres of excellence' approach. Instead, it has tried to move forward in an incremental way so that all disabled students can learn and live in an environment which is fully and continuously aware of their needs and which tries to meet these needs as routinely and as unobtrusively as possible.

Policy and development: issues for the future

At the same time as these developments have been occurring within education, there has been a more widespread concern with disability discrimination in British society. The Bill, which had the support of many disabled people, emphasised civil rights as opposed to discrimination, and so was much stronger. In the end it was 'talked out' of the House of Commons in July 1995 since there was insufficient time to discuss all the proposed amendments. The other Bill, the one sponsored by the government, was less radical and was directed towards ending discrimination on grounds of disability, particularly in employment and access to public transport, and goods and services. Education was not mentioned in the proposals but pressure on the government did force it to do something.

The Disability Discrimination Act became law in 1995. In relation to this, the government proposed two amendments to existing education law. The first intended to place a statutory duty on the higher education funding councils to "have regard for the needs of disabled students in its allocation of funding". The second amendment wanted to impose on institutions the duty to publish Disability Statements. When these amendments were made known, there were many protests. For example, the CVCP felt that the changes would be harmful to the traditional autonomy of institutions. The debates in the House of Lords also revealed the extent of resistance (see Hurst 1996 for more details). However, despite the opposition, changes were made. All higher education institutions had to publish a Disability Statement by January 1997. In fairness to the funding councils, they had engaged in a consultation process during 1996 and so the institutions have had some impact on the format, content, and timing of the Statements (see HEFCE 1995b). Institutions must provide information on their present policies, their current provision, and their future plans. The intended target readers are prospective disabled students. The information has to be reviewed and up-dated at least once every three years.

Moving away from concerns more narrowly associated with developing policy and provision for disabled students, there is a more widespread debate about the entire field of higher education in the United Kingdom. This has been prompted by a coalescence of public concerns - the duration of undergraduate first degree programmes, the efficient use of resources, the content and relevance of the curriculum, and the current high proportion of public expenditure. The government is also concerned and announced in late Summer 1996 that there would be a National Committee of Inquiry into Higher Education. This was to be chaired by Sir Ron Dearing who has become associated with two other recent committees which have looked at the National Curriculum in schools and vocational qualifications for school-leavers. The terms of reference require the Committee to consider the definition and purposes of higher education, teaching and research, the shape, size, and structure of the system, the wider contribution of higher education to national life, and funding issues. In the more detailed advice, a number of student groups are mentioned, but there is nothing said about disabled students. At the very least this is surprising given the progress made since 1992 and given the increased visibility of disability in connection with the Disability Discrimination Act. It is also very worrying since the Committee's report, which is due to appear in Summer 1997, is likely to influence higher education for the next 20 years or so. If disabled students are not considered now, there could be difficulties later in any new system introduced post-Dearing. In response to the neglect of disabled students, many people took every opportunity to remind the Committee that it ought to consider them. Skill submitted very detailed evidence and others wrote offering their own personal views. As a consequence of these activities, Skill was invited to send a small delegation to meet the Committee early in 1997. At least, it seems that disability is now on the agenda.

Meanwhile, other developments are taking place which will have an impact before any recommendations from the Dearing Committee can be put into operation. The HEFCE, for example, has indicated that in future allocations of funding to institutions based on student numbers, disabled students will have a premium rating. At the time of writing, it is not clear when this will be introduced, or indeed how the additional money will be calculated. As noted at the start of this chapter, collecting accurate numbers has always been a major problem. However, the fact that the additional costs incurred by institutions recruiting disabled students is being recognised is a move in the right direction, although it must be recognised that this additional income will be a part of the block grant allocated to the institutions and is not necessarily to be used specifically for policy and provision for disabled students.

Conclusion

Since 1992, much has happened and significant progress has been made in policy and provision for disabled students. This is something to celebrate and to be proud of - and yet it would be foolish and short-sighted to think that the gains made so far are secure. There are threats from all sides and the change of government in 1997 is unlikely to reverse what is already in train - for example in relation to the funding of higher education in general and financing students in particular. Regression is a distinct and unwelcome possibility as the United Kingdom approaches the Millennium.

References

Cooper, D. & Corlett, S. (1996), 'An Overview of Current Provision' in Wolfendale, S. & Corbett, J. (eds) (1996), *Opening Doors: Learning Support in Higher Education*, Cassell: London.

Department of Education and Science (DES) (1978), 'Special Educational Needs: Report of the Warnock Committee', HMSO, London.

Further Education Funding Council (FEFC) (1996), 'Inclusive Learning: Report of the Learning Difficulties and/or Disabilities Committee' (The Tomlinson Report), FEFC, Coventry.

Higher Education Funding Council for England (HEFCE) (1993a), 'Circular 9/93 Special Initiatives to Widen Participation', HEFCE, Bristol.

HEFCE (1993b), 'Circular 22/93 Special Initiatives to Widen Participation: Funded Projects', HEFCE, Bristol.

HEFCE (1994a), 'Circular 8/94 Special Initiatives to Encourage Widening Participation', HEFCE, Bristol.

HEFCE (1994b), 'Circular 20/94 Special Initiatives to Encourage Widening Participation Funded Projects', HEFCE, Bristol.

HEFCE (1995a), 'Access to Higher Education: Students with Special Needs - An HEFCE Report on the 1993-94 Special Initiatives to Encourage Widening Participation for Students with Special Needs', HEFCE, Bristol.

HEFCE (1995b), 'Circular 3/95 Proposed Specification for Disability Statements to be Required from Institutions', HEFCE, Bristol.

HEFCE (1996), 'Access to Higher Education: Students with Learning Difficulties and Disabilities - A Report on the 1993-94 and 1994-95 HEFCE Special Initiatives to Encourage Widening Participation for Students with Disabilities', HEFCE, Bristol.

Hurst, A. (1993), *Steps Towards Graduation: Access to Higher Education and People with Disabilities*, Avebury: Aldershot.

Hurst, A. (1996), 'Equal Opportunities and Access 1990-1995' in Wolfendale, S. & Corbett, J. (eds) (1996), *Opening Doors: Learning Support in Higher Education*, Cassell: London.

Patton, B. (1990), 'A survey of the Disabled Students Allowances', *Educare 36,* March 1990, pp. 3-7.

Scottish Higher Education Funding Council (1994), 'Access to Success for Students with Disabilities in Higher Education in Scotland', HEFC, Edinburgh.

Times Educational Supplement (1996), 'The cost of imperfection', *Times Educational Supplement* (February 16th 1996, TES2 p. 7).

16 Disability awareness-raising and disability awareness-training in higher education in the United Kingdom

Alan Hurst

Introduction

As might be inferred from the title, this chapter examines two distinct but inter-related matters concerned with disability and the initial and continuing professional development of staff. There is also another important dual dimension to the chapter. This concerns the provision for those working with disabled students in all higher education institutions throughout the sector as opposed to opportunities for training and development within a single institution. The chapter will start by looking at issues about the development of training opportunities for the sector and then look at what is happening in one institution, the University of Central Lancashire.

Part one: the national level

The context and the need for a national staff development programme

It is possible to identify several factors indicating not only the need for a programme of professional development for staff working with disabled students but also that the time is right to promote such a development.

Within the national context there have been some important changes. Firstly, since late 1995, the Disability Discrimination Act has become law. The focus of this is to ensure that disabled people do not encounter discrimination based on their disabilities when applying for jobs or when seeking access to a range of services (e.g. shops, entertainment centres, public transport). The government decided to exclude 'education' from its provisions. However, universities and other institutions will have to comply with the law in their roles as employers.

This could bring benefits and progress for disabled students as well as disabled staff. The decision to exclude education met with opposition from many sources, including Skill: National Bureau for Students with Disabilities. Perhaps as a result of these protests the government did make changes within education, the most significant being the requirement that all institutions must produce and publish a Disability Statement.

Responsibility for the implementation was passed to the national higher education funding councils, each of which approached the issue slightly differently. The Higher Education Funding Council for England (HEFCE) had already established a small Advisory Group on Students with Learning Difficulties and Disabilities (more comments about this follow below) and this acted as a consultative group about the form and content of the proposed Disability Statements. After discussions with the sector, the formal requirement was communicated to the institutions in Summer 1996 indicating that the Statements should be sent to the HEFCE by early January 1997. For the purposes of the discussion on staff development, the important point to note is that the specified content ensured that the compilation of the Statement involved many staff, thereby making them more aware of disability issues. More significantly perhaps, the format necessitated the close involvement of very senior staff. Past experience has suggested that progress is made where this occurs and where there is a lack of involvement, there is a corresponding lack of progress (see Skill 1996 a).

The Disability Discrimination Act and the Disability Statements were really two factors which contributed to a continuation of the momentum already started as a result of the activities of the national funding councils. Discussion of this is available already (see Hurst 1996; and Cooper and Corlett 1996). In brief, in both 1993-94 and 1994-95, additional funding was made available to support projects to widen the participation of disabled people in higher education. Part of the successful bid from the University of Central Lancashire in 1994-95 was for financial support for the development of the training programme to be discussed below. Having paused for a short time to evaluate the progress made, the HEFCE allocated a further £6 million to the work. Of the 87 bids, 31 were selected (see HEFCE 1996 for details.). As with the earlier bid, the concern of the project being undertaken at the University of Central Lancashire is the focus of this chapter and will be discussed later. The point to make about all three special initiatives and the projects which were funded is that many of them have involved the recruitment of a significant number of staff, many of whom were coming to this work without a strong foundation of knowledge or experience. Hence, the need to provided opportunities for initial and on-going training and professional development became more crucial.

Apart from these system-wide policy-based stimuli, there were other compelling reasons indicating the need for staff training and staff development. These are linked with the desirability of ensuring that whatever provision was being made, it was of high quality. Secondly, there is the importance of the status accorded to working with disabled students. One way in which status could be gained is via the successful completion of an accredited programme of training. Certainly, this was the case for staff working to support students in other ways. For example, student counsellors have their own professionally-recognised training courses as do staff offering careers guidance. Many staff supporting disabled students are based within their institution's student services section. For many, this means working alongside carers advisers and student counsellors. Both of the latter groups have means of obtaining professional recognition for their work through the availability of courses and qualifications. There were no similar opportunities for staff in disability services.

It should be noted that the roles and responsibilities of staff working with disabled students are wide-ranging. Services and support are offered prior to entry, during the course, and at the point of leaving higher education. The kinds of services offered to students include: advising about learning support strategies, proposing modifications to assessment regimes, managing staff, working with other agencies, developing policies and provision, raising disability awareness, and initiating and participating in staff training. As stated earlier, apart from the desirability of professional recognition, a major issue concerns the importance of monitoring the work done, ensuring that the practices employed are of good quality and that the knowledge and experiences are disseminated widely. These aspects can be facilitated by the creation of specialist courses and qualifications.

Having outlined the context and demonstrated the need for and the potential value of a specialist course and qualification, it is appropriate to look next at how the programme of courses was devised.

The development of the programme of specialist courses and qualifications

As stated already, financial support for the development of the programme came from the HEFCE. The way in which the development moved forward was something rather unusual. In a period when the emphasis in higher education appeared to be more on institutional competition and rivalry, the programme was created as a result of colleagues from many institutions and organisations working together. The University of Central Lancashire acted as leader and co-ordinator but the meetings to discuss the proposals were funded by the HEFCE. The involvement of colleagues from outside the University was seen as being of particular importance and was intended to give the programme credibility and respect throughout the sector. It was an open acknowledgement that high quality expertise existed in a number of places and for everyone to benefit, this pool of practices needed to be used.

The actual method of involving others used systems in place already. Firstly, in England, Skill: National Bureau for Students with Disabilities plays an important role working for progress for disabled students in all forms of education after the end of compulsory schooling.   Skill's Higher Education Working Party is composed of colleagues from institutions throughout the United Kingdom who are regarded as being at the leading edge of policy and provision.   Hence, members of this national group were invited to participate.   Secondly, Skill operates throughout the country at regional level in that staff working with disabled students in these regions meet each other once each term to discuss matters of mutual interest and to share ideas and experiences.   Thus, members of the group in which the University of Central Lancashire participates, were also invited to join the course development group.   All travel and subsistence costs were paid for by the funding received by the University from the HEFCE.

Normally, when course developments are proposed within the University, a course development committee is established and a series of regular meetings follows usually for two hours or so weekly or fortnightly.   Clearly, given the close involvement of other colleagues from outside the University, many of whom would have to travel great distances to participate, this pattern was inappropriate and inefficient.   Instead, the course development group met for intensive discussions on a number of week-ends in a hotel in Preston.   At the initial meeting the structure of the University's system of awards and qualifications was outlined and decisions taken about how any proposals would need to fit in with the modular structure.   Putting the courses and programme together took around six months and so it was in late October 1995 that the programme underwent the final stage of its development, namely validation. This involved the course development group in a day-long meeting with staff from within the University plus two external representatives with knowledge and experience of disabilities.   At this meeting, the group was asked to justify and explain the reasons for its decisions etc.   This was completed successfully and the programme was given formal approval to operate for five years from January 1996.

The higher education disability services programme: clientele and structure

It is possible to identify two different client groups for whom the availability of the programme should prove attractive.   Bearing in mind the developments in policy outlined at the start of the chapter, there are many staff being recruited to working with disabled students who need a basic introduction to what is involved. Hence, within the programme, there is the opportunity to gain an initial qualification. There are also many staff already in post who wish to seek formal recognition and accreditation for the work that they have done previously and are continuing to do. The flexibility of the University's modular structure allows those interested in the programme to join and leave at points suitable to their own needs and career paths. The highest level of qualification is the Post-Graduate Diploma. For some, this is seen as an important marker in terms of moving on to even further advanced study since the completion of the Post-Graduate Diploma can be regarded as the half-way point on the route towards a Master's degree.

It is possible to provide some other illustrative examples of the flexibility of the programme. For example, an adviser for disabled students with some experience but who changes jobs before completing the full programme might leave with the award of a University Advanced Certificate (completion of two modules plus the introductory one). An adviser for disabled students who seeks accreditation only for what has been achieved already could be awarded a University Diploma (completion of four modules).

For all those coming to the programme with some prior experience, there is a system in place through which they can seek accreditation for this and thereby exemption from some of the modules. In particular, it is anticipated that many experienced staff will seek and be granted exemption from the introductory overview module at the very least.

The higher education and disability services programme: aims and content

The overall aim of the programme is to produce competent practitioners who offer advice and support to disabled students in higher education and who co-ordinate services and develop policy and provision for disabled students efficiently and effectively. The overall learning outcomes include both the theoretically-based and the practically-oriented, the intention throughout the course being to promote the inter-relationship of the two. Having completed the full programme, course members will be able to:

(a) analyse logically and make informed judgements about issues relating to disabled students;

(b) assess critically the nature of the processes involved in developing policies and provision for disabled students;

(c) examine critically the nature of the relationships between policy and provision for disabled students and other aspects of policy and provision both institutionally and nationally;

(d) establish mutually supportive relationships with others working with disabled students in higher education;

(e) contribute to the embedding of policy and practice regarding disabled students within the institution; and

(f) participate in improving the quality of the student experience by initiating change in the institutional structures, systems, culture and environment.

The programme consists of six modules in total. Within the University's academic programmes, the introductory module is seen as being at a level commensurate with the second level of undergraduate studies whilst four other modules are at the level commensurate with final year undergraduate honours degree work. The sixth module involves an individual investigation/project and this is seen as having the status equivalent to post-graduate research.

The six modules are:

Module One - Higher Education and Disability : An Introduction and Overview
(offering an introduction and overview of both the individual and institutional aspects of developing policy and provision for disabled students in higher education).

Module Two - Disability and Society
(exploring issues relating to definitions and meanings of 'disability', the importance of language both to the development of the individual's self-concept and group identity, and also as the major force in the creation of social reality; reference is made to rights and equal opportunities and to developments concerned with an inclusive society and the ending of discrimination).

Module Three - Disabled Students in Higher Education
(considering aspects of policy and provision from the perspective of students at undergraduate and post-graduate levels and including both academic and non-academic concerns).

Module Four - Disabled Students: Institutional and National Policies and Provision
(looking at the development of policy and provision in institutions, and set within the context of national policy; trends and change in educational policy are examined in terms of their effects on disabled students e.g. changes to student funding).

Module Five - Developing Professional, Managerial, and Interpersonal Skills
(reflecting on the roles of staff as professionals working within a particular
context, looking at their strengths and identifying aspects of their work for which
they need further development).

Module Six Project/Dissertation
(providing the opportunity to undertake independent study in an area of choice
and personal relevance).

Each module is assessed to the same extent (i.e. assignments equivalent to 5,000
words). However, the assessment strategy differs for each module and is
intended to be of a kind that is the most appropriate. The project/dissertation is
between 15,000 and 20,000 words long.

*The higher education and disability services programme: organisation and
delivery*

The organisation and delivery of the modules does vary but underpinning
everything is recognition that the programme is aimed at a national rather than a
local market. Hence strategies have been devised which provide for efficient and
effective use of time both for those involved as tutors and those participating as
course members.

The semester structure provides greater flexibility for clients to join and leave
the programme in that it is possible to start at two points rather than one during
an academic year. For those who take all modules and who cannot gain
accreditation/module exemption on the grounds of prior work, the normal
duration of the programme is five semesters minimum. Offering two modules
simultaneously each semester can mean that some course members who have
been granted the maximum exemption can complete the programme to Post
Graduate Diploma level in 18 months (three semesters).

Each module is covered during two weekend residential meetings, one towards
the start of the module/semester, the other towards the close. Attendance at these
weekends is compulsory. During the weekend there are formal inputs from
visiting tutors, there are opportunities to meet with tutors on an individual basis
to discuss progress on assignments, and there are seminars, workshops, and other
small-group learning activities. The actual teaching and learning makes use of a
range of approaches - the focus being more on learning rather than teaching and
thus the strategies employed try to involve the course members actively in their
own learning.

Throughout the period of their enrolment as a course member, individuals are allocated to a mentor. This person is someone who already has some experience of working with disabled students in higher education and who is based in an institution near to that of the course member. The overall role of the mentor is to offer help and advice particularly with the assessed assignments.

The introductory module is organised differently. Because of the limited background of the course members, it is necessary for meetings to be held on a more regular basis and to adopt a more formal classroom approach (this does not imply a more presentational strategy). Those enrolled for this module are required to attend the University for six half-day sessions over the period of one academic year. The longer duration of this module is to allow course members more opportunities to gain experience whilst taking the module.

In terms of administration, there is a Programme Leader and an External Examiner - both of these are in accordance with standard University procedures. In relation to monitoring and quality control, a course steering group is responsible, membership of this comprising course members, University-based staff, and representatives from other institutions and organisations.

The higher education disability services programme: resources and costs

Whilst the University of Central Lancashire has adequate resources, it should be remembered that the nature of the programme means that course members will be in a position to draw upon whatever is available to them at their workbase. Hence the customary issues of library books, access to IT, etc. which are important when securing course validation had to be treated on a more general basis. Course member are encouraged also to explore and use the materials available in print and via computer networks.

The programme is delivered on a full-cost basis. This means that the fees (£400 per module) have to incorporate the costs of two residential weekends, a contribution towards the payment of the expenses of visiting speakers, a sum to cover the cost of the fee paid to those colleagues acting as mentors, and all other costs associated with the administration, support, and assessment of courses in continuing professional development. There might be other additional costs relating to the provision of special services (e.g. personal assistants for disabled course members, sign-language interpreters, etc.).

The higher education disability services programme: progress report

Unfortunately, since being validated, it has not proved possible to start the programme. There are a number of reasons for this:

(a)   whilst there have been applications from a number of individuals, the total overall number has not reached the level deemed by the University to make the courses viable;

(b)   some of the shortfall in numbers might result from the lack of widespread publicity - only in March 1997 were the official, standard University information sheets ready for distribution;

(c)   without doubt, a major issue is the cost of the Programme which has been developed at a time when there is a growing effort to cut expenditure in institutions;

(d)   one way in which costs might be reduced and also viable groups created would be to obtain recognition from the European Commission and to open the Programme to colleagues working in Europe - although this might require some amendments being made to what has been validated; and

(e)   one short-term strategy which is being introduced is the use of the Introductory Module as part of the staff development programme within the University of Central Lancashire itself - which leads into the second part of this chapter.

Part two: the institutional context

Staff training and staff development within an institution: a case study

Background Earlier in this chapter, reference was made to the additional funding made available by the HEFCE. The project put forward for consideration from the University of Central Lancashire involved support for a programme which aims to approach staff training and staff development on a much more systematic, developmental way than has been the case previously. Currently, several key staff are involved with offering sessions usually in the lunch break and in the form of single "one off" events with no further follow-up. Also, given the sudden growth in the number of students whose first language is British Sign Language (BSL - currently there are around 15) it was decided to include a specific dimension about Deafness. The title of the project submitted was "Towards a 'Whole Institution' Approach on Disability and Deafness". The University was informed in late November 1996 that the HEFCE had agreed to give financial support of £166,000 for the three-year project. However, prior to discussing this, it is important to note that within the UK there are some important general issues concerned with staff development and disability.

Disability awareness-raising and training: some issues

One method of considering these issues is to use a number of questions:

(a)   who needs awareness-raising/training?

One answer to this is that everyone needs it - from the most senior to the most junior staff irrespective of their work responsibilities. However, this might seem to be a formidable task and so another answer is that those who need it can be targeted, perhaps because they are in a situation where they encounter disabled people (e.g. tutors on particular courses, staff in student accommodation, etc.);

(b)   who should be involved in awareness-raising/training?

There are several possible sources of expertise: individual specialists within the institution itself, staff within the institution responsible for all other staff training, individual outsiders with knowledge and expertise, outside organisations, and disabled people themselves. Within the UK, there is a very strong view that the last-mentioned are the most appropriate sources of knowledge, expertise, and experience - although this leads on to questions about the training of these trainers;

(c)   when should the awareness-raising/training occur?

Awareness-raising/training could be provided before the first contact with disabled students but this might mean that the limited background and lack of prior experience is a problem. On the other hand, it has the advantage that people are well-prepared before this first encounter. Alternatively, if awareness-raising/training occurs after people have had some experience of disability, it could mean that they themselves can identify issues they would like to find out more about. The disadvantage with this is that action at this point might come too late. Another important dimension is how the timing of sessions is allocated. A series of regular, developmental sessions should accomplish more than the repetition of single, very basic sessions. The likelihood is that there will be a need for both the 'one-off' and the progressive approaches;

(d)   what methods and strategies can be used in disability awareness-raising/training?

In the past, some trainers have used simulation exercises - and feedback from participants has suggested that this has had some success. However, more recently, there has been some reluctance to employ this approach (see French 1992). Also, today, more and more commercially-produced resources are available but these might need to be supplemented by materials produced in-house with a specific context in mind; and

(e) what should be included in disability awareness-raising/training?
The debate here is between a more general coverage where the emphasis is on the "education" of the participants and a more specific programme which provided "training".

The HEFCE project at the University of Central Lancashire 1996-1999

Both the 1993-94 and the 1994-95 HEFCE-funded projects were subject to regular internal monitoring and end of year external evaluation. The latter made use of an experienced, external consultant and her recommendations were used to direct future actions, including the 1996-99 project. Whilst a key to the successful implementation of policy and provision at the University has been the high level of specialist staff allocated to this work, if the underlying philosophy of a "whole institution" approach is to be successful and if the progress made is to endure, it is important to ensure that staff in all sections and departments are fully aware of the needs of students with disabilities and/or learning difficulties. In her 1994-95 report, the consultant commented several times on the need for staff training and staff development. For example she stated that "there is still a need to continue to seek ways and means of improving the general levels of awareness of all staff in the University".

It would be misleading to give the impression that little was being done to provide staff training and staff development opportunities. On the contrary, within the broader context, the University has an effective policy for individual staff development which affirms the institution's intentions to develop its human resources. The major responsibility for ensuring that this policy is implemented lies with the Training and Development Section (TDS) of Personnel Services. TDS provides a number of routes through which this can take place including in-house courses, conferences, workshops, and so on. With regard to disability, and as stated above, sessions have been provided in a fairly ad hoc manner primarily because the specialist staff who are best qualified to deliver them do not have training and staff development as their primary role and thus can fit in these sessions only when they themselves have free time. Given this, prior to the HEFCE project, there was a lack of progression in terms of depth of knowledge. Again, this is not to deny that training and development does take place in a systematic and organised way. Indeed, there are induction programmes for new staff along with equal opportunities training in a number of formats, all of which do include references to disability issues.

Apart from the need for these general and broad-based programmes, there was a more specific need for training resulting directly from the University's success in recruiting increasing numbers of deaf students. This has several dimensions: where the deaf student is expected to learn from non-deaf lecturers via the mediation of an interpreter/communicator, all three participants require situation-specific advice and training in order to make the most effective use of classroom learning opportunities. Experience gained at this University can be supported by evidence from elsewhere.

The application for financial support from HEFCE, then, had two strands which might be described as "generalist" and "specialist". The focus of this chapter is mainly on the former and so the latter will be described and discussed only briefly when appropriate.

The need for a more effective approach has been outlined already. It should be recalled too that the passing of the Disability Discrimination Act (1995) gave added importance to disability issues. Much of the basic content of a systematic, developmental programme is already available in the form of the Introductory Module within the Higher Education and Disability Services Programme described earlier. What this new project proposes is to refine and adapt this in conjunction with staff from the Disabilities Office in Student Services, staff from TDS, and representatives from every academic department and service in the University. This builds on a structure which is already starting to emerge as a result of an initiative taken by the Property Services Section which has designated one of its staff as having responsibility for disability issues.

In connection with the design and delivery of the training programme, the University wanted to make more effective use of an important staff resource, namely the writer of this chapter. Over the years I have gained knowledge and expertise relating to disability issues in higher education. My background as a teacher and my work within the University's Department of Education Studies has meant that I am aware of educational principles about course design etc. Prior to the start of the project, I was seconded to the Disabilities Office for the equivalent of one day each week. In order to provide time to participate fully in the staff development programme, arrangements have been made to take away most of my duties within the Department. Thus, the bid to HEFCE was for financial support to facilitate my secondment almost full time to the Disabilities Office. Money was needed also for the appointment of two full-time project officers to implement the more specialist dimension relating to deaf students. The three staff intend to work closely to create a training package concerning deaf students. This will be based on some initial research and will then be implemented and tested at the University of Central Lancashire before it is made available to a wider audience.

The HEFCE project: the first three months (January - March 1997)

The University was informed in late November that its application for financial support had been successful. Since term ended in mid-December followed by the Christmas vacation, there was little that could be done until January. In fact, much of what has happened since then has taken the form of planning and administration and it will be from the start of the next academic year that any signs of clear progress become evident. However, it is important to report on what has happened so far and to point out what the plans are for the immediate future.

Apart from the more practical issues like moving rooms and appointing someone to take over my teaching in Education Studies, an important matter was to set down some key principles on which the staff awareness-raising/training is to be based.

Working with colleagues already involved with students with disabilities and/or learning difficulties There is a very experienced team of people working within the Disabilities Office and within the Specialised Learning Resources Unit in the Library; it will be appropriate and necessary to make use of their skills, for example when discussing classroom support for blind or for deaf students.

Working with colleagues already involved in aspects of training and development for academic and support service staff The intention is to ensure that all induction programme cover disability issues and that any staff who have a particular interest can pursue this and seek certification for it (via the Introductory Module in the Higher Education and Disability Services Programme).

Working with colleagues with relevant special expertise Within the University there are individuals and groups of staff whose academic interests and work relates to disability issues - for example within the Department of Organisation Studies, at least two colleagues have already run workshops on the anti-discrimination legislation in relation to human resource management and personnel matters.

Working with colleagues and with students who have first-hand experience of disability A number of staff with disabilities which are obvious have been approached and have agreed to become involved; the close involvement of students is more problematic since whatever they do must not harm their studies. Staff with disabilities which are not obvious are an important resource and it is hoped that they might be willing to become more involved although by doing so, they might need to disclose something which until then had been hidden.

Working with Faculties, Departments, and services to devise programmes to meet the needs as they themselves define them   Rather than try to impose something from the centre, the strategy is to ask the various parts to identify what they feel they need - for example, if they are encountering deaf students for the first time, they might decide that the focus first of all should be on deafness.

Developing a programme which is progressive and which leads to the award of certification/qualification   An incentive for some colleagues could be that by completing a short course, they can be awarded a certificate which itself might be useful in relation to future career plans.

Developing materials which can be used by others both within the University and outside it   An important aspect of the application for funds from the HEFCE was the commitment to create materials in various formats which can be made available for use elsewhere, either in conjunction with staff from the University of Central Lancashire who can be used as paid consultants, or independently.

Developing a programme which is congruent with the University calendar   As an initial strategy, it is being suggested that a programme is made available to various sections within the University at particular points in time which fit with the annual cycle of events - for example, given that new students arrive at the University in September, it might be appropriate that a programme is targeted at the accommodation service just in advance of this time.

Working in co-operation with other institutions   Another important agreement set down in the original application is to keep in close contact with other institutions both those whose projects were funded by the HEFCE and those who were either unsuccessful or made no application. There are systems and structures in place already to accomplish this (for example the regional and national work of Skill). It should be noted, too, that the HEFCE has decided to appoint a National Co-ordinator for Disabled Students for the duration of the projects; clearly it will be important to ensure that the person appointed is in touch with what is happening at the University of Central Lancashire. (See Skill 1996b for information about dissemination.)

In addition to drawing up and gaining support for the principles, a number of other actions have taken place, involving the advertising and recruitment of staff for the Deaf Awareness part of the project. Another task which is underway is the establishment of a Consultative Group to oversee and comment on the progress of the project. This will involve not only staff and students from the University but also representatives from other institutions and organisations. Thirdly, links have been made with TDS to consider how the proposals can be fitted into the institution's overall staff development programme most effectively.

Between April and June, it is planned to deliver a number of sessions which can be used as trial efforts for what is to follow. For example, a session has been built into the Post-Graduate Diploma in Higher Education, the in-house training course for academic staff new to teaching. A similar session will be delivered at a national conference for university administrators which is being hosted by the University of Central Lancashire. Both of these are in the form of single 90 minute sessions. Before the end of June, it is planned to deliver half-day long events for a small number of services and academic departments. (The Lancashire College of Health and Nursing which has joined with the University in recent months has asked for a programme to be devised - this could be an interesting location to start since there are issues about medical and social models of disability and also about access to health professions for people with disabilities and/or learning difficulties.)

Conclusions

Higher education in the UK in 1997 is the subject of a very important committee of inquiry set up by the government and due to report in Summer. This was prompted by a number of concerns. The committee has been asked to look at and make recommendations on the future scope of higher education (i.e. size), the future structure, future standards and quality, and future funding. All of these have implications for staff and students with disabilities and/or learning difficulties. When the terms of reference for the committee were announced, whilst other under represented groups were identified, there was no mention of disabled people. Many people drew attention to this and the committee has met a delegation from Skill, invited Skill to participate in a seminar, and received a considerable amount of documentary evidence. However, given the huge brief and the pressure from a large number of interest groups, it will be a sign of progress if disability is mentioned at all! Thus, perhaps the answer to ensuring further development and efficient, effective and permanent high quality provision lies in promoting and maintaining high levels of awareness amongst all those involved in higher education.

References

Cooper, D. and Corlett, S. (1996), 'An overview of current provision' in Wolfendale, S. and Corbett, J. (eds), *Opening Doors: Learning Support in Higher Education,* Cassell: London.

French, S. (1992), 'Simulation exercises in disability awareness training : a critique', *Disability, Handicap and Society,* Vol. 7, No. 3.

Higher Education Funding Council for England (HEFCE) (1996), *Special Initiative to Encourage High Quality Provision for Students with Learning Difficulties and Disabilities (SLDD): Funded Projects (Circular 23/96),* HEFCE: Bristol.

Hurst A. (1996), 'Equal opportunities and access: developments in policy and provision for disabled students 1990-1995', in Wolfendale, S. and Corbett, J. (eds) op.cit.

Skill: National Bureau for Students with Disabilities (1996 a), *Making Change Last : Strategies for Ensuring Effective Embedding of Developments and Improvements in Provision for Students with Disabilities in Higher Education,* Skill: London.

Skill (1996 b), *Sharing the Gains: Strategies for Effective Dissemination of Good Practice in Provision for Students with Disabilities,* Skill: London.

17 Higher education and disability in the United States of America: the context, a comprehensive model, and current issues

Betty Aune

Introduction

The American educational system has made significant progress in the past twenty years to make its schools, colleges, and universities more accessible to students with disabilities. However, much remains to be done. This chapter will provide an overview of the educational system in the United States: changing perspectives of disability; disability services at the secondary and post-secondary level; an example of how one university has structured its disability services; and finally, unresolved issues concerning disability in American higher education.

National context for higher education in the United States

The United States offers free public education from kindergarten (age 5) through Grade 12. Attendance is mandatory to age 16. Traditionally, schools were organised as elementary (kindergarten-6), junior high (7-9), and senior high (10-12). Now, many school systems are organised with a middle school for students in grades 6-8. Senior high schools typically offer general education, prevocational, and college preparatory courses. Those who are preparing for college often have the option of taking honours or advanced placement courses. Advanced placement courses offer college credits if the student passes a national exam at the end of the course. In an effort to integrate schools racially, many urban systems offer magnet schools. These schools offer specialised and advanced courses in a particular area of study (e.g. sciences, arts). Although the majority of American children attend public school, there are also private schools at both the elementary and secondary levels, many of which were founded by religious institutions.

The U.S. Department of Education reported that in the autumn of 1993, 14.4 million students were enrolled in the nation's 3,600 accredited higher education institutions (Facts and Figures in U.S. Higher Education, 1996). Two-year community or technical colleges (both public and private) offer associate degrees or the option to transfer to a four-year institution. The U.S. has 1,400 two year institutions enrolling 5.6 million students. Four-year public and private colleges and universities offer baccalaureate degrees (B.A., B.S.) and in some cases advanced degrees, such as master of arts (M.A.), master of science (M.S.), doctor of philosophy (Ph.D.), and doctor of education (Ed.D). Professional schools offer degrees in specialised areas (e.g., fine arts, technology). The nation's 2,200 four-year institutions enrol 8.8 million students. The make-up of the student body in American colleges and universities has been changing in recent years, with increasing numbers of part-time, "non-traditional" students, who are 25 years of age or older, commuting to school, and non-degree seeking (Otuya & Mitchell, 1994).

Selectivity of colleges and universities ranges from open enrolment (only a high school diploma or equivalent required) in many two-year colleges to highly selective in some four-year institutions. Selective schools consider grade point average, college admissions test scores, class rank, involvement in co-curricular activities, and evidence of specific talents or leadership skills.

According to the U.S. Department of Education, tuition fees for the 1993-1994 school year averaged $1,100 at public two year institutions, $2,500 at public four year institutions, and $11,000 at private four year institutions (Facts and Figures in U.S. Higher Education, 1996). Financial aid is available through a variety of scholarships and government grants and loans. A standard financial aid application is used throughout the country, which determines the need of the student. Individual colleges then put together a financial aid package based on results of the application and, in some cases, taking academic or athletic achievement into account. Most financial aid awards require full-time student status, which is problematic for some disabled students. In some cases, the full-time status is waived as an accommodation for a disabled student.

National context for disability in education

Disability, according to the Americans with Disabilities Act of 1990, is defined as a physical or mental impairment that substantially limits one or more major life activities. Included in this definition are mobility impairments, learning disabilities, developmental disabilities, psychiatric disabilities, acquired brain injuries, chronic illnesses, hearing and visual impairments, blindness, and deafness. This definition reinforces the one outlined in the regulations for Section 504 of the Rehabilitation Act, which were issued in 1973. (For further discussion of the two Acts, see the chapter by Saucier and Gagliano).

The changing paradigm of disability

The traditional medical model defines disability as a deficit within the individual. However, the medical model has been criticised in recent years (Booth, Swan, Masterton, & Potts, 1992; Gill, 1987, 1992; Hahn, 1985, 1988; Oliver, 1990) because it suggests that the limitations are entirely within the individual, when in fact, limitations result from the interaction between the disabled person and society. The "interactional model" (also referred to as the "civil rights" or "minority group" model), proposed by those criticising the medical model, implies that the major difficulties in having a disability are the barriers constructed by society. This shift in paradigms, from the medical to the interactional model, compels educational institutions to consider how the institution must change to accommodate a diverse population of students (Aune, 1995; Smith, 1989). Aune and Porter (in press) explain the important implication of this perspective for educators.

> This "interactionist" view of disability ... shifts analysis from immutable factors such as the medical impairments of students to dynamic processes that are controllable, such as how Faculty and students ... can work together to optimise educational progress and minimise educational disability ... Resolving disability does not mean "fixing" the impaired learner, but redesigning the learning task and instructional approach in light of learner characteristics and curricular goals" (Aune & Porter forthcoming).

The interactional model also has implications for student services staff. Instead of focusing on services to assist the student in adapting to an inaccessible environment, the service provider focuses on steps to make the environment more accessible (Kroeger & Schuck, 1993). This model is gradually gaining influence on the development of policy and practice in American educational institutions.

Disability in the kindergarten-grade 12 system

Public schools are required to provide a free appropriate education to students with disabilities. Since 1975, when the Education for All Handicapped Children Act (EHA) was passed, and now IDEA the Individuals with Disabilities Education Act of 1990 (IDEA) schools have been required to identify students with disabilities, determine their needs, and provide them with an appropriate education in the least restrictive environment. All students deemed eligible for services are required to have an IEP (Individual Education Plan). Parents must be given the opportunity to participate in the development of the plan. Currently, school districts receive money from state and federal government to partially cover the cost of these programs, depending on the number of students identified as having a disability.

Special education services and approaches vary widely among different states. Typically, students are provided various levels of service, depending on their ability to function in regular classes. Services include simply monitoring the student in the regular program, offering support for mainstream classes, providing certain academic courses through special education, and keeping the student in a self-contained program in which all or almost all of a student's classes are provided in a special education setting. The trend is moving from separate programs and towards mainstreaming or inclusion, in which special education students participate in regular education for most or all of the day. Ideally, special education teachers or paraprofessional aides assist in accommodating these students in the regular classroom.

Since 1984, the U.S. Department of Education has placed a special emphasis on the transition of students from high school to adult life. Each student's IEP must include transition objectives as well as objectives for in-school achievement. A number of funding competitions have been held by the U.S. Department of Education to encourage the development of improved transition services for students with disabilities. A major effort on the part of these transition programs has been to develop the self-advocacy skills of students, so that they will be able to identify themselves and request appropriate accommodations in college and in the workplace.

In 1985, the U.S. Department of Education commissioned a five year study of 8,000 special education students - the National Longitudinal Transition Study of Special Education Students (NLTS). This study found that 14 per cent of students with disabilities compared to 68.3 per cent of the general population enrolled in post-secondary education within two years of leaving high school (Wagner, D'Amico, Marder, Newman, & Blackorby, 1992). Further, only 3.7 per cent of high school graduates with disabilities in the NLTS study enrolled in four year colleges and universities compared to 33.7 per cent of non-disabled graduates (Fairweather & Shaver, 1990).

Disability in the higher education system

Despite the low participation rates noted by the NLTS, the number of students with disabilities attending post-secondary education is definitely increasing. From 1978 to 1994, the percentage of college freshmen reporting a disability rose from 2.6 per cent to 9.2 per cent (Henderson, 1995). Those with learning disabilities represented the largest group (32.2 per cent). In addition, learning disabilities represents the fastest growing group and currently makes up the largest group using disability services at many colleges and universities. Another report (Otuya & Mitchell, 1994) indicates that the percentage of students with disabilities varies by type of institution. Community colleges (two year public institutions) have an 8 per cent enrolment of students with disabilities, public four year institutions 5 percent, and independent four year institutions 6 percent. Based on the enrolment figures reported by the U.S. Department of Education (Facts and Figures in U.S. Higher Education, 1996), these percentages indicate that about one million students with disabilities are enrolled in higher education in the United States.

Laws governing disability in kindergarten-grade 12 are different from those governing post-secondary education. Under IDEA which governs special education in elementary and secondary education, the *school* is responsible for identifying disabled students, determining what services they need, and then providing those services. Under Section 504, Subpart E, of the Rehabilitation Act of 1973, which governs disability access to post-secondary education, *students* are responsible for disclosing their disability and requesting services and accommodations through appropriate channels. In addition, teacher-student contact decreases, academic competition increases, and more independence is expected (Dalke & Schmitt, 1987; Ness, 1989). Before the recent efforts to improve transition from high school to college, little was done to prepare students to take on the active role expected of them in the post-secondary setting.

Since 1977, post-secondary institutions receiving federal funds have been under the guidelines of Section 504 of the Rehabilitation Act of 1973. The ADA extended coverage to the private sector and heightened awareness of the rights of people with disabilities. Essentially these two laws require that educational institutions do not discriminate against students with disabilities in terms of admissions and in access to programs and services of the institution. The ADA addresses non-discrimination in employment, public accommodations, state and local government services, transportation, and telecommunications. All colleges and universities are required to have someone designated to facilitate compliance with Section 504 of the Rehabilitation Act 1973 and the ADA. In addition, each institution was required to conduct a self-study and develop a plan for meeting the requirements of the ADA by 1993. For further discussion of how these laws affect higher education, see Heyward (1993), Jarrow (1993), and Rothstein (1991).

Aspects of policy and provision

Admissions and recruitment

Post-secondary institutions are expected to provide equal opportunity for students with disabilities in the application process. No questions regarding disability are allowed on the application form and no quota can be set on the number of disabled students an institution might accept. Students with disabilities who are "otherwise qualified" must be considered on an equal basis with other applicants; that is, students cannot be denied admission on the basis of their disability, but they must meet the same criteria for admission as any other student. The two most common college entrance tests are the SAT (Scholastic Aptitude Test) and the ACT (American College Test). Students with documented disabilities can request accommodations when taking the tests, such as extended time, alternative print, or a reader when taking the test. The fact that they received accommodations is indicated on the results, but post-secondary institutions are not to use this information as a factor in deciding whether to admit the student. Admissions offices may consult with the disability services office on campus to review disability documentation when uncertain as to whether a disabled student is otherwise qualified, or when providing accommodations in the admissions process. For further discussion of the concept of "otherwise qualified", see Scott (1990).

Disclosure and documentation

Post-secondary institutions are required to make reasonable accommodations in their academic programs for students with disabilities. If students with to receive accommodations, they must disclose their disability and in some cases, provide documentation of the disability, either from high school records or from a private diagnostic assessment made by an appropriately licensed professional. These confidential records are kept in the disability services or Dean's office. Access to the information is generally limited to those directly involved in addressing the student's request for accommodations.

Types of services offered

A wide range of services may be offered for disabled students, depending on the resources and size of the school. Some schools provide services to disabled students through a learning centre that is available to all students, disabled or not. Most schools have a Section 504/ADA officer, and many have a disability services office. Disability services offices (a) review documentation to determine eligibility; (b) determine in consultation with the student what accommodations might be reasonable, considering the essential skills and knowledge needed for a particular course of study or co-curricular activity; and (c) assist in arranging for those accommodations where necessary. Regardless of where these services are housed, schools are expected to provide reasonable accommodations for eligible students. Occasionally, Faculty or staff may not agree that a particular accommodation is reasonable, if it fundamentally alters the nature of the course, results in a safety risk to the individual or others, or causes an undue financial hardship on the institution. If the student, Faculty or staff, and disability services staff can not come to an agreement, the ADA co-ordinator decides whether the accommodation is appropriate. Listed below are accommodations typically provided:

- Alternative test arrangements, such as extended time, taking the test in a separate room, having the test read out loud, having a scribe for the test.
- Re-assignment of a class to an accessible location (e.g. moving the class to another building if the building is not physically accessible).
- Alternative assignments (e.g. preparing an oral report instead of a paper).
- Sign language interpreter.
- Assistive listening devices, such as FM transmitters/receivers.
- Laboratory assistant for laboratory classes.
- Course substitution, if the course is not integral to the student's course of study (e.g., taking French history instead of French language).
- Materials provided in alternative print (e.g. Braille, large print, tape, disk).
- Early registration (e.g. being allowed to register before other students to address disability-related issues).
- Extended time to complete class assignments.
- Permission to tape record lectures.

Some schools have programs that go beyond these mandated accommodations, typically offering tutoring, paid note taking services, intensive academic counselling and case management, and support groups. These programs are frequently supported either by special fees or by grants to the institution from the government or a private source.

Some colleges and universities also offer transition programs to assist students in the transition to post-secondary education. The first of these was funded by the U.S. Department of Education as part of the transition initiative described earlier. Activities include outreach to high schools to encourage students with disabilities to enrol in post-secondary education, and preparation activities such as selecting and applying to a college, developing study strategies, and practising self-advocacy skills needed in the post-secondary setting to obtain necessary accommodations.

Since 1991, the U.S. Department of Education has also funded demonstration programs to improve students' transition out of post-secondary education and into the workplace. Such programs provide career services specifically geared to students with disabilities, and work with employers, particularly in understanding the requirements under the ADA.

Schools are expected to provide adaptive equipment, hardware, and software, comparable to that available to all students as reasonable accommodations for eligible students. The amount of equipment available and its location varies by school. Adaptive equipment might be found in a designated accessible laboratory, in the libraries, or in the disability services office. Some schools have a staff person designated to assist students in selecting and learning how to use appropriate adaptive technology.

In addition to programs specifically for disabled students, many colleges and universities offer training and consultation for faculty and campus staff regarding students with disabilities. Training typically covers general information about students with disabilities, legal requirements, and reasonable academic accommodations. Consultation is often regarding a particular student the Faculty member has in class.

Division of rehabilitation services

Every state has an agency that provides rehabilitation services to eligible individuals. The primary goal of this agency is to assist disabled individuals to develop and implement a career plan appropriate to their abilities. When a post-secondary education appears to be a realistic goal and is necessary for the student to implement his or her career plan, rehabilitation services may provide all or part of the tuition and fees for the student. In some cases, a representative from the agency has an office on campus. In others, the agency seeks to co-ordinate services with the disability services office on campus. Recent changes in eligibility requirements for receiving rehabilitation services have resulted in fewer college potential students receiving these services.

The University of Minnesota Disability Services Office

The University of Minnesota is a large research university where most of its 40,000 students live off campus and commute to class. The Disability Services Office at the University of Minnesota offers more comprehensive services than disability offices on most campuses. The office was established in 1978 as part of University Counselling Services. In 1989, it became a separate unit within Student Affairs, and in 1995, it moved to the Academic Affairs Division. The office receives its funds from central administration of the University.

In 1993, the office expanded and re-organised. Currently, there are 52 staff members (33 full-time, 19 part-time) plus 10-15 hourly staff organised in five areas: administration, student services, employee services, auxiliary services, and research/training. Due to space limitations, Disability Services is housed in three buildings and shares data via a computerised local area network. Contacts with students and consultations with professionals are recorded in a database which direct service staff can access but which provides for confidentiality. Staff communicate via e-mail and share files through a common server.

Specialists in the student services area document disability, determine reasonable accommodation, consult with Faculty and staff, and develop plans for the provision of accommodations. Although diagnostic assessment is not offered, the office does conduct screening for learning disabilities and refer students for assessment. In the 1994-95 fiscal year the office served 1,100 students. These students either referred themselves or were referred by a tutor, a high school teacher, a parent, or a representative of a community agency. The largest group served were those with learning disabilities (37 per cent), the next largest were those with psychiatric disabilities (16 per cent). Other disabilities represented included blindness and low vision, brain injury, mobility impairments, hearing loss (deaf and significant), speech impairments, and systemic conditions (Disability Services 1995a).

In 1993, Disability Services established the employee services area to assist disabled Faculty and staff in obtaining or retaining positions at the University. Staff from this area work with individual Faculty or staff members, supervisors, union representatives, and/or human resource representatives in documenting disability and recommending appropriate accommodations. Staff also provide training on legal guidelines in employing people with disabilities. In 1994-95, 214 employees were served.

The auxiliary services area provides academic assistance (e.g., taped text books, proctored exams with accommodations, laboratory assistants), document conversion (conversion to Braille, large print, tape, disk), and interpreter services (sign language interpreting for classes, meetings, and events). In the 1994-95 school year, interpreter services provided 15,000 hours of classroom interpreting and 1,900 hours of non-classroom interpreting. Staff also proctored 520 exams, and taped 130 texts for students.

The administrative area provides leadership for the unit, handles personnel matters, co-ordinates technology used by the unit, and offers technical assistance to University departments on physical access issues. A specialist conducts on-site surveys, reviews architectural drawings, and advises departments on new construction and remodelling projects.

The research and training area goes beyond mandated services, developing innovative models to improve career advancement and leadership opportunities for students with disabilities. External funding is obtained for the following projects from state and local government with matching funds provided by the University:

- *Career Connections/DRS Liaison* provides career development services to University Students with disabilities, liaison between the Division of Rehabilitation Services (DRS) and University offices, and education/consultation to campus staff and community employers.
- *Careers On-Line* provides on-line career-related services through World Wide Web on the Internet.
- *Project LEEDS* (Leadership Education to Empower Disabled Students) provides national leadership training to teams of disabled students and student affairs professionals.
- *Engage: Disability Access to Student Life* provides training to teams of disabled and non-disabled student leaders and student activities staff on how to make co-curricular activities more accessible and welcoming to students with disabilities.

The research and training area also provides training, consultation, and printed/on-line information to the University community. In 1995, the office distributed to all deans, directors, and department heads two guidebooks outlining policies and procedures regarding students and employees with disabilities (Disability Services, 1995 b & c). The student guidebook is geared for Faculty and staff who have disabled students in class or in programs and activities. The employee guidebook is geared for supervisors who have disabled employees on staff. The unit offers training sessions based on the guidebooks. In addition, Disability Services provides training and consultation to the local and national community through conference presentations, workshops, correspondence, and phone consultations.

Disability Services works collaboratively with Distributed Computing Services to make computer laboratories on campus accessible to students with disabilities. A technical expert co-ordinates adaptive technology services. One laboratory serves as a demonstration lab, with state of the art adaptive hardware, software, furniture, and equipment. Students receive assistance on selecting technology to meet their needs and also receive training on how to use the technology. Two other laboratories have a range of adaptive devices. The libraries also are equipped with basic adaptive equipment and software. Other equipment is placed at various locations on campus depending on individual student needs.

Other disability related organisations on the University of Minnesota campus include the ADA Co-ordinating Committee and the Disabled Student Cultural Centre. The ADA Co-ordinating Committee oversees University policies, procedures, and services concerning disability legislation and the implementation of the recommendations made by a campus ADA task force. The mission of the cultural centre, which was established in 1991, is to foster and develop community and pride. The centre sponsors discussion groups and cultural events to further this mission.

Current issues regarding disability and higher education

Many issues remain unresolved regarding students with disabilities in higher education. These issues fall into four main areas: specific populations, services, access, and program evaluation. The issues discussed below are by no means an exhaustive list, but represent the range of issues currently being discussed (See the chapter by Saucier and Gagliano for discussion of additional issues).

Specific Populations

Higher education institutions are currently addressing the needs of a diverse population of students with disabilities. Three groups in particular have raised issues about the institution's responsibilities - students with psychiatric disabilities, students with learning disabilities, and students of colour with disabilities.

a) *Students with psychiatric disabilities.* The increasing population of students with psychiatric disabilities attending post-secondary institutions has led to many questions about what accommodations and services are appropriate for this group. Unger (1992) points out that disability service providers may have difficulty separating treatment issues from academic issues. She recommends that disability services offices address only educational issues and that treatment issues should be referred to other agencies or units. Students with psychiatric disabilities need a support network, but the disability services office cannot be the sole source of such support. Higher education Faculty and staff sometimes have difficulty determining appropriate limits for a student with psychiatric disability and may mistakenly stretch limits for this particular group (Unger, 1992). It is therefore important that disability services staff work to remove not only these misguided practices but also the stigma associated with the disability by educating campus faculty and staff about myths commonly associated with psychiatric disabilities. It is also important for colleges and universities to have a code of conduct in place for all students. This code can serve as a guide in handling behavioural issues which may arise from a psychiatric disability.

b) *Students with learning disabilities.*   Students with learning disabilities frequently make up one-third to one-half of disabled students served on many college and university campuses. Although efforts have been made to educate Faculty about students with learning disabilities, many misconceptions still exist among Faculty regarding this group of students. Some Faculty question whether students with learning disabilities should be in their classes and hesitate making accommodations for them, thinking it unfair to other students. Faculty and staff continue to question how to handle situations in which a particular graduation requirement, such as a second language or a mathematics course, is problematic due to the limitations of a student's disability, yet is an integral part of the student's course of study. Admissions offices have difficulty determining whether a student with a learning disability is "otherwise qualified", when their college admissions test scores and high school transcripts do not meet the criteria for admission. Such issues require close collaboration between academic departments and the disability services office, and frequently must be resolved on case-by-case basis.

To further compound the difficulty of resolving these issues there is the fact that the services provided by the institution may not be administered by someone trained in learning disabilities. Professional staff serving college students with learning disabilities come from a wide range of education backgrounds, as no certification or licensure is required. Furthermore, these staff have little empirically based literature to draw on in making decisions about practice, as limited research exists concerning students with learning disabilities at the post-secondary level (Brinckerhoff, Shaw, & McGuire, 1993).

Students with learning disabilities also have fewer community resources to draw on than students with other types of disabilities. The Division of Rehabilitation Services has recently changed its eligibility guidelines, which has resulted in fewer students with learning disabilities being eligible for their services. For further discussion of issues related to students with learning disabilities, see Block (1993) and Brinckerhoff, Shaw, and McGuire (1993).

c) *Students of colour with disabilities.* These students experience double stigma as members of two minority groups - people of colour and people with disabilities. Students of colour with disabilities are under represented in many disabled service programs (Ball-Brown & Frank 1993). Cultural and language barriers may prevent students from seeking services. Students of colour also may be hesitant to seek out assistance because of bad experiences in special education at the elementary and secondary level. Studies have shown that minority children are disproportionately represented in special education and experience lower expectations on the part of special education teachers (Ball-Brown & Frank 1993).

Programs which emphasise reaching minority students often do not consider the unique aspects of minority cultures and do not change their approaches to different cultures (e.g., for Asian students to ask for assistance many mean losing face - teaching self-advocacy to this group involves a different approach than one would take with white students; in some minority cultures the extended family is as involved in a student's life as the parents - hence events typically held for parents should include other family members). The ways in which disability is socially constructed within a specific culture also must be acknowledged (O'Connor, 1993). Efforts are being made both at the secondary and post-secondary levels to educate Faculty and staff on multicultural issues, which will hopefully improve the climate for both disabled and non-disabled students of colour.

Services

Issues currently being discussed relate to accommodations for students with disabilities including funding for interpreters, the availability of diagnostic assessment, and responsibility for career services for disabled students.

a) *Funding for interpreters.* The rising cost of interpreters is an issue on most campuses, especially in light of recent changes in rehabilitation services policy. In some states, rehabilitation services interprets the ADA to mandate that schools provide these services. Colleges in rural areas find it difficult to obtain the services of qualified interpreters and smaller schools cannot afford to hire full-time interpreters. Agencies provide freelance interpreters, but this option becomes expensive if used extensively. Disability services offices have difficulty obtaining adequate funding for interpreters, partially because administrators look at it from the perspective of cost per student. Undoubtedly, students who need interpreters cost more to educate, but the law is clear that such an accommodation must be provided.

b) *Diagnostic assessment.*   Another unresolved service issue is diagnostic assessment for learning disabilities and ADD (Attention Deficit Disorder). Many adults are returning to school who attended elementary or secondary school before much as known about learning disabilities and ADD.   Some of these students come to realise while in college that they might have a learning disability.   However, very few post-secondary institutions provide diagnostic assessments and the cost of obtaining the assessment can be prohibitive for many students.   Some agencies offer assessments on a sliding fee scale and some students can obtain medical insurance to cover the cost.   Disability services offices generally approve limited accommodations prior to diagnosis, if the student is in the process of getting an assessment.   Another compounding factor related to assessment is that there is little agreement as to what constitutes adequate assessment and documentation of a learning disability.   A wide range exists in the quality of assessment reports and in their usefulness for determining student needs.

c) *Career services.*   For college students with disabilities, career development is crucial, as the outlook for employment after graduation remains limited.   A study by Frank, Karst, and Boles (1989) indicated that American graduates with disabilities have a lower employment rate, require more time to obtain employment, and are more likely to be employed outside of their chosen field than are graduates without disabilities.   The issue of who should provide career services for students with disabilities and what those services should include also is currently being debated.   Disability services offices are not required to offer specialised career services, but the college or university must make regular career services accessible to students with disabilities.

Regardless of where career services are housed, it is generally agreed that there are some unique aspects of providing effective career services for this group. The U.S. Department of Education has funded demonstration projects since 1991 to address career issues specific to students with disabilities including learning about one's rights and responsibilities under the employment title of ADA, considering the limitations of the disability in selecting a career, and planning for workplace accommodations. Career services offices seldom have expertise in the area of disability. However, disability services seldom have expertise in the area of career development.   It is crucial, therefore, that these two offices work collaboratively to provide effective career development services to students with disabilities.

Access

Issues still remain regarding disabled students' access to post-secondary education and to the co-curriculum. Kroeger and Shuck (1993) highlighted the fact that mainstream campus activities are often inaccessible, due to physical, programmatic, informational, and attitudinal barriers, and that creating access must address *all* of these aspects.

> Access to higher education means much more than being able to get into a building, move around in it, use the rest rooms and drinking fountains, and park close by or use the transit service. Creating barrier-free environments means attending not only to grounds and buildings but also attitudes and information as well (Kroeger & Schuck, 1993, p. 105).

It is perhaps more important to address the limitations of the environment than to address the limitations of the individual with a disability. Non-disabled Faculty, staff, and students unwittingly put up physical, informational, programmatic, and attitudinal barriers by the environments they create. Education for and collaboration with non-disabled groups is essential for meaningful access to occur. A concept gaining favour is that of universal design, in which environments are designed to be accessible to all. Accommodations that were originally made to provide access for a person with a disability are seen to also provide better access to non-disabled individuals.

a) *Access to post-secondary education.* Throughout the practitioner literature is the assumption that special education and disability services personnel should assist disabled students with college preparation, tacitly exempting mainstream guidance and admissions personnel from the loop of inclusive preparation and outreach. Yet, typically, special education and disability services personnel do not have information about post-secondary education options, application procedures, campus visits and the like. Conversely, the guidance office, and the admissions office have little information on disability.

In high school, there is very little co-ordination between special education and guidance offices. In colleges and universities, the same is true of admissions and disability services, in spite of the fact that in some systems more students are identifying themselves as disabled during the application process. The literature emphasises the importance of collaboration among high school staff and between high school post-secondary staff (Aune & Johnson, 1992; Hartman, 1993; Seidenberg, 1986), yet the dominant pattern is one of professionals labouring in isolation from each other to the further disadvantage of students. Thus access to opportunities for post-secondary education is sometimes limited for students with disabilities because of lack of awareness among mainstream service providers - in high school, guidance counsellors, and at the post-secondary level, admissions recruiters - regarding disability issues and support services available for disabled students. Awareness among these individuals is especially critical, since they are the ones with the information and expertise on post-secondary opportunities (Allard, Dodd, & Peralez, 1987).

This general lack of information and training leads not only to a gap in the information flow at the critical point of matriculation, it also creates or exacerbates attitudinal barriers. These barriers appear as assumptions among guidance counsellors and admissions recruiters that disabled students are not "college material.". More subtly, this surfaces as a critical lack of flexibility in admissions criteria to accommodate disability. Traditional admissions criteria (e.g. Grade Point Average, precollege coursework, SAT scores) cannot effectively determine which students are likely to achieve success (Ryan & Heikkila, 1988). For students who are both disabled and members of ethnic or cultural minority groups, the problems in this area are dramatic and compounded by racism (e.g. Dodd & Nelson, 1989; Joe & Locust, 1987; O'Connor 1993; Ramirez, 1989).

b) *Access to technology.* Once students enrol in post-secondary education, procedures for ensuring access to academic programs in higher education are quite well established. However, other aspects of the college experience need further attention. Students with disabilities frequently do not have equal access to technology, often because appropriate adaptive technology is not available or the student has not been trained in how to use the technology. Also, with the development of highly graphic programs, students with visual impairments frequently cannot access the information efficiently. With the rapidly increasing use of technology in all aspects of society, it is crucial that students with disabilities have equal opportunity to develop skills in this area (Brown, 1993).

c) *Access to student life.* Access to co-curricular activities has received little attention, despite legal mandates of Section 504 and convincing research demonstrating the positive effects of overall student development. For example, studies by Pascarelli and Chapman (1983) emphasised the academic and social integration of students as major factors in retention.

Student activities co-ordinators and key student leaders often do not have the resources or training to build student activities programming this is inclusive of students with disabilities. The result is that many students with disabilities are not integrated into the co-curriculum, participate in student activities functions at low rates, and reap few of the benefits of the co-curriculum which have been shown to support the success of their non-disabled peers. In a survey completed by 78 disabled students at the University of Minnesota (Kroeger, 1992), 69 per cent had never belonged to a club or group while at the University.

In addition, few opportunities exist for students with disabilities to develop leadership skills. Alison Breeze, Director of the National Clearinghouse for Leadership Programs, reports that the clearinghouse has no materials which specifically address "the leadership interests, identities, and skills of students with disabilities" (personal communication, January 12, 1994). Although international experiences are becoming an important part of many students' leadership development, students with disabilities are not a proportionate part of this trend. According to Mobility International U.S.A., only 1 per cent of students participating in international exchange are disabled. The development and implementation of programs designed to foster leadership among young adults with disabilities is critical to ensure that individuals with disabilities are available to assume leadership positions within society at large and disability-related fields (Abery & York, 1992).

Astin conducted a study of the most important influences on college students' development. He found that the peer group was "the most potent source of influence on growth and development during the undergraduate years" (Astin, 1992, p. 398). Unfortunately, students with disabilities often miss out on this important peer group interaction. Non-disabled students continue to experience little interaction with disabled students and thus perpetuate existing stereotypes, not only in campus life but also once they enter the workplace. A study conducted by Susan Foster and Paula Brown (1989) at the National Technical Institute for the Deaf at Rochester Institute of Technology (RIT) found that for hearing impaired students at RIT, academic integration generally had been more successful than social integration. Participants in the study were generally positive about their mainstream academic experience. However, mainstream social integration of these students was much less developed, and "close and sustained friendships with hearing students were rare" (Foster & Brown, 1989, p 88.)

Students with disabilities report experiencing a climate of exclusion from campus life in general. West, Kregel, Getzel, Zhu, Ipsen, and Martin (1993) identified this as one of the major barriers faced by students with disabilities in higher education. They conducted a survey of 761 college and university students with disabilities in Virginia and reported that "a large number of students with disabilities centred on the social isolation, ostracism, or scorn they felt from their instructors and fellow students, either because of their disabilities or because they requested accommodations to which other students were not entitled" (West et al, 1993, p. 462.)

d) *Program Evaluation.* With the shrinking resources that almost all post-secondary institutions are experiencing, accountability is becoming increasingly important. Very few programs keep extensive data on demographics, services provided, and outcomes. Follow-up of students after leaving or graduating from the institution is seldom conducted. Kroeger and Schuck (1993) suggest that both process evaluation and outcome evaluation be conducted. Much work remains to be done to evaluate thoroughly the impact and effectiveness of disability services provided in higher education institutions. One step that has been taken is the development of standards and guidelines for disability programs. These guidelines are in the appendix to the CAS Standards and Guidelines for Student Services/Development Programs (Council for the Advancement of Standards for Student Services/Development Programs, 1988). See Brinckerhoff, Shaw, and McGuire (1993) for further discussion of evaluation of disability services programs.

Conclusion

Because of landmark legislation governing all levels of education (IDEA, section 504 of the Rehabilitation Act (1973),& ADA), students with disabilities in the United States are guaranteed the right to equal access to education. However, implementation of this legislation is not complete and many unresolved issues remain. Educators, administrators, and students must work collaboratively to achieve the full integration of students with disabilities into higher education.

Note

The author would like to acknowledge the following individuals who reviewed the manuscript: Barb Blacklock, Terry Collins, Gayle Gagliano, Rhona Hartman, Sue Kroeger, Sue Lasoff, Barbara Robertson and David Schrot.

References

Abery, B., & York, J. (1992), 'Learning to lead - leading to learn: Facilitating the leadership of young adults with disabilities. Proposal to Office of Special Education Programs', U.S. Department of Education, Institute of Community Integration, University of Minnesota.

Allard, W.G., Dodd, J.M., & Peralez, E. (1987), 'Keeping LD students in college', *Academic Therapy, 22* (4), pp. 359-365.

Astin, A. (1992), *What matters in college: Four critical years revisited,* Jossey-Bass: San Francisco.

Aune, B. (1995), 'The human dimension of organisational change', *The Review of Higher Education, 18,* (2) pp. 149-173.

Aune, B. & Johnson, E.P. & Johnson, J. (1992), 'Transition takes teamwork! A collaborative model for college-bound students with LD', *Intervention in School and Clinic, 27,* (4), pp. 222-227.

Aune, B. & Porter, J. (in press), 'Disability in higher education: Alternative organisational approaches', in Makas, E. & Schlesinger, L. (eds), *End Results and Starting Points: Expanding the Field of Disability Studies,* Portland, ME: The Society for Disability Studies and the Edumund S. Muskie Institute of Public Affairs.

Ball-Brown, B. & Frank, Z.L. (1993), 'Disabled students of colour', in Kroeger, S. & Schuck, J. (eds), *Responding to Disability Issues in Student Affairs.* New Directions for Student Services series, Number 64, Jossey-Bass: San Francisco.

Block, L. (1993), 'Students with learning disabilities', in Kroeger, S. & Schuck, J. (eds), *Responding to Disability Issues in Student Affairs.* New Directions for Students Services series, Number 64, Jossey-Bass: San Francisco.

Booth, T., Swann, W., Masterton, M., & Potts, P. (eds), *Policies for Diversity in Education,* Routledge: London.

Brinckerhoff, L.D., Shaw, S.F., & McGuire, J.M. (1993), *Promoting Postsecondary Education for Students with Learning Disabilities: A Handbook for Practitioners,* Pro-Ed: Austin, TX.

Brown, C. (1993), 'Assistive computer technology: Opening new doorways', in Kroeger, S. & Schuck, J. (eds), *Responding to Disability Issues in Student Affairs.* New Directions for Student Services series, No. 64, Jossey-Bass: San Francisco.

Council for the Advancement of Standards for Student Services/Development Programs, (1988), *CAS Standards and Guidelines for Student Services/Development Programs,* Athens, GA: American College Testing Program.

Dalke, C., & Schmitt, S. (1987), 'Meeting the transition needs of college-bound students with learning disabilities', *Journal of Learning Disabilities, 20* (3), pp. 176-180.

Disability Services, University of Minnesota (1995a), *Disability services annual report (1994-1995),* Minneapolis, MN.

Disability Services, University of Minnesota (1996b), *Access for employees with disabilities: Policies, procedures, and resources,* Minneapolis, MN.

Disability Services, University of Minnesota (1995c), *Access for students with disabilities: Policies, procedures, and resources,* Author: Minneapolis, MN.

Dodd, J.M. & Nelson, J.R. (1989), 'Leaning disabled adults: Implications for tribal colleges', *Journal of American Indian Education, 28,* pp. 31-38.

Facts and Figures in U.S. higher education (1996, January 2-8), *Academe this Week* [On-line], Available: http://chronicle.merits.edu/almanac/.links.html.

From the Almanac Issue of *The Chronicle of Higher Education,* 1 September 1995.

Fairweather, J.S. & Shaver, D.M. (1990), 'A trouble future? Participation in post-secondary education by youths with disabilities', *Journal of Higher Education, 61* (3), pp. 332-348.

Foster, S., & Brown, P. (1989), 'Factors influencing the academic and social integration of hearing impaired college students', *The Journal of Post-secondary Education and Disability,* 7, pp. 78-96.

Frank, K., Karst, R., & Boles C. (1989), 'After graduation: The quest for employment by disabled college graduates', *Journal of Applied Rehabilitation Counselling,* 20 *(4),* pp. 3-7.

Gill, C.J. (1987), 'A new social perspective on disability and its implications for rehabilitation', in Cromwell, F.S. (ed), *Sociocultural Implications in Treatment Planning Occupational Therapy,* Haworth Press: New York.

Gill, C.J. (1992), 'Valuing life with a disability: New models for modern medicine', paper presented *at Americans with Disabilities: Introduction to an Emerging People,* University of Minnesota, Minneapolis, MN.

Hahn, H. (1985), 'Towards a politics of disability: Definitions, disciplines and policies', *The Social Science Journal,* 22 (4), pp. 87-105.

Hahn, H. (1988), 'The politics of physical differences: Disability and discrimination', *Journal of Social Issues,* 44 (1), pp. 39-47.

Hartman, R. (1993), 'Transition to higher education', in Kroeger, S. & Schuck, J. (eds), *Responding to Disability Issues in Student Affairs,* New Directions for Student Services series, Number 64, Jossey-Bass: San Francisco.

Henderson, C. (1995), *College freshmen with disabilities: A triennial statistical profile',* American Council for Education, HEATH Resource Centre: Washington, DC.

Heyward, S.M. (1993), 'Students' rights and responsibilities', in Kroeger, S. & Schuck, J. (eds), *Responding to Disability Issues in Student Affairs,* New Directions for Student Services series, Number 64, Jossey-Bass: San Francisco.

Joe, J.R. & Locust, C. (1987), *Government Policies and the Disabled in American Indian Communities,* Native American Research and Training Centre, University of Arizona: Tucson, AZ.

Kroeger, S. (1992), [Disabled student survey results]. Unpublished raw data.

Kroeger, S. & Schuck, J. (1993), 'Moving ahead: Issues, recommendations and conclusions', in Kroeger, S. & Schuck, J. (eds), *Responding to Disability Issues in Student Affairs*, New Directions for Student Services series, Number 64, Jossey-Bass: San Francisco.

Ness, J.E. (1989), 'The high jump: Transition issues of learning disabled students and their parents', *Academic Therapy*, 25 (1), pp. 33-40.

O'Connor, S. (1993), *Disability and the Multicultural Dialogue*, Syracuse University: Syracuse, NY.

Oliver, M. (1990), *The Politics of Disablement*, MacMillan: Houndmills, UK.

Ortiz, A.A. & Ramirez, B.A. (eds), (1989), *Schools and the Culturally Diverse Exceptional Student: Promising Practices and Future Directions*, The Council for Exceptional Children: Reston, VA.

Otuya, E. & Mitchell, A. (1994), 'Today's college students: Varied characteristics by sector', *Research Briefs*, 5 (1), pp. 1-10.

Pascarella, E.T. & Chapman, D. (1983), 'A multi-institutional, path analytic validation of Tinto's model of college withdrawal', *American Educational Research Journal*, 20, pp. 87-102.

Rothstein, L.F. (1991), 'Students, staff and faculty with disabilities: Current issues for colleges and universities', *Journal of College and University Law*, 17 (4), pp. 471-482.

Ryan, A.G. & Heikkila, M.K. (1988), 'Learning disabilities in higher education: Misconceptions', *Academic Therapy*, 24 (2), pp. 177-192.

Scott, S.S. (1990), 'Coming to terms with the "otherwise qualified" student with a learning disability', *Journal of Learning Disabilities*, 23, pp. 398-405.

Seidenberg, P.L. (1986), 'The high school-college connection: A guide for the transition of learning disabled students', Long Island University Transition Project, Position Paper Number 8.

Smith, D.G. (1989), 'The challenge of diversity: Involvement or Alienation in the Academy?' ASHE-ERIC Higher Education Report No. 5, School of Education and Human Development, George Washington University: Washington, D.C.

Unger, K.V. (1992), 'Adults with psychiatric disabilities on campus', (Resource Paper), HEATH Resource Centre: Washington, D.C.

Wagner, M., D'Amico, R., Marder, C., Newman, L., & Blackorby, J. (1992), 'What happens next? Trends in postschool outcomes of youth with disabilities', *The Second Comprehensive Report from the National Longitudinal Transition Study of Special Education Students*, Menlo Park, CA: SRI International.

West, M., Kregel, J., Getzel, E., Zhu, M., Ipsen, S.M., & Martin, E.D. (1993), 'Beyond Section 504: Satisfaction and empowerment of students with disabilities in higher education', *Exceptional Children*, 59 (5), pp. 456-467.

18 Serving students with disabilities in higher education in the United States of America

Cheryl T. Saucier and Gayle V. Gagliano

Introduction

In the developing area of higher education and disability, the United States of America (USA) has made some notable contributions through the enactment of landmark legislation for people with disabilities and the development of service delivery systems for students with disabilities. This paper examines the major pieces of federal legislation affecting higher education and disability, reviews the most prevalent models of disability service delivery in post-secondary educational institutions, and concludes by discussing issues of contemporary concern to service providers. The terms post-secondary education and higher education are used interchangeably and signify institutions which provide training beyond the high school level including technical or trade schools, two-year junior or community colleges, four-year colleges, and comprehensive universities.

Legislative and historical perspective

The early history of serving students with disabilities in higher education in the USA can be traced as far back as the early 1800s. A school for the blind was established in Baltimore in 1812 as one of the first institutions serving a need-specific population. Gallaudet University was then founded in 1817 as a liberal arts college for the deaf (Shapiro, 1993). In 1918, the first vocational rehabilitation program was mandated to provide retraining services to veterans disabled in World War I. In 1920, the Smith-Fess Act extended vocational rehabilitation services to individuals injured in industrial accidents and otherwise.

Subsequent to World War II, several colleges and universities initiated programs and services to ensure their campuses were accessible for disabled veterans. The first of these programs was established in 1947 at the University of Illinois at Urbana-Champaign (UIUC) and focused on providing physical access, medical services, and daily living support to veterans using wheelchairs (Jarrow, 1993). Their initiative is generally considered the first of the modern day Disabled Student Services (DSS) programs.

The disability-rights movement and independent-living philosophy gained momentum in the 1960s spurred by the success of the civil-rights movement for African Americans and women. This push for alternatives to institutionalisation translated into increased access to higher education for individuals with disabilities.

The Rehabilitation Act of 1973

Built on the foundation of the 1964 Civil Rights Act *(Public Law 88-352)* and previous vocational rehabilitation legislation, the Rehabilitation Act of 1973 *(Public Law 93-112)* significantly improved access to society for individuals with disabilities, especially to employment and education (see Appendix A). This Act had a major impact on higher education.

Section 504 of Title V of the Rehabilitation Act of 1973 is a "program access" statute and mandates covered entities ensure equal access for people with disabilities. The term "program access" means that although all facilities may not be architecturally accessible, all programs must be offered in architecturally accessible locations, even if it means moving the program or event. (Jarrow, 1993). Section 504, in part, states: "No otherwise qualified handicapped individual in the United States shall, solely by reason of his or her handicap, be excluded from participation in, be denied the benefits of, or be subjected to discrimination under any program or activity receiving federal financial assistance" (29 U.S.C. 794) (see Figure 1).

Term	Definition
Individual with a Disability	A person who has a physical or mental impairment which substantially limits one or more **major life activities**, has a record of such an impairment, is regarded as having an impairment, or has **physical or mental impairment** that substantially limits **major life activities** only as a result of the attitude of others toward such impairment.

Qualified Individual with a Disability	With respect to educational institutions, a person who meets the academic and technical standards requisite to admission or participation in the educational program or activity.
Major Life Activities	Functions such as caring for oneself, performing manual tasks, walking, seeing, hearing, speaking, breathing, learning and working.
Examples of *Physical or Mental Impairments*	Includes, but is not limited to: alcoholism; attention deficit disorders; blindness or visual impairments; cancer; cerebral palsy; contagious diseases; deafness or being hard of hearing; diabetes; drug addiction; epilepsy; heart disease; HIV-positive status; mental retardation; multiple sclerosis; muscular dystrophy; orthopaedic impairments; perceptual handicaps such as dyslexia, developmental aphasia, and specific learning disabilities; speech impairments; and traumatic brain injury.

Source: Section 504 Compliance Handbook, Washington, DC: Thomson Publishing Group.

Figure 1:   Selected Definitions of Terms Related to Section 504 of the Rehabilitation Act of 1973

Section 504 and higher education

Subpart E of Section 504 of the Rehabilitation Act of 1973 specifically addresses equal access to higher education and is the most prominent governing policy for post-secondary institutions receiving federal financial assistance. According to Section 504, post-secondary educational institutions cannot discriminate against qualified people with disabilities during recruitment, admission, or treatment after admission. The provisions in Subpart E of Section 504 contend that post-secondary education cannot:

1.   Limit the number of students with disabilities admitted.

2.   Make pre-admission inquiries as to whether or not an applicant is disabled.

3. Use admissions criteria or tests that inadequately measure the academic qualifications of disabled students.

4. Exclude a qualified student with a disability from financial assistance or otherwise discriminate in administering scholarships, fellowships, internships, or assistantships on the basis of handicap.

5. Counsel a student with a disability towards a more restrictive career.

6. Measure student achievement using modes that adversely discriminate against a student with a disability.

7. Establish rules and policies that may adversely affect students with disabilities.

The provisions further indicate that post-secondary institutions may be required to make modifications for students with disabilities such as:

1. Removing architectural barriers.

2. Providing services such as readers for print disabled students (e.g., blind or learning disabled); interpreters for deaf students; and notetakers for deaf, hard of hearing, mobility impaired and/or learning disabled students. Colleges and universities are not required to provide aids, devices, or services of a personal nature such as personal care assistants, wheelchairs, hearing aids, or adaptive aids required for personal study time.

3. Extending the time permitted to earn a degree.

4. Developing course modifications, substitutions, or waivers.

5. Allowing extra time to complete examinations and assignments.

6. Providing adapted examinations (e.g., individually proctored, orally read, dictated, or typed).

7. Increasing the frequency of tests or examinations.

8. Using alternative forms for students to demonstrate course mastery (e.g., a narrative tape instead of a written journal).

9.   Providing adaptive aids such as four-track recorders, word-processors, or spell-checkers.

Even though the mandates do not require post-secondary educational institutions to establish separate special programs or services for students with disabilities, many colleges and universities have established offices to co-ordinate mandated services. Moreover, all existing programs and services such as student organisations and academic programs must be accessible to students with disabilities (Jarrow, 1993). Institutions which are not in compliance with Section 504 are subject to losing federal funds, which is critical to public higher education in the USA.

Other legislation affecting students with disabilities in higher education

Individuals with Disabilities Education Act (Public Law 94-142).   The Individuals with Disabilities Education Act (IDEA), formally known as The Education of all Handicapped Children Action of 1975, mandates that all children, regardless of disability, are entitled to a free and adequate public education through graduation from high school, or age 21, whichever comes first (see Appendix C).   IDEA fostered a climate that encouraged educational adaptations for students in elementary and secondary education. As a result, the first generation of students educated under IDEA is entering post-secondary educational institutions increasing numbers and placing much greater demands on these institutions.

Americans with Disabilities Action of 1990 (Public Law 101-336).   The Americans with Disabilities Act (ADA) is a comprehensive piece of legislation that focuses on eliminating discrimination against people with disabilities.   The ADA secures the right of equal access to employment, public goods and services, transportation, and telecommunications (see Appendix B).   While the ADA reaffirms and expands the requirements of Section 504, it does not supersede it. For those post-secondary institutions already in compliance with Section 504, passage of the ADA requires minimal changes as noted in "ADA/504 and Institutions of Higher Education" (Heath, 1992, p. 7):

> Colleges and universities will have to make the necessary adjustments
> in terms of employment and access to buildings, transportation, and
> telecommunications. For colleges and universities, however, making
> these changes will be less drastic and more subtle than for others
> (entities other than post-secondary education under this mandate);

most institutions already comply with Section 504 requirements, many of which are the same as those in the ADA. (See appendix 18.3.)

Perhaps, the most significant change in higher education brought about by the passage of the ADA is the refocused of attention on the need for increased access to higher education for students with disabilities (Brinckerhoff, Shaw, & McGuire, 1993).

The impact of this legislation since the early 1970s has been a dramatic increase in the number of students with disabilities attending post-secondary institutions and in the number of programs established to serve these students (Schuck & Kroeger, 1993). According to Higher Education and the Handicapped (HEATH) the percentage of entering freshmen reporting a disability rose from 2.6 per cent to 8.8 per cent between 1978 and 1991 (Henderson, 1992).

State of practice: current service-delivery models and practices in the USA

The legal mandates do not specify *how* institutions must meet the legislative requirements. For this reason, a variety of service-delivery models are represented in this country. The following is the authors' interpretation of the most common of those models.

Informal services model

The informal services model exists at some institutions where no co-ordinated services are available. When a student attending one of these institutions has an accommodative need, a contact staff person may or may not be available to assist the student. Often, serving students with disabilities is an added task that is not closely related with the employee's primary responsibilities (Schuck & Kroeger, 1993). Providing services at these institutions may be the responsibility of staff from student affairs or services, the dean of students office, academic affairs, or the library. Policies and procedures associated with providing accommodative services may not exist, thus services are provided piecemeal through students' petitions to existing university resources. The students often rely on convincing self-advocacy skills and good fortune to find sympathetic staff to get the accommodations needed.

Centralised services model

The centralised services model provides institutional access by meeting all needs for students with disabilities within one department. This department administers these services whether or not they are disability related. These services typically can include: financial aid planning, academic advising, housing, transportation, tutoring, career counselling services, as well as disability-related academic accommodations.

Once held as an ideal by the DSS profession, this model had more of a "caretaker" connotation where the DSS office seemed to say to the rest of the campus, "We'll take care of this student". As the philosophical paradigm of service delivery has shifted from "caretaker" to student empowerment, independence, and inclusion, this model has become less prevalent and/or acceptable (Jarrow, 1993).

There are some universities, sometimes under this model, that offer services beyond mandated services. These departments offer programs and services such as adaptive physical education programs, adaptive athletics, specialised tutoring and academic skills remediation, adaptive driving evaluation and training, wheelchair repairs, and social organisations. Funding for these programs is often supplied through federal grants, endowments, or fees for those services that go beyond mandated services.

Centrally co-ordinated services

The centrally co-ordinated services model differs from the preceding model in that students are referred to DSS for direct, disability-related services such as testing accommodations, reader and scribe services, and sign language interpreters. Generally, DSS offices are managed by a full-time staff member who co-ordinates programs and services for the department. For traditional needs such as housing and financial aid, the DSS co-ordinator directs students to appropriate departments. These departments are obligated to ensure their existing services are accessible to all students including students with disabilities. This model seems to be the most prevalent model found in this country (Jarrow, 1993).

Services available through the Disabled Student Services office (DSS) at the University of New Orleans (UNO) illustrate this model and typifies many DSS programs in the USA. Governed by a university-wide administrative policy, DSS acts as a liaison between the student and the University and provides a limited number of direct services (see Figure 2). Students with all kinds of documented permanent and temporary disabilities, including sensory, motor, psychological, and health impairments; learning disabilities; and age-related disabilities are eligible to register with DSS. Services begin when registered UNO students contact the DSS office, provide documentation of disability, and request assistance. The package of services offered to each student depends upon the student's documented, disability-related needs, and is determined jointly by the student and Co-ordinator of DSS on a case-by-case basis. These services can be altered throughout the course of the students' education. Services end when the student leaves the University or requests removal from the DSS active student files (Lyn, 1995).

In the 1994-95 school year, the UNO DSS budget totalled approximately $77,500, most of which was used for human resources. The staff consists of one full-time co-ordinator with a master's degree and four to five student workers and/or graduate assistants. Administrative functions are conducted in the co-ordinator's office. Direct services are administered a converted classroom with individual testing carrels and assistive technology carrels. DSS served approximately 350 students during the 1994-95 school year. For purposes of comparison, the Disabled Student Services Data Bank is compiled annually by Dr. William Scales at the University of Maryland, College Park.

In addition to the DSS Office, UNO has a specialised Training and Resource Centre for clients of Louisiana Rehabilitation Services (LRS), the state vocational rehabilitation agency. Many UNO students with disabilities are clients of LRS. The Centre offers a variety of enhanced services, including computer and vocational evaluations, an array of assistive devices from low-tech daily living aids to advanced computer technology, training, job placement, and community outreach programs. The Centre also spearheaded the 1992 and 1995 Innsbruck Conferences on higher education and disability, published an international guide to accessible university programs and services, and has sponsored international exchanges. While such a Centre is not a typical feature on USA campuses, it offers a special dimension to college life for UNO students with disabilities. In 1997 the Centre moved into a new purpose built accommodation, the building itself being considered for prizes for its design and accessibility to user of all impairments.

Decentralised services

A new movement in DSS service provision, decentralised services, has grown in popularity over the past decade (Brown, 1994). Decentralised DSS services are limited only to verifying disability, recommending appropriate accommodations, and educating all university departments on administering these accommodations independently. Successful implementation of this model requires students to be effective self-advocates. Students should be able to approach their instructors to discuss their accommodative needs, the rationale, the options for delivering these accommodations. Equally as important to success is the participation of faculty and staff.

Category	Services
Classroom Accommodations	- Adaptive furniture - Volunteer notetaker service - Tape recorded lectures - Personal amplification devices - Sign Language interpreters - Textbook recording service
Testing Accommodations	- Extended time - Reader - Oral proctors - Alternative media such as brailled or large print testing materials - Access to computers - Assistive technology - Alternative test formats such as essay instead of multiple choice
Advocacy	- Liaison between student and University Faculty and staff - Promotes ongoing improvements in physical, programmatic, and academic accessibility
Information and Referral	- Extensive library of disability-related materials - Tutor referral service - Referrals to campus and community resources
Technology	- Synthesised speech - Large print programs - Optical character recognition systems - Braille technology - Closed circuit television magnifiers - Availability at various campus locations
Campus and Community Outreach	- Disability awareness workshops - Newsletters and other publications - Presentation and lectures

Adapted by permission from the UNO DSS general informational brochure

Figure 2: **Services available to students with disabilities through DSS at the University of New Orleans**

For this model to work, faculty and staff members must not only be well-versed in disability-related issues, accommodations, and legislative mandates, but they must also be willing participants in the accommodative process.

While this model is philosophically appealing to many professionals in the field, its practicality is questionable (Lawton, 1995). The institution is ultimately responsible for ensuring that appropriate accommodations are available to those students who are eligible for them. In many instances, institutions cannot rely on individual faculty members to provide adequate and appropriate accommodations that meet a high enough standard to ensure institutional compliance.

For example, the policy for a given university might call for a student with a disability to approach a faculty member for a distraction-free testing environment as an accommodations. The faculty member willingly agrees to provide this accommodation and places the student in his/her office for the test. During the test, the phone rings, the computer beeps indicating an incoming e-mail message, the faculty member steps in and out of the office a number times. The student fails the test and contends an appropriate accommodation was not made. If that student seeks legal recourse, the institutional policy, and therefore the institution, will be under scrutiny instead of the individual faculty member who was following institutional policy.

If services are totally decentralised, the questions become: can individual faculty and staff members meet the institutional obligation to provide reasonable and appropriate accommodations? Or, is it a better idea to involve faculty in the process, but to administer some accommodations such as distraction-free testing in a controlled and standardised setting with specially trained staff?

As the previous discussion indicates, it is evident that each institution needs to have a plan for accommodating students with disabilities, even though the means by which they decide to do so can vary. As Simon (1995) contends, "No one model of providing services to students with disabilities fits all campuses or institutional settings". One disadvantage of this variability is the inevitable discrepancies in services. Just as institutional policies for admissions criteria differ, institutional policies for eligibility for access to accommodation differ (Schuck & Kroeger, 1993). If a student with a learning disability chooses to transfer from one university to another, it is possible the two institutions will have different criteria for access to accommodations. For example, the student may be eligible for extended test-taking time at one university but not at another university. Standards for basic accepted components of service delivery are an important consideration and are being addressed through various professional organisations including the Association of Higher Education and Disability (Brinckerhoff, 1995).

Current issues in serving students with disabilities in higher education

The issues in serving this growing population of students with disabilities are varied and complex. A review of current literature, as well as recent teleconference topics and professional conference session topics, reveals a number of current concerns professionals in the field. The following discussion covers some of these issues.

Determining reasonable accommodations

Prior to mandated services, requests for accommodations were few and far between. These initial requests generally came from students with obvious disabilities, such as deafness or blindness. The accommodative needs for these students were typically easy to identify, such as readers and brailled materials for students who are blind. As the population of students with disabilities has grown, it has also become more diverse. Students with invisible and/or more complex disabilities, such as learning disabilities and psychological impairments, are attending colleges and universities in increasing numbers. For this reason, determining reasonable accommodations has become more complicated (Jarrow, 1993). Institutions struggle to balance a need to preserve the academic integrity of their programs while ensuring the equal opportunity for students with disabilities.

Salome Heyward, an attorney specialising in disability law, suggests a number of factors to consider when determining reasonable accommodations. First, the student is obligated to make a specific and direct request for accommodations. The institution is not under any obligation to accommodate a student unless that student has identified him/herself to the institution according to the institution's well-documented and publicised policies and procedures. Next, the student must provide documentation that indicates there is a disability and supports the need for the requested accommodation with sufficient information. Finally, the institution must conduct an individualised assessment of the skills, abilities, and needs of the student. The student's preference for accommodation must be considered; however, the institution may choose an alternative accommodation if it can demonstrate the alternative accommodation is equally as effective as the accommodation requested by the student (Heyward, 1995).

Faculty often contend that accommodations interfere with academic integrity. The purpose of accommodations is to provide equal *opportunity* rather than preferential treatment in educational programs. As Heyward (1993) further notes, "The regulations do not preclude or interfere with the right of institutions to impose and enforce acceptable criteria and standards".

Cost of services

Since the regulations of Section 504 of the Rehabilitation Act of 1973 were issued, institutions of higher education have been concerned with the costs of providing access as mandated in the regulations. Although it appears to be clear in Section 504 that the institution bears primary responsibility for reasonable accommodations, a continuous debate exists among agencies and institutions. The federal agency that underwrites the college expenses of many students with disabilities in Rehabilitation Services Administration (RSA), located in the USA Department of Education. RSA has Vocational Rehabilitation (VR) offices in each state that provide services on the local level, services which can vary significantly state by state. The ongoing attempt to distinguish the fiscal responsibilities of the university DSS office from those of the VR agency has at times resulted in contention and confusion. Depending on the policies of a particular state VR office, VR clients may be eligible for an array of services and support such as tuition and fees, readers, assistive technology, interpreters, personal care attendants, room and board, and mental health counselling.

While there are a number of components to this debate, the most controversial issue is who is responsible for paying the high cost of interpreter services for students who are hard of hearing or deaf (Heyward, 1995). To date, the USA Department of Justice (DOJ), which is charged with enforcing the regulations, has given little guidance as to who bears responsibility for providing funding for interpreters. For this reason, the means by which interpreters for students in higher education are paid varies from state to state. Results from at least two early cases (i.e., *Schornsteing v. New Jersey Division of Vocational Rehabilitation* and *Jones v. Illinois Department of Rehabilitation Services*) suggest VR bears responsibility for the costs. Other cases (i.e., *United States v. Board of Trustees of the University of Alabama*, *Barnes v. Converse College, Crawford v. University of North Carolina*) support the contention that the institution is responsible.

Due to the rising number of students with disabilities and costs for accommodations, colleges and universities will continue to look for external funding to offset these costs. The Section 504 regulations also reveal post-secondary institutions are not required to incur the costs of services of a personal nature such as personal attendant care or accommodative aids for personal study time.

Students with learning disabilities

Perhaps one of the most difficult issues for disabled student services administrators today is serving students with learning disabilities (LD). The term "learning disabled" in the USA generally refers to individuals who are of average or above average intelligence but who have an impairment (e.g., dyslexia, dysgraphia, dyscalculia) caused by dysfunction in one or more of the cognitive areas. It is not considered the same thing as mental retardation. The individual with a learning disability often experiences difficulty in academic functioning, social interaction, and daily living skills in spite of "normal" or high intelligence (Scheiber & Talpers, 1987).

While great strides have been made in this field over the past two decades, this population continues to be particularly difficult to serve for a number of reasons. One of the most significant problems lies in defining LD (Brinckerhoff & McGuire, 1994). Definitions of LD vary from state to state and from post-secondary institution to post-secondary institution. There is also great variability in how the definition is placed into operation (i.e., which combination of numbers or scores indicates LD, how severe must a weakness be before it is called LD). To address this problem, the National Joint Committee on Learning Disabilities (NJCLD), composed of representatives of organisations committed to the education and welfare of individuals with learning disabilities, offers this widely recognised and accepted definition:

> Learning disabilities is a general term that refers to a heterogeneous group of disorders manifested by significant difficulties in the acquisition and use of listening, speaking, reading, writing, reasoning, or mathematical abilities. These disorders are intrinsic to the individual, presumed to be due to central nervous system dysfunction, and may occur across the life span. Problems in self-regulatory behaviours, social perceptions, and social interaction may exist with learning disabilities but do not by themselves constitute a learning disability. Although learning disabilities may occur concomitantly with other handicapping conditions (for example, sensory impairment, mental retardation, serious emotional disturbance) or with extrinsic influences (such a cultural differences, insufficient or inappropriate instruction), they are not the result of those conditions or influences (National Joint Committee on Learning Disabilities, 1990, p. 65).

Brinckerhoff, Shaw and McGuire suggest the definition put forth by the NJCLD is the "definition of choice at the post-secondary level" (Brinckerhoff, et al., 1993).

A second area for concern is assessment and diagnosis of LD. Currently, in the USA, there are no universally recognised standards or credentials required for a professional to assess and diagnose individuals with learning disabilities. Some feel only a licensed psychologist can offer a diagnosis, while others feel a diagnosis can be derived by a speech and language pathologist, vocational rehabilitation counsellor, special education assessment teacher, or a physician. Similarly, there is not a universally recognised battery of tests or evaluative procedure for assessing LD.   In addition, the assessment instruments and procedures used for children are inappropriately used to evaluate adults.

One final related difficulty in serving this population is that of determining reasonable accommodations. Due to the heterogeneous nature of this population, accommodations must be tailored for every individual. There should be a clear link between a students' documented weaknesses and the type of academic accommodations for which they are eligible. Further, the weakness must be severe enough to be classified as a true learning disability: providing accommodations for "learning weaknesses" or "learning differences" is not appropriate. Unfortunately, reports documenting LD vary widely and often do not contain enough information to ascertain what accommodations are necessary and equitable. As Brinckerhoff and McGuire (1994, p. 77) note, "Not every recommendation contained in a student's documentation need be implemented, unless it is supported by the diagnostic data". Finally, even when requests are legitimate and well documented, some faculty question the existence of LD and attempt to deny requests for course modifications.

At least one state, Georgia, has developed a state-wide policy that standardises the definition and assessment of LD, the credentials and training professionals must possess before they perform LD assessments, and the means by which reasonable accommodations are determined and administered. This policy affects all institutions of higher education in Georgia. Other states are expressing interest in adopting this policy as well (University of Georgia, 1994).

Conclusion

Legislation, service models and issues relating to the area of higher education and disability are diverse and complicated. This complexity grows as one moves from state to state within the United States, then across national borders. The recent trans-national networks that have been established among university administrators, educators, and service providers and events like the two Innsbruck Conferences will help to develop services and opportunities for students with disabilities. This increased international attention and the experiences of various nations and cultures are enriching the body of knowledge, standards of practice, and legal solutions for a population long neglected in higher education.

References

ADA/504 and Institutions of Higher Education (1992 March-April), *Information for HEATH*, pp. 1, 7-8.

Brinckerhoff, L.C. (1995), 'From the President', *AHEAD Alert*, January, p8.

Brinckerhoff, L.C. & McGuire, J.M. (1994), 'Students with Learning Disabilities', in McCarthy, D.R. & McCarthy, M. (eds) *A Student Affairs Guide to the ADA and Disability Issues, 17*, National Association of Student Personnel Administrators: Washington D.C.

Brinckerhoff, L.C., Shaw, S. & McGuire, J. (1993), *Promoting Postsecondary Education for Students with Learning Disabilities: A Handbook for Practitioners*, Pro-Ed: Austin, TX.

Brown, J.T. (1994), 'Effective Disability Support Service Programs' in McCarthy, D.R. & McCarthy, (eds) M. *A Student Affairs Guide to the ADA and Disability Issues, 17*, National Association of Student Personnel Administrators: Washington D.C.

Carney, N. (1995), *Support Services for Students with Disabilities in Postsecondary Education Settings*, (Teleconference), Mississippi State University: Starkville, MS.

Heyward, S.M. (1995), *Support Services for Students with Disabilities in Postsecondary Education Settings*, (Teleconference), Mississippi State University: Starkville, MS.

Henderson, C. (1992), *College Freshmen with Disabilities: A Statistical Profile*, HEATH Resource Centre, American Council on Education: Washington, D.C.

Jarrow, J. (1993), 'Beyond Ramps: New Ways of Viewing Access' , in Kroeger, S. & Schuck, J. (eds), *New Directions for Student Services, No. 64: Responding to Disability Issues in Student Affairs*, Jossey-Bass: San Francisco.

Lawton, D. (1995), Letter to the author.

Lyn, J.G. (ed.) (1995), *The University of New Orleans, Office of Disabled Student Services* (brochure), available from University of New Orleans Disabled Student Services, UC Room 260, New Orleans, LA 70148.

National Joint Committee on Learning Disabilities (1994), 'Learning Disabilities: Issues on Definition', *Collective Perspectives on Issues Affecting Learnign Disabilities: Position Papers and Statements*, National Joint Committee on Learning Disabilities: Austin, TX.

Scheiber, B. & Talpers, J. (1987), *Unlocking Potential: College and Other Choices for Learning Disabled People - A Step-by-Step Guide*, Adler & Adler Publishers: Bethesda, MD.

Schuck, J. & Kroeger, S. (1993), 'Essential Elements in Effective Service Delivery', in Kroeger, S. & Schuck, J. (eds), *New Directions for Student Services, No. 64: Responding to Disability Issues in Student Affairs*, Jossey-Bass: San Francisco.

Section 504 Compliance Handbook (1992), Thompson Publishing Group: Washington, D.C.

Shapiro, J.P. (1993), *No Pity: People with Disabilities Forging a New Civil Rights Movement*, Times Books: New York.

Simon, S. (1995), *Support Services for Students with Disabilities in Postsecondary Education Settings* (Teleconference), Mississippi State University: Starkville, MS.

University of Georgia (1994), *Academic Affairs Handbook*, available from University of Georgia Learning Disabilities Centre, 528 Aderhold, Athens, Georgia, 30602-7155.

Appendix 18.1

Title V of the Rehabilitation Act of 1973

This act was the first federal legislation to recognise the disabled as a protected class.

Section	Description
Sections from Title V of The Rehabilitation Action of 1973	
Section 501	Covers discrimination claims for "federal" employees
Section 502	Establishes facility standards for accessibility - Minimum Guidelines and Requirements for Accessible Design (MGRAD)
Section 503	Requires the implementation of affirmative action plans by federal contractors
Section 504	Defines key terms and definitions that were incorporated into the ADA. Mandates that any recipient, direct of indirect, of federal funds must make their programs and activities accessible to individuals with disabilities. Virtually all institutions of higher education are covered here.

Appendix 18.2

The Americans with Disabilities Act of 1990, (P.L. 101-336)

The Americans with Disabilities Act (ADA) is a federal civil rights law that prohibits covered entities - both public and private - from excluding people from jobs, services, activities or benefits based on disabilities.* The ADA has five titles.

The Americans with Disabilities Act of 1990

Title	Description
Title I: Employment	Prohibits discrimination against a qualified individual with a disability in the employment process.
Title II: Public Services	State and local governments may not refuse a person with a disability to participate in a service, program, or activity simply because the person has a disability.
Title III: Public Accommodations	Private entities operating public accommodations, businesses and services cannot discriminate on the basis of disability in the full and equal access to their goods and services.
Title IV: Telecommunications	ADA mandates telecommunications relay services be offered by private companies and includes services operated by states.
Title V: Miscellaneous	Various explanations and exemptions are included. For example, the ADA prohibits retaliation against an individual filing an ADA claim of discrimination.

* It should be noted that while higher education must comply with the ADA, Subpart E of Section 504 of the Rehabilitation Act of 1973 specifically addresses accessibility of programs and services in higher education.

Appendix 18.3

Comparisons between IDEA, Section 504 of the Rehabilitation Act, and ADA

	The IDEA	Section 504	The ADA
Mission	To provide a free, appropriate, public education (FAPE) in the least restrictive environment.	To provide persons with disabilities, to the maximum extent possible, the opportunity to be fully integrated into mainstream American Life.	To provide all persons with disabilities broader coverage than Section 504 in all aspects of discrimination law.
Scope	Applies to public schools.	Applies to any program or activity that is receiving any federal financial assistance.	Applies to public or private employment, transportation, accommodations, and telecommunications, regardless of whether federal funding is received.
Coverage	Only those who are educationally disabled, in that they require special educational services, ages 3-21 years.	All qualified persons with disabilities regardless of whether special education services are required in public elementary, secondary, or post-secondary educational settings.	All qualified persons with disabilities, and qualified non-disabled persons related to or associated with a person with a disability.

Appendix 18.3 continued

Disability Defined	A listing of disabilities is provided in the act, including specific learning disabilities.	No listing of disabilities provided, but includes any physical or mental impairment that substantially limits one or more major life activities, having record of such an impairment, or being regarded as having an impairment.	No listing of disabilities provided. Same criteria as found in Section 504. HIV status and contagious and non-contagious diseases recently included.
Identifica-tion Process	Responsibility of school district to identify through "Child Find" and evaluate at no expense to parent or individual.	Responsibility of individual with the disability to self-identify and to provide documentation. Cost of the evaluation must be assumed by the individual, not the institution.	Same as Section 504.
Service Delivery	Special education services and auxiliary aids must be mandated by Child Study Team and stipulated in the Individualised Education Plan (IEP).	Services, auxiliary aids, and academic adjustments may be provided in the regular education setting. Arranged for by the special education co-ordinator or disabled student services provider.	Services, auxiliary aids, and accommodations arranged for by the designated ADA co-ordinator. Requires that accommodations do not pose an "undue hardship" to employers.
Funding	Federal funds are conditional to compliance with IDEA regulations.	No authorisation for funding attached to this Civil Rights statute.	Same as Section 504.

Appendix 18.3 continued

Enforce-ment Agency	Office of Special Education and Rehabilitative Services in US Department of Education.	The Office for Civil Rights (OCR) in the US Department of Education.	Primarily the US Department of Justice, in conjunction with the Equal Employment Opportunity Commission and Federal Communications Commission. May overlap with OCR.
Remedies	Reimbursement by district of school-related expenses is available to parents of children with disabilities to ensure a FAPE.	A private individual may sue a recipient of federal financial assistance to ensure compliance with Section 504.	Same as Section 504 with monetary damages up to $50,000 for the first violation. Attorney fees and litigation expenses are also recoverable.

Source: Brinckerhoff, et al., 1993.

19 Students with disabilities and international exchanges

Alan Hurst

Introduction

One of the most interesting developments to occur in recent years is the growth in international student mobility. To have the opportunity to spend an extended period of time living and working in a foreign country is a valuable educational experience in itself. For students of modern languages, time abroad speaking the language has been a compulsory element of the course. A wide range of other courses have come to involve a period of study abroad. As a medical student, my son spent a short period in San Francisco and a much longer period in the Falkland Islands whilst my daughter has had to spend one complete year in France as a student of French. There have been many long-standing partnership arrangements between different countries and there have also been organisations willing to give financial support to students keen to take part. Within Europe, further stimulus has come as a result of initiatives associated with the European Union. Programmes such as ERASMUS, TEMPUS, and LEONARDO have enabled many students to study abroad. What is not clear is how these opportunities have been open to students with disabilities and how many have taken the chance to travel and live in another country. The rest of this chapter explores a number of issues associated with ensuring that this group of students are not denied opportunities to participate. The discussion is structured around five questions. These are followed by brief descriptions of some students with disabilities based in the university where I work who have studied abroad.

Who is involved in international exchanges and study abroad?

The simple answer to this question is that any student irrespective of impairment and programme of study should be able to participate if they so choose. In practice, the situation is more complex. For example, some students enrolled on courses of training for a profession might find opportunities limited. In England, student taking courses in initial teacher training might find that the structure of the courses does limit possibilities. There might also be difficulties for part-time students who have full-time jobs from which they cannot be released. Some part-time students have responsibilities outside their studies - for example as parents and partners - which would be hard to escape. Part-time students might also have more problems with financial support.

All of the above considerations apply to students with disabilities as much as to their non-disabled peers.

The question is not only about students - it is about the involvement of others. Thus, academic and faculty staff have a role to play in advising about study programmes in other institutions in other countries. For students with disabilities, the specialist support staff are often members of networks of practitioners both at national and international levels and so they can give advice about aspects associated with support needs. As with any student who would like to spend time in a foreign country, the institution's office which handles this will have an important role to play. This could involve help with administrative requirements such as the obtaining of a visa for some countries.

A third group of people with some stake in the taking up of opportunities to study abroad are the student's family. Most parents and friends experience some degree of worry for their loved ones, irrespective of whether they have an impairment. The impairment can be an additional source of concern. In some cases, perhaps where the students are relatively young, have limited experience of foreign countries, and who appear to need a considerable level of support, it is important to ensure that any anxieties and worries are made public and attempts made to provide answers to questions and to offer some general reassurance.

When should the period spent abroad take place?

In England, most undergraduate programmes take three years to complete. The pattern which has become most common is for the period abroad to take place during the second year. Many universities have introduced semester systems and credit accumulation/modular structures which have contributed to making the process more congruent between the different countries. This has been helpful to students irrespective of having an impairment. For the sake of completeness, perhaps it is necessary to repeat what was said in the introduction that there are some courses where study abroad is a requirement and where the time when this occurs is already fixed.

Where should the foreign study take place?

One can begin to address this question by suggesting that the student should be free to choose. In practice the range of opportunities is more limited. However, what is important is that if students with disabilities wish to spend time overseas, their opportunities should be as free or as limited as their non-disabled peers. Many institutions have partnership agreements with institutions in other countries and these have been operating successfully for many years. In its simplest form, there are regular exchanges of students. Because of the formal partnership agreement and because of the growing experience, arranging exchanges has become routine and problem free. However, this might not always be the case if students with disabilities wish to participate. It could be that the overseas partner does not have policy and provision which would enable the needs of the student with the impairment to be met. One obvious example is where buildings and living accommodation have not been adapted and are inaccessible to wheelchair users. If a situation such as this arises, it might be possible to arrange a period of study abroad on an ad hoc basis with another institution where policy and provision has been developed. Exchanges with institutions which are not partners will take much more time to arrange and will involve giving attention to some aspects which are taken for granted where partners are involved. For example, one issue to be resolved could concern finance, particularly tuition fees Exchanges between partners normally mean that each will teach students from the partner without charge. This is not usually the case if the study abroad is at an institution with which the home base has no formal links.

How can exchanges be supported and facilitated?

The comments which follow in this section are in the form of suggestions intended to alert people to the various processes and stages which have to be negotiated when arranging study abroad for students with disabilities. All students, whether disabled or not, will need to find out if there are government regulations for entry to the country - for example a visa or financial guarantees might be needed. For some countries, there are medical requirements such as immunisation.

To begin with, students with disabilities need information about what is available in other countries. In recent times there have been several developments which have made this easier to get. In Europe, as a result of a project undertaken within the European Forum for Student Guidance (FEDORA) organisation and with the support of the European Commission and the Catholic University of Leuven, Belgium, a guide has been produced which lists what is available at a number of universities in the countries which are members of the European Union (Van Acker 1996a). Whilst this is not totally comprehensive, it is an excellent foundation. A parallel development has taken place in the USA and a similar guide has been published which covers universities there (Gagliano and Moore 1997). On a more global scale, since 1995, Mobility International USA (MIUSA) has established the National Clearing House on Disability and Exchange (NCDE) for disabled students. Not only has a very thorough guide been produced (NCDE 1997), there is also a regular newsletter which updates information and contains accounts written by disabled students who have studied abroad. MIUSA have worked with students with disabilities in different structures which go beyond study exchanges. These include home-stay experiences, community service, and work placements. They have a growing knowledge of cross-cultural issues, and legal and travel issues Moving back to the national level, some countries have some kind of national guide which can be used by students with disabilities - for example in England Skill is responsible for the annual publication "Higher Education and Disability" (Skill 1997). Similar publications exist in France and Germany. Individual institutions do publish information specially for students with disabilities. Since 1997, in England all universities have had to compile and publish a Disability Statement which summarises policy, describes provision, and identifies future changes. The Disability Statements can be seen on the internet as a result of the work of the CANDO Project based at the University of Lancaster.

All of the above is about the giving of information and the institutions and organisations making information available. Despite all of these helpful approaches, individual students still need to check for themselves the extent to which universities in other countries can meet their needs. In the past, this might have been made more difficult because of language barriers. A second dimension of the FEDORA Project mentioned above was the development of a very comprehensive questionnaire which students with disabilities can use when making initial contact with overseas institutions(Van Acker 1996b). Much time was spent by the team working on the Project to produce a list of questions which covered as many aspects of policy and provision as possible and would be useful to students with different impairments. Having agreed on the questions, all were translated into the different languages of the member countries by native speakers. This means that students can copy the questions into the language spoken in the country which they would like to visit and because all questions are the same and in the same order, they can find out more easily what the position is.

Having obtained the information and taken some initial decisions the second stage is to explore some of the academic dimensions. These would include the calendar of the overseas university and the start and finish of teaching programmes, the study programmes available, their level and credit ratings, the transferability and acceptability of the credits at the home institution, and the nature of formal assessment and examinations which have to be passed if the programme is to be completed successful. Students with mobility impairments will also have to think about physical access to teaching rooms, the library, and the general nature and layout of the campus. Blind and deaf students need to consider how they will access learning and the curriculum. All groups will need to think about special arrangements for assessment and examinations. (Often these are called "accommodations" and whilst this is an appropriate term to use, it can lead to some confusion since the word is used in some countries to refer only to student's residential requirements). If special arrangements will be required, this could raise the issue of the evidence judged appropriate to support the changes. In this instance, the requirements vary in the different universities and vary too according to the nature of the impairment.

If the concern is to process students with disabilities in the same way as non-disabled students as much as possible, these might take precedence. If that is the case, we move to the third stage although in reality disabled students might need to consider aspects of life outside the classroom at the same time as the more academic issues. Where the student will live is of major importance and so for wheelchair users, accessible, adapted rooms in halls of residence or flats in the local community will have to be arranged. Special facilities will need to be taken into account when blind and deaf students are choosing where to live. If the living quarters are on campus, some of the potential difficulties associated with travel are minimised but where the residences are located at some distance from where the course is delivered, attention will have to be paid to how students will travel to and from the university. Some students might require personal assistance, possibly on a continuous basis. This must also be explored.

One aspect which underpins much of the above is finance. Studying abroad can lead to lots of additional expense and so students will need to find out where there are sources of funding. Apart from some of the costs associated with aspects mentioned already, sometimes a significant additional expense results from the need for medical and health insurance. It is advisable for students with disabilities to determine exactly what the additional disability-related costs are and to include these in their financial planning.

To organise all of the above and to be confident of some success does take considerable time, lots of effort, and a degree of persistence. However, there is a growing number of students with disabilities who are taking opportunities to study abroad. In the next section, some examples will be described.

Students from the University of Central Lancashire and studying abroad

As one of the so-called 'new universities' which changed their names in 1992 as a result of the Further and Higher Education Act the University does not have the long-established links with overseas institutions which some of the older, traditional universities do. Also, given this situation, the new universities like Central Lancashire tried to explore partnerships with new countries. Thus, in the case of Central Lancashire, very good relationships have developed with parts of China, the Far East, and some of the countries in eastern Europe which were formerly under strong Soviet influence. In many of these countries, societal development is at a different stage from that of Western Europe and consideration for the needs of their disabled citizens seems to have very low priority. For students with disabilities wishing to study abroad, the partnerships with institutions in these countries are almost impossible to arrange. It would be a very brave student who would wish to pioneer the way in some of the more provincial areas of Rumania, Poland, or China.

It would be wrong to convey a picture which is too negative. As with all other universities, students studying foreign languages have to meet the requirement for residence abroad. In recent years, a blind student has spent time studying French at the University of Caen whilst a different blind student has spent time at the University Kassel as part of his German course. The experiences of both students were relatively problem-free although one possible complication could have occurred. Both of these students used a long cane to aid their mobility and independence. As an alternative, they might have chosen to use a guide dog. Fortunately, they did not since if they had taken their dogs with them to France and Germany, they would have had to adhere to national regulations about quarantine on their return. They would have been deprived of the services of their dogs for a significant period of time.

The University of Central Lancashire has acquired a national reputation for its policies and provision for students who are deaf or hard-of-hearing. Since 1993 the number of these student has grown considerably and in 1997, there were around 20 students whose first language was British Sign Language (BSL) and needed the services of interpreters and notetakers. Experience of deaf students studying abroad is very limited so far. In 1997, one deaf student spent a semester in Madrid although the experience was shared with another student pursuing the same course.

Students who use wheelchairs have taken part in international exchanges. Some years ago a History student spent a semester at the University of New Orleans whilst at the time of writing a Health Studies Major student is in the middle of a one year period at the same university. As a result of these experiences, the two universities are considering making a formal partnership agreement. When this is signed, many of the tasks which staff in both institutions have had to tackle in order for student exchanges to take place should become less onerous.

Closing comments

Students with disabilities and the staff who work with them on international programmes have gathered a lot of experience and expertise which most are willing to share with others coming new to this work. These same students and staff will have many stories of things that went wrong! Some of the difficulties can be overcome by following some general guidelines.

To begin with, first hand knowledge of the institutions and their staff is very useful if it is possible. Site visits are extremely useful although they are expensive. At the very least, good personal contacts are necessary. Secondly, planning for a visit to an institution overseas needs to start as soon as possible - there is much to do. Thirdly, whilst forward planning is necessary, it is also necessary for all those involved to adopt a flexible approach and to be creative when confronted with unforeseen difficulties. Fourthly, the preparation of students going abroad needs to take into account the possible culture shock which will occur. Sometimes, there are very marked cultural differences, even between societies which appear to be at similar stages of development. For example, students from the USA coming to spend time in England might be surprised, frustrated and annoyed by some of the barriers they meet, barriers which would not be allowed in the USA following the various anti-discrimination laws. At the same time, an English student spending time in the USA might wonder why other people do not rush to offer assistance as they might do at home. The student would need to be aware of the impact of the disability rights movement in the USA and the notions both of independence and also fear of litigation if the help leads to an accident. Finally, there is a need to "expect the unexpected". There will always be problems to address. It is by doing this that we acquire experience so that, as time goes by, the difficulties being faced are fewer. The challenge is to overcome these so that students with disabilities who pursue the opportunities to study abroad in the same way as their non-disabled peers have an experience of the highest quality. The fact that at the many conferences there appear to be workshops and presentations about students with disabilities involving those keen to promote international education is a positive sign that progress is being made.

References

Gagliano, G. and Moore, N. (1997), *Studying Abroad: A Guide to Accessible University Programs and Facilities for Students with Disabilities - The United States and Canada*, University of New Orleans: New Orleans.

National Clearing House on Disability and Exchange (1997), *Building Bridges: Including People with Disabilities in International Programs*, MIUSA, Eugene, Oregon.

Skill (1997), *Higher Education and Disability; The Guide to Higher Education for People with Disabilities*, Skill: London.

Van Acker, M. (1996a), *Studying Abroad: 2 European Guide for Students with Disabilities*, FEDORA/KU Leuven: Leuven.

Van Acker, M. (1996b), *Studying Abroad: 1. Checklist of Needs for Students with Disabilities*, FEDORA/KU Leuven: Leuven.

Note: "*A World Awaits You*": A Journal of Success in International Exchange for People with Disabilities' published by MIUSA and available free of charge, is a useful source of information.